COVENANT AND COMMUNICATION

*A Christian Moral Conversation
with Jürgen Habermas*

Hak Joon Lee

University Press of America,® Inc.
Lanham · Boulder · New York · Toronto · Oxford

Copyright © 2006 by
University Press of America,® Inc.
4501 Forbes Boulevard
Suite 200
Lanham, Maryland 20706
UPA Acquisitions Department (301) 459-3366

PO Box 317
Oxford
OX2 9RU, UK

Library of Congress Control Number: 2005935827
ISBN 0-7618-3373-0 (paperback : alk. ppr.)

To
My wife, Jackie, and my sons, Jonathan and David,
Whose prayers and support made this work possible

TABLE OF CONTENTS

FOREWORD

Dr. Lee is one of the intellectual leaders among that new generation of outstanding younger scholars who are taking up questions of "Public Theology." He and a number of other talented thinkers seek not only to address social and political issues in theological and theological-ethical terms, they argue that a philosophical theology is neither an esoteric discipline nor simply a megaphone for irrational religious belief. Rather, when carefully thought through, it is a useful, indeed, an indispensable, way of talking reasonably about normative matters in an age of fragmented philosophical discourses and of multiple religious orientations.

The apparent fragmentation and pluralism of much contemporary thought has plunged many into a de-constructive nihilism, a romantic traditionalism, a militant fundamentalism, or a belief in an inevitably clash of cultures and civilizations. Many, in despair, have thus inclined to a militant rejection of modernity, of liberal thought, of democratic ideals, of a regard for universal human rights, of progressive efforts to bring about greater justice with freedom, or of any religion that speaks about "truth" with conviction on any of these matters. Lee is convinced that we need not be so pessimistic and we must not reject these highly desirable aspects of modernity's legacy; although the "legitimation crisis" Habermas identified needs to be overcome.

Building on his "highest honors" dissertation of several years ago, Dr. Lee argues with compelling suggestiveness that contemporary theology should attend to Jürgen Habermas' philosophy of communicative action more than it has to date. He notes that Habermas (and his sympathetic critics, such as Seyla Benhabib) largely avoids the difficulties that "post-modern" thinkers such as Foucault, MacIntyre, Rorty, etc., say they find in "modernity" and "liberalism"—terms that have become terms of reproach or contempt far too often At the same time, Lee holds that Habermas' views need a deeper grounding if they are to be sustained over time. This deeper grounding can, Lee argues, be best supplied by key themes in Christian theology that inevitably focuses on the power of the communicative "word," on the concrete formation of communities of ethical commitment, and on an awareness of that ultimate reconciling diversity that alone is by definition universal – the triune God. In short, he offers a careful, systematic conversation between a key representative of post-foundational modern, liberal social philosophy and several key classic motifs in Christian doctrine to form a fresh proposal for a strengthened and publicly accessible philosophical theology, one more likely able to provide a viable ethic for a globalizing world than any one of these developments alone.

It is well known that in his earlier work, Habermas was quite dismissive of religious and theological perspectives; but he softened his views over the decades due to conversations with various theologians in Germany and America, and has become quite open to a more dialogical appreciation of religion. It is not clear, however, that he has made any substantive use of key theological resources. Lee shows that this is not only possible, but critically important for both his philosophy and contemporary theology. Especially significant, he says, are certain ontic implications of the doctrine of the Trinity and certain major social implications of the doctrine of Covenant. These are not only compatible with the central intent of Habermas' project, but give some of his formalistic thought and abstract arguments greater amplitude and concreteness.

Lee's argument is essentially systematic. He makes reference to the possibility that some historical continuities can be discerned, but the fuller historical connections between the classical theological traditions and the best of modern philosophy has yet to be fully traced out. Still, several developments in regard to the doctrine of the Trinity by such diverse theologians as Karl Barth, Paul Tillich, Catherine M. LaCugna, and Jürgen Moltmann suggest a wide and broad recognition of a communitarian understanding of the very being of God. This doctrine also has implications for the nature of human nature, made for relationship in accord with the "image of God." Further, he draws on the analysis of social and political implications of covenantal motifs, as traced historically and cross-culturally by the noted Jewish scholar Daniel Elazar and systematically by a number of Reformed social theorists who followed the great (but too-often neglected) Protestant political philosopher, Althusius. One doctrine has to do with the very nature of the divine beyond and within humans, and the other has to do with the kind of bondings between peoples and groups that can create and sustain non-coercive communities of edifying discourse, even in the face of disagreement. Such motifs strengthen, and partially correct, Habermas' case.

All of this issues in a proposal for a liberal-progressive ethic, based in a Trinitarian-Covenantal philosophical-theology. This proposal illustrates that liberal-progressive thought is not, as some say, passè, nor is it all merely an accommodation of faith and reason to cultural trends. On this basis, he not only criticized some of the post-modern philosophers mentioned above, he turns his critical-appreciative eye to two leading Christian ethicists—the widely-read Methodist communitarian essayist, Stanley Hauerwas, and the highly-regarded Catholic social thinker, David Hollenbach. In each case he identifies what their work offers to such an effort and shows how his proposal could also, in fact, strengthen and modulate their efforts as well.

In brief, we are offered here a constructive vision of a more genuine communicative ethic that is more profound than the anti-cosmopolitan and anti-theological philosophers of our day or the theological dogmatists who would ignore philosophy and social theory. Altogether, this is a major intellectual, and faithful, achievement.

Max L. Stackhouse
Rimmer & Ruth deVries Professor of
Reformed Theology and Public Life
Princeton Theological Seminary
February 22, 2005

PREFACE

Christianity has enjoyed a long history of public engagement from its inception. It has not been afraid of interacting with the dominant philosophical ideas, ethical values, and cultural trends of various historical times in preaching and sharing the truth of the gospel. Through these engagements, Christianity has enriched and expanded its understanding of God, humanity, mission and moral responsibility, and in the process, emerged as a major culture-shaping, civilization-forming force in human history.

Christianity today is equally demanded to engage with dominant philosophies, values and cultures in order to share the truth, moral insights, and visions of the gospel for the renewal of our social life and the enhancement of the common good. This task is not unusual. For example, St. Paul preached and defended the gospel to the Greco-Roman world using a Greek stoic philosophy; Augustine relied on neo-Platonism to defend the truth of the gospel against heretical teachings and dominant socio-political misunderstandings; Aquinas used the Aristotelian metaphysics and ethics to explain the divine nature and economy to his contemporaries. Recently, liberation theology has utilized Marxist social theories to uphold the Christian social responsibility for the oppressed.

In this work, I chose Jürgen Habermas, a renowned German philosopher and social scientist, as my conversation partner for Christian public engagement. Habermas' critical social theory is useful in dealing with the question of social order and publicity in a pluralistic society: how is social order possible today, and what constitutes a fair, just and reciprocal discourse? His theory provides a reasonable and practical alternative to the two unattractive options of decimating relativism and rigid foundationalism. Furthermore, his concern for social justice, respect for freedom, public good, and democratic discourse deeply resonates with the Reformed Christian sensibilities. In particular, his notion of communicative action is useful in expanding and revising a Christian understanding of covenantal discourses and the Trinitarian economy. However, this work is not an uncritical adoption of Habermas' theory. It is my conviction that Habermas' theory can be refined and improved through engagement with the rich social philosophical tradition of Christianity, just as the Christian moral understanding can be expanded, deepened, and revitalized by Habermas' theory.

This book was possible through the contributions of many faithful people whose presence and acquaintance have been a blessing for me. I first want to express my gratitude to my teachers, as this book has grown out of my Ph.D. dissertation. I am blessed by having two of the best ethicists in the U.S. today as my teachers: Drs. Peter Paris and Max Stackhouse. As chief advisor of my dissertation committee, Dr. Paris supported me with his unfailing moral encouragement, probing questions, and thoughtful suggestions beyond the responsibility of advising a dissertation. His scholarship and dedication to social justice have been a model for my own intellectual and spiritual life.

I am also deeply indebted to Dr. Max L. Stackhouse in many ways. His conviction on the public theological task of Christianity was influential for my intellectual growth. Through him, I was able to learn the depth and richness of Reformed Christianity which I could not find in any other places. I am truly grateful for his continuous moral and intellectual support for my scholarship, as demonstrated by his graciousness to write the Preface for this book. I am honored by his contribution.

I am also grateful to Dr. Mark Taylor whose seminar on Theory and Praxis stimulated me to study Habermas seriously. I still remember his advice that a Christian ethicist needs to company one good social theorist for adequate social analyses and policy formulations. My choice was Habermas. Similarly, Dr. Nancy Duff's Seminar on Paul L. Lehmann inspired me to expand my understanding of Christian ethical methodologies and to deepen my concern for social justice.

I want to express my gratitude to Joanne Noel, E. J. Emerson, Lynn Berg, Chuck Chamberlayne, and others who carefully read the manuscript and provided fruitful editorial suggestions, comments, and critiques. Yet, the responsibility is entirely mine for any mistake or error.

My greatest indebtedness goes to my family, my wife, Jackie, and two sons, David and Jonathan. I must confess that the writing of this book demanded that I sacrifice the joy of sharing my love and friendship with them. They not only bore my occasional absences from family events with grace but also sustained me with unceasing prayer and encouragement. In particular, I am so grateful to Jackie for gracefully filling in my parental–covenantal responsibilities with her uncommon wisdom, patience, and commitment. My family deserves equal credit with me for the completion of this book. Therefore, I dedicate this book to my wife and two sons.

It is my humble wish that this book may inspire a few minds to have a better understanding of the communicative and covenantal nature of the trinitarian economy and the richness and stability of Christian moral existence shaped by it.

To the Triune God be the honor and glory forever!

Hak Joon Lee
New Brunswick, NJ.
Easter Sunday, 2005

INTRODUCTION

CHRISTIAN PUBLIC ENGAGEMENT IN A GLOBAL SOCIETY

I. Liberal Democracy and a Global Society

In his highly acclaimed and disputed work, *The End of History and the Last Man*, Francis Fukuyama states that the collapse of Communism has brought about the "unabashed victory of economic and political liberalism, the end point of mankind's ideological evolution and the universalization of Western liberal democracy as the final form of human government." Our global society, with the exception of Cuba, North Korea, several countries in Africa, and the Middle East, witnesses liberal democracy as the dominant political system, pluralism as an expanding cultural-social reality, and human rights as the international standard of morality.

Liberalism, as a Western political and social philosophy, literally means the belief in freedom. Yet, liberalism indicates a very complex and multifarious system of thoughts which are still embodied in various social institutions and practices. It has diverse traditions and ideological strands within it, such as utilitarianism, Kantianism, and social contractualism. Any easy, fixed definition of liberalism is difficult because it is still very much a living and changing phenomenon. Liberalism exhibits several of the following salient characteristics despite internal variations:

1) Liberalism takes the rights of individuals to equal treatment and respect as the fundamental morality. What ultimately counts is the freedom of individuals. The idea that the individual freedom is the ultimate and final source of authority means that the claims of individuals have more authority than those of institutions and society. Political and social institutions are evaluated by their impact on individuals. Social institutions and the government must be organized and arranged in a way to protect individual rights. This emphasis on individual freedom reflects the historical ethos of the movement which emerged to protect individuals against the tyranny and the abuse of religious and political authorities.

Historically, liberalism emerged as a movement against arbitrary authority, both religious and monarchical/aristocratic powers. The development of liberalism has also been accelerated by the situation of religious pluralism of the European society since the Reformation. Instead of the traditional authority of religious powers, superstition, and aristocratic lineage, liberalism discovered human reason as the source of true morality and knowledge. Liberalism attempted to secure the social order on universal, abstract, impersonal, and indiscriminate laws founded upon rational principles.

2) Liberalism emphasizes equality among human beings. It denies any natural moral or political hierarchy and any intrinsic inequality among human beings. Humanity shares a single moral status. This idea is closely associated with the idea of rule by laws. That is, the laws must be applied indiscriminately and impersonally.

3) In liberalism, the right is prior to the good. This emphasis is the result of liberalism's historical response to the plurality of religious and cultural life. Historically, liberalism emerged as a political theory to deal with pluralism. The development of liberalism, in its current form, was greatly affected by religious wars in a European society. It is based on the realization that since human beings hold different and often conflicting cultural and religious convictions about the ultimate good, any collective effort to implement a comprehensive idea of the good through law would inevitably violate some individuals' rights to freedom and equal respect. Liberalism attempted to solve the problem by instituting rationality, not revelation or tradition, as the basis of morality. In doing so, it relied on the idea of natural rights which contends that by virtue of their very human nature, there are weighty duties and rights that are owed to all human beings regardless of their cultural, religious, and historical orientations and memberships. The principle of justice does not depend on any vision of the good; it is independently established by reason, free from various parochial affiliations and religious ends.

4) The idea of endless progress characterizes liberalism. Human society and institutions are to improve infinitely by the use of human critical reason despite their present imperfections.

These core political and social beliefs are expressed in the system of democracy which inscribes the rule of the majority under the constraint of the law. They are also codified judicially in the idea of human rights which protects basic civil and political human activities such as freedom of expression, freedom of association, freedom of conscience, free exercise of religion, and so on. These beliefs are sustained by institutional pluralism which acknowledges and protects the relative authority of various social institutions in their assigned social functions within a complex social relationship.

Ironically, however, in its most glorious moment of ascendance, liberalism has come under severe philosophical criticism under the rubric of postmodernity.[1] The sociology of knowledge, anthropology, linguistics, ethnography, and postmodern social and philosophical theories challenge the very foundation of liberalism, the ideas of liberal rationality, autonomy, and justice. For instance, Richard Rorty, a renowned American philosopher of pragmatism, severs the foundational link between Enlightenment rationality and liberal democracy, thus reducing liberal democracy to an aspect of political habits and the ethnocentric lifestyle of Western society. Michel Foucault finds in the liberal ideas of rationality and autonomy a subtle form of subjugation exercised through the disciplines and scientific knowledge of various mediating institutions of society. On the other hand, communitarianism challenges the foundationalistic presuppositions of liberalism. Communitarians such as Alasdair MacIntyre, Charles Taylor, Michael Walzer, and Michael Sandel, challenge the incoherence of liberal ideas of "the unencumbered self," neutrality, legislative rationality and autonomy, and universal morality. They contend that all ethics and morality are historically constituted and culturally situated. Therefore, the liberal ideas of freedom, autonomy, and inalienable rights, far from being universal, are historical, cultural products of a particular community.[2]

The challenge for liberal philosophy and institutions does not cease with the philosophical and intellectual challenge posed by postmodernity. The conventional functions of liberal institutions to maintain peace and order come under strains through a massive transformation taking place in contemporary society: globalization. Today, we are experiencing an increasing exchange, migration, and trade of peoples, cultural images and practices, and goods among different societies through the time-space compression made possible by technological-scientific innovations and advances. This situation of exchange and interconnectedness is conducive to the rise of religious, ethnic, and cultural pluralism in a society.[3] Globalization—and its ensuing pluralism—disrupts the taken-for-granted moral universe of a traditional society, challenging moral certainty, self-evident truth, routines, and the regularity of life in that society. This disruption inevitably evokes the senses of uncertainty, ambiguity, and dissonance. As various forms of values and beliefs move beyond their traditional boundaries and interact with each other, they are relativized. Unreflective spontaneity has disappeared and is replaced by constant demands of reflection, deliberations, and decisions. There is no available center of authority or a unified tradition to which individuals can easily resort for direction and accompanying guidelines. Society in this sense is turning into a religious and philosophical supermarket. Thus, there is validity to Peter Berger's assertion that "[w]hat previously was self-evident fact now becomes an occasion to choose....[T]he individual who is compelled to make choices is also compelled to stop and think. The more choices, the more reflection."[4]

At a glance, the process of globalization entails two seemingly contradictory reactions: global cosmopolitanism and local conservatism. On the one hand, through the expansion of communication technology, commerce, and popular culture, the world is experienced as an increasingly homogenized place. On the other hand, this process gives rise to a new challenge and threatens to disrupt each individual's religious, ethnic, and cultural tradition and identity. Struggles exist on the local or regional level for the confirmation and protection of traditional identity and beliefs. The surge of religious fundamentalism and conservatism is evidence of this phenomenon. On the global level, facing various forms of ethnic and religious conflict, we feel an urgent need for a universally-defined common moral standard. On the local level, however, we experience an intense need for confirmation of identity and tradition in reaction to the universalizing forces of technology and commercialism.

Without doubt, as the September 11, 2001 tragedy indicates, this condition generates a high possibility for conflict and clashes among religious and ethnic groups as religious groups protect their identities by asserting their boundaries. The world has increasingly witnessed the rise of religious and ethnic conflicts. These paradoxical phenomena of pluralism, relativization of values, and the rise of religious fundamentalism are associated with globalization, in one way or the other.

These intellectual and structural challenges raise serious questions for the problem of social order and justice for a global community: Can liberal democracy and human rights still continue their proper functions when their traditional philosophical foundation has collapsed? If liberal projects are dismissed as purely historical episodes or artifacts, what should be their alternative? That is, if liberal institutions are rejected, where can we find a viable institutional form, structure, and rule of order and justice?

The question of order and justice is an immediate and pressing concern to our society for the common survival and well-being of humanity. Global peace and justice, and, more fundamentally, the common survival of humanity, are not possible without a certain common moral ground which adjudicates conflicting claims among various religious and social groups. The philosophical paradigm change of postmodernity and structural transformation of globalization force us to reevaluate the historical role and function that liberal institutions have played for the order and justice of a human society in today's social context.

There are many critiques which dismiss the liberal institutions as Western cultural products and ideological constructs. There is some historical and philosophical validity for this claim. However, I contend that liberal institutions of democracy and human rights still provide some viable moral political elements for peace and justice in a global community. Despite many problems, one cannot simply disregard the positive functions and roles which liberal institutions are playing for the maintenance of order and justice today. It seems that the peace and order of a global society are inevitably associated with the status and value of liberal political institutions (especially democracy and human rights). The outright rejection of all liberal institutions, such as basic human rights, democracy, institutional pluralism, and rule of law, is not only absurd but also dangerous for the common well-being of society. Liberal institutions represent a collective human wisdom gleaned from painful experiences of religious wars, genocide, and struggle against absolutist states and monarchies. Liberal political projects have played a critical role for the adjudication of conflicts and the maintenance of peace and order. The social function of liberal institutions is indispensable as contemporary social conflicts move beyond the boundaries of Western societies. Today, whether one likes it or not, the liberal political institutions are increasingly adopted as prevalent political and legal systems of a global society. For example, human rights are emerging as the moral *lingua franca* of a global society, and there is a rising agreement that among many political experimentations, democracy is the best political system that human societies have so far invented. This implies that the collapse of liberal foundational philosophy is not equivalent to the abolishment of entire liberal institutions. In order to reconstitute liberal institutions in a new socio-cultural context, an alternative moral philosophy is desperately needed.

Liberal institutions face another challenge: religious conflicts. Because of this additional challenge, the relationship of liberal institutions and social order attains different, and more complicated, dynamics than in previous generations. The rise of religious fundamentalism and ensuing conflicts increasingly threaten the order and peace of many societies. As Hans Küng proclaims, there would not be any authentic world order or justice without peace among religious communities.[5] This implies that the questions of democracy, human rights, justice and order cannot be adequately dealt with unless religious communities are included as authentic partners of public discourse. Furthermore, as a postmodern critique of the foundationalist fallacy of a modern philosophy shows, there is no intellectual basis for secularists to dismiss religious belief or moral claims as simply private or personal opinions or ideas. These postmodern philosophical and societal changes warrant that religious communities have a legitimate place and claim in the public realm. In short, the relationship of religion and liberal institutions has become one of the most serious political and moral problems today. Global justice and peace are closely related to the question of how religious groups have to come to terms with liberal political institutions.

As the struggles of many Arab nation-states indicate, the situation today urgently requires reconceptualization of the relationship that religious communities have with liberal institutions. Christian communities in America are not exceptions to this challenge. There is an unceasing tension between religious communities and liberal institutions. The volatile moral situation forces Christianity to rethink its relationship with liberalism and its political institutions: what should be the shape of the relationship between liberalism and Christianity in a pluralistic society? Can Christian ethics embrace the liberal project without distorting its theological convictions and communal traditions? What should be the philosophical and theological bases of reconstruction? What are the philosophical and theological bases for postmodern Christian engagement in the public sphere? Does the post-liberal situation provide an intellectual free pass for Christians from public scrutiny and defense of their truth claims? Are liberal institutions necessarily detrimental to Christian convictions, and thus entities to be completely abandoned? Or is there still something to be critically appropriated by Christians? The attempt to answer these questions compels Christians to revisit the very foundations of their moral understandings and historical traditions. That is, these questions cannot be adequately addressed without a critical engagement and self-reflection on the theological and philosophical foundations of Christian ethics, which ultimately boil down to the question of Christian ethical methodology.

A Christian ethical methodology is concerned with the way a Christian reaches a decision, and it includes the process of evaluating and examining the options and courses of actions. This means that the process of decision-making inevitably engages with authoritative sources, such as Scripture, tradition, reason, and experience. Christian decisions acquire a theological legitimacy through their reference to these normative sources.

On the other hand, an ethical methodology must address the issues raised by a contingent situation. In a postmodern, global society, as discussed above, that is, through a varied accenting and weighing of the four sources of ethics (Scripture, tradition, reason, and experience) in response to the problems raised in a situation, a moral decision is reached. Ethical methodology in this process presents a rational way of discerning moral issues and guiding individual and collective human actions. Different methodologies of Christian ethics imply the different emphases and focuses on the four sources. This means that different Christian ethical methodologies inevitably carry in them different accents and nuances on the understanding of God, the world, moral agents, the relationship of individual and society, and the relationship of faith and reason.

In dealing with Christian approaches to liberal political institutions in a pluralistic context, this study intends to develop a new methodology of Christian ethics which is instrumental for Christian public engagement. The methodology of Christian public engagement must address the several distinctive challenges posed by intellectual, cultural and social changes. That is, Christians are challenged to deal with the question of how to celebrate their convictions in a religiously and culturally pluralistic society, without disregarding the presence and contributions of other religious traditions, yet at the same time, actively participating in the public life. Christians are invited to cooperate with other religious and cultural communities in order to serve and enhance the common well-being of humanity.

II. Thesis
I believe the liberal political project of democracy and human rights can be reconstructed on a new philosophical ground, despite the collapse of a foundational moral edifice. I contend that there are certain political and moral elements within liberalism which cannot be easily dismissed or abandoned, despite the collapse of its foundational philosophy. The construction of political and ethical methodology around these elements could be productive for the reconstruction of liberal institutions and consequently peace and justice in our society. These elements, which I call communicative requisites, could be retrieved on a non-foundational philosophical basis. Toward this end, Jürgen Habermas offers one of the most plausible philosophical methods to reconstitute liberal political institutions on a postfoundational philosophical ground. Habermas' project is characterized by how to reconstruct modern ideals—human rationality, democracy, subjectivity, and emancipation—on a postmodern philosophi-

cal basis. His achievements in the fields of contemporary philosophy and
social science are impressive. His work encompasses a variety of topics
and interdisciplinary fields, such as modernity/postmodernity, historical
materialism, hermeneutics, rationality, philosophy of language, public
discourse, system theory, etc.[6] Habermas is especially relevant because he
deals with various philosophical, political questions that bear upon communitarianism and liberalism. Habermas' communicative ethics provides
a philosophical and political alternative to the antithesis of communitarianism and liberalism. Habermas' theory synthesizes the communitarian
insights of situated moral reasoning and the liberal idea of universalizability of moral principles. Through a communicative model of ethical adjudication, his ethics responds to the concerns of the common morality and
historical contextuality, simultaneously.[7]

In this book, I contend that Jurgen Habermas' communicative ethics
provides a significant philosophical insight for a constructive methodology
of Christian ethics and a productive Christian relationship with liberal
institutions. Specifically, I contend, when appropriated into a covenantal-
trinitarian theological framework, a communicative ethical methodology
presents a plausible model of methodology for Christian ethics for public
engagements. The incorporation is possible because:

1) Habermas' communicative ethic shares theological and moral
presuppositions of the Reformed idea of covenant: freedom, equality, and
reciprocity. Covenant requires the participation of all concerned in the
process of a decision-making, and the grant of fair opportunity to each
party to mutually address and criticize common social problems and issues.

2) His formal-pragmatic methodology of communicative reasoning
exhibits dynamics and mechanisms which are strikingly similar to covenant. Covenant is arrived at through communication between different
parties. Covenanting includes the process of intersubjective practical reasoning to reach mutual understanding. Covenant is based on the agreement of people through the intersubjective process of presentation of
claims, mutual critique, argumentation, and acceptance. In short, communicative ethics employs a method of covenanting.

3) A covenantal religious tradition is not alien to liberal political
institutions or a modern project. Historically, the Reformed idea of covenant and its ecclesial institutions and practices (especially in the Free Calvinist Church tradition) played a formative role in the rise and
development of liberal politics and institutions in the West.

4) Communicative ethics implicitly envisions and privileges a form

Introduction 9

of life which is commensurate with the Christian ideal of the trinitarian Kingdom of God. The Trinity, as espoused by social trinitarian theologians, shows analogous communicative dynamics of freedom, equality, and reciprocity among the three trinitarian persons of Father, Son, and the Spirit. Specifically, I shall show how this communicative-covenantal action of God has a root in God's trinitarian perichoresis. This discovery has a profound implication for a constructive Christian theological ethics of communication. If covenant is the primary mechanism God uses in relating to humanity, and if covenant occurs through communicative engagement, then God's covenantal action with humanity also will take a communicative form.

Rooted in the doctrine of the Trinity and covenant, a new constructive Christian ethics, called covenantal-communicative ethics, responds to the demand of Christian public engagement without sacrificing particular Christian theological convictions. Covenantal-communicative ethics is constructive in reconceptualizing the relationship between liberal institutions and Christianity. It provides a theologically coherent and practically effective Christian approach to liberal political institutions. The idea of covenant, reconstituted in a communicative ethical framework, presents a relevant Christian methodology of public engagement in a more thoroughly democratic, inclusive, intersubjective manner than a classical covenantal theology by overcoming its difficulties (e.g. foundationalistic, hierarchical, and exclusivistic tendencies).

III. Order

This book consists of six chapters. Chapter 1 studies the tenets of Jürgen Habermas' theory of communicative action with the focus on communicative ethics. Engaging Habermas with liberals and communitarians, the chapter attempts to show the strengths and merits of Habermas in dealing with the challenges posed by a postmodern, global society, especially for the construction of common morality. The chapter also offers a critique of Habermas' limitations, especially his refusal to ascribe a positive role and function to religious discourse and communities for civil society and democratic politics.

Chapter 2 studies the covenantal theology of the Free Calvinists as a Christian political theory. Through the survey of the historical relationship of covenantal theology and liberal institutions, especially around the writings of H. R. Niebuhr and Max L. Stackhouse, it shows how the covenantal theological tradition has informed the rise and development of liberal institutions in America. After surveying the limitations and problems of a traditional covenantal theology, the chapter engages covenantal theology with Habermas' communicative ethics. The engagement between the two shows not only their compatibility, but also certain methodological consonance and commensurability which is instrumental for a constructive Christian ethics of public engagement which I call a covenantal-communicative ethics.

Chapter 3 further explores the significance of the idea of communication in conversation with the social doctrine of the Trinity. The chapter shows that the idea of communication does not merely pertain to the procedural-adjudicative aspect of a Christian life, but is integral to a Christian understanding of God's economy. A free, equal, and reciprocal communication reflects the structure of inner Trinitarian life, namely perichoresis. Perichoresis refers to a dynamic nature of God's trinitarian self-communication. Communication refers to the mode of God's action in history as God relates to humanity. The discussion identifies communication as a significant mechanism of divine-human, human-human interaction, and covenant as a structure of this communication. By showing the integral, organic interconnection among covenant, communication, and communion (perichoresis), the chapter demonstrates that covenantal-communicative ethics is justified by the most distinctive and unique Christian theological doctrine, namely the Trinity.

Chapter 4 explicates the tenets of covenantal-communcative ethics—its methodology, basis, and application. It will show the important contributions which covenantal-communicative ethics makes to Christian engagements in social spheres by reconstructing various themes of a traditional covenantal theology such as special grace, conscience, and the church.

Chapter 5 tests the merits and plausibility of the new ethics in conversation with other prominent contemporary Christian methodologies of ethics, notably Stanley Hauerwas' narrative ethics, David Hollenbach's Catholic theory of human rights, and liberation ethics.

The volume concludes with the assessment on how the discovery of communication, as a core moral process of divine-human and human-human interaction, contributes to Christian public engagement in a postmodern, global society.

Notes

1. "Postmodernity" is an extremely elusive term to define. It pertains to a major philosophical, cultural, and aesthetical sea-change taking place today. It roughly describes the currents of ethos underlying the thoughts and practices which celebrate differences, otherness, and contingencies, rejecting any idea of determinacy, metaphysics, canon, foundation, and universal morality. These traits are often identifiable in areas of creative expression such as art, including sculpture and architecture as well as literature and music, affirming indeterminacy, fragmentation, decanonization, hybridization, and so on. Yet, when we shift our focus to other realms, such as a political, economic, and institutional realm, the vagueness intensifies. In this volume, I use the term more in a descriptive sense than an evaluative one.

2. According to communitarianism, every moral knowledge and understanding is situated in history. The nature and structure of moral reasoning is dependent on a particular community's history, narrative, and convictions. There is no universal epistemological standpoint which is independent of the history and tradition of a particular community. Ethics always draws its basic premises, such as the ideas of the self, the world, and God, from a particular history and tradition of the community. Communitarianism emphasizes a practical constitutive power of a particular community, history and tradition for the formation of one's moral understanding and practices. A person is essentially a social being. A person's biographical history and social bonds are constitutive of selfhood. They identify liberalism as the primary source of moral erosion and fragmentation of self-identity. Therefore, in communitarianism, the good is prior to the right. The question of how a person ought to live depends on what kind of a community, history and tradition the person belongs to. A socially shared idea of the good, the common good, delineates how a society should be organized and how persons should live and be taught in virtue. However, since this is not a viable option today because of the radically pluralistic nature of our cultural life, some communitarians contend that for the time being, we must concentrate on raising a virtuous people in local communities.

3. *Globalization* is a widely used, fashionable word today. Although its technical definition is highly disputed together with its exact nature, scope and implication (Cf. world system theory, neo-liberal theory), it generally refers to the enduring patterns and tendencies of growing interconnectedness in the world through the rapid increase of political, economic, cultural, and social exchanges and interactions. That is, globalization refers to the historical-structural process through which the world is experienced as a single place and, thereby, various religious, cultural, and ethnic views and ideologies are brought into mutual

exposure, examination, and competition. It is questionable when and how exactly this phenomenon started. However, one cannot deny that the advance of productive forces has greatly contributed to this process. That is, the advance of science and technology, especially in the areas of communication, satellites, transportation, and trade has made the movement and exchange of people, goods, culture, symbols across borders, growing both in pace and in magnitude. Politically, the collapse of the Soviet Union and subsequent surge of capitalism and democracy as ubiquitous political economic institutions also dramatically intensified the discussion of this issue. In this volume, the idea of globalization will be used as a purely descriptive term, not as an evaluative or judgmental term which advocates the neo-liberal values of deregulation, free market, and exchange.

4. Peter L. Berger, *The Heretical Imperative: Contemporary Possibilities of Religious Affirmation* (Garden City, N.Y.: Anchor Press, 1979), 20.

5. Cf. Hans Küng and Karl-Josef Kuschel (eds.) *A Global Ethics* (New York: Continuum, 1993).

6. His work has been also widely discussed among Christian theologians and ethicists. Cf. Helmut Peukert, *Science, Action, and Fundamental Theology: Toward a Theology of Communicative Action* (Cambridge: M.I.T. Press, 1982), David Tracy, *Plurality and Ambiguity: Hermeneutics, Religion, Hope* (San Francisco: Harper & Row, 1987), Paul Lakeland, *Theology and Critical Theory: The Discourse of the Church* (Nashville: Abingdon Press, 1990), Don S. Browning & Francis S. Fiorenza, eds., *Habermas, Modernity, and Public Theology* (New York: Cross Road, 1993).

7. Cf. Seyla Behabib, *Situating the Self: Gender, Community and Postmodernism in Contemporary Ethics* (New York: Routledge, 1992) Behabib, in a Habermasian vein, contends that the concrete and situated individuality and the universality of principle are not mutually exclusive.

CHAPTER 1

JÜRGEN HABERMAS' COMMUNICATIVE ETHICS

I. Jürgen Habermas and Modernity/ Postmodernity

A. Communicative Ethics and Pluralism

Jürgen Habermas' communicative ethics responds to the pressing needs of social order and a common ground of moral adjudication in a pluralistic society. It provides a methodology to procure the minimal moral consensus which is indispensable for any society. It is grounded on the premise that the possibility of mutual understanding or agreement among diverse forms of life still strongly exists in spite of the radical diversity of human cultures and the plurality of life forms. Habermas contends that social order is practically possible on the basis of legitimately achieved norms and arranged institutions. Every speech-act has a built-in symmetrical structure of communication which makes mutual understanding possible, and provides the empirical ground for coordinated intersubjectivity with enormous implications for the renewal of human social life.

Habermas begins with the recognition that our world is inhabited by an irreducible variety of different forms of life and different concepts of what constitutes the good. The plurality of the good and their conflicts amounts to a threat to common human existence. Any society which lacks a shared morality is unable to maintain its order and life. The plurality of the good raises a question for social order: How is a rational adjudication of moral claims and a nonviolent resolution of conflicts possible? In a pluralistic society, according to Habermas, the basis of the social cooperation and social order can no longer rest upon a single conception of the good or a single metaphysics. The disruption of the lifeworld[1] has become a permanent characteristic of our life. The prospect for consensus on one historical form of the good is no longer promising. Instead, we must seek a way to harmonize the multiple existence of the good with the demand for social cooperation. To live in a pluralistic society raises the question: How should diverse groups regulate their social interactions? Cooperation is not to be understood as a categorical imperative but as a practical necessity. Some form of social cooperation is necessary for common human existence in order to cope with common problems facing society. For this process, conversation and compromise are indispensable elements. Habermas contends,

> That is why the radical skeptic's refusal to argue is an empty gesture. No matter how consistent a dropout he may be, he cannot drop out of the communicative practice of everyday life, to the presuppositions of which he remains bound. And these in turn are at least partly identical with the presuppositions of argumentation as such.[2]

How is cooperation possible? What is its basis? Habermas argues that the situation of pluralism forces us to be morally and ethically more reflective in searching and evaluating their moral perspective in comparison to other claims. A pluralistic society demands that one look beyond his or her own particular ethnic, religious, and cultural attachments, to understand the claims of other peoples. The reflective procedure becomes the indispensable and necessary aspect of ethical reflection. It is a unique dimension of a pluralistic, but highly interactive, and interdependent world. It is inevitable in order to deal with the plurality of conflicting claims, and the need to meet the demands of order and justice. Confronting each other, the religious and cultural communities also become more reflective in examining their traditions in dialogue with others.

> When culture has become reflexive, the only traditions and forms of life that can sustain themselves are those that bind their members while at the same time subjecting themselves to critical examination and leaving later generations the option of learning from other traditions or converting and setting out for other shores.[3]

Participants propose their needs and interests in the language of others; this requires a certain degree of imaginative abstraction from one's cognitive frames and linguistic interpretations, and, at the same time, the ability to understand other positions. Habermas says, "[T]he languages and vocabularies in which we interpret our needs/wants and explicate our moral feelings must be porous to one another."[4] This situation raises the questions of "(i) whether a reason that has objectively split up into its moment can still preserve its unity, and (ii) how expert cultures can be mediated with everyday practice."[5]

In a pluralistic society, moral decision is no longer made in unquestioned appeal to the authority of tradition or in reliance on the transcendental moral structure or the comprehensive idea of the good. Rationally motivated agreement is the only way to avoid the settlement of differences and conflicts by force and violation. Under the practical challenge of various conflicts, communication—not violence—is the ultimate answer to the problem. And public ethics inevitably turns on the question of justice because adjudication among the diverse forms of life and values is almost impossible. They are perceived to be equally legitimate. One cannot expect to resolve the problem of value conflicts by asking, what is good for me? but rather, what is good for us all? That is, one must ask, what is a generalizable, common interest for all of us?

B. Conflict Resolution

One can see that the methodology of Habermas is designed to deal with pluralism and conflict in the situation of the absence of a commonly-shared moral ground. For Habermas, practical discourse constitutes the alternative to violence, coercion, and manipulation. If one cannot convince others of the validity of claims by offering good reasons, then violence, coercion and evils of similar kinds are unavoidable consequences of public life. It anticipates non-violent strategies of conflict resolution yet without necessarily excluding the possibility of using violence as the last resort. It encourages cooperative and associative methods of problem solving.[6]

> Like all argumentation, practical discourse resembles islands threatened with inundation in a sea of practice where the pattern of consensual conflict resolution is by no means the dominant one. The means of reaching agreement are repeatedly thrust aside by the instruments of force. Hence action that is oriented toward ethical principles has to accommodate itself to imperatives that flow not from principles but from strategic necessities.[7]

The question of justice is raised when society requires the general assent on its basic social institutions and arrangements. Habermas contends that the question of justice can be resolved only in equal, impartial terms on the basis of the consent of all affected. For Habermas, "justice" is more a question of validity and cogency rather than of value. Questions of general interest are those that are recognized as valid by all affected. Thus, the scope of communicative ethics is limited to public moral conflicts. The questions of the good have their relevant place in an individual, private realm.

C. Critique of Liberalism and Communitarianism

In many ways, communicative ethics continues a Kantian project of a universal morality in a postmodern vein. Yet communicative ethics approaches the principle of universalizability in intersubjective, not subjective, terms. The principle of universalizability rests on intersubjective critique and the redemption of validity claims. Like Immanuel Kant, Habermas refuses to reduce morality to by-products of conventions, contingencies of culture, and traditions. He distinguishes rational justification from expedient political decision or bargaining of interests.

Unlike Kant, Habermas rejects the liberal idea of the unencumbered self and its foundational idea of reason and autonomy. He refuses to draw moral principles from the autonomous will of the individual. Rather, he places the possibility of universal moral adjudication on an implicit *telos* of language, i.e., understanding. With communitarians, he believes that our ethical cognition and moral motivation are shaped and conditioned in history. Social relations and bonds exist prior to individual autonomy and freedom. There can be no moral standpoint which stands outside history and tradition. Nor is there any transcendental morality which is predetermined and given for every person.

On the other hand, Habermas differs from communitarians in arguing that this priority of history and tradition does not mean relativism. Whereas many communitarians reduce the question of truth and morality to that of convention and historical custom, Habermas believes in the possibility of the rational adjudication and redemption of validity claims of truth and morality. This is important for our reconstructive project because it implies that Habermas still embraces some tenets of the Enlightenment and liberal democracy. Guarding against nihilism and relativism implicit in communitarianism, he refuses to completely relinquish the idea of reason and its emancipatory potency. He believes in the critical and emancipatory as well as unifying role of reason for social criticism and social cooperation. He believes that the possibility of the universalizable moral principle in postmodern society is critical for the sake of just order, democracy, and the common survival of humanity. Historical contingency and contextuality do not abolish the possibility of the universal redemption of validity claims. Yet, he attempts to reconstitute the unity of reason on a different ground, i.e., the intersubjective-procedural ground.

Habermas upholds the redemptive potential of intersubjective human discourse which may enable each participant to be critical of his or her own religious traditions, ethnic loyalties, and cultural conventions in adjudicating conflicting claims and arguments in the process of reaching necessary forms of social coordination. In short, he thinks that universalizability is still possible through public conversation and agreement. It implies that any proposition of truth or the claims of rightness can be judged and assessed only by the criteria of cogency.

This belief in universalizability is based on his observation that communitarians do not realize that one's pursuit of happiness or the good inevitably affects others, especially in a highly interdependent society such as ours. Therefore, individuals must figure out how to adjudicate differences. The communitarian approach suffers from the total deficiency of any objective standard or criteria of adjudicating normativity and truth. Humankind needs some criteria upon which to base our judgments of understanding and misunderstanding. Secondly, communitarians present an uncritical view of tradition, authority, and community. Relationality, or sociality, is subject to distortion by power. There is no pure form of symbolic exchange. Language also can be the medium of domination and manipulation, tradition and authority, when it is uncritically used or accepted. It distorts and destroys human dignity and solidarity. One, therefore, has to examine how the realities of domination, subjugation, and manipulation interfere with the process of ethical interpretation, reasoning, and schooling, and how one's particular social location constrains one's understanding of identity, values, and meanings of tradition. Hence, nonlinguistic forms of social constraints such as economic relationship and political domination must be considered in social analysis and ethical reflection. Individuals should not exclude the possibility that it is possible to share relatively objective standards of social action and relationality. A critical, trans-communal perspective is required to keep the necessary distance from destructive and oppressive aspects of one's convention. Habermas claims that the task of communicative ethics is to reconstitute the unity of reason and the possibility of common morality, together with a critical-reflective capacity of the self, on an intersubjective ground. As such, he believes, it can overcome the foundational fallacy of liberalism and the historical relativism of communitarians.

II. Communicative Action Theory

A. Types of Action

Habermas regards language as a constitutive aspect of human social life. Language shows that human beings are social beings, that is, not isolated, self-sufficient, self-enclosed subjects. Language is intersubjective by nature. Language obtains its currency and influence through the use of society. Human perception of reality is mediated by language. Social relations are established and maintained by language. Our perception of the world is constructed by language acts. Language exercises a formative power in shaping human individual and cultural identity. It constitutes the "universal medium" of human social life.

Habermas identifies two prominent modes of human speech interaction: strategic action which is oriented toward success, and communicative action which is oriented toward mutual understanding. Strategic action understands human relationship in terms of a means-ends relationship with a primal objective in a technological, bureaucratic control and domination of nature and system. Contrary to this, human interaction becomes communicative "when the participants coordinate their plans of action consensually, with the agreement reached at any point being evaluated in terms of the intersubjective recognition of validity claims."[8] Communicative action, oriented toward mutual understanding, is possible intersubjectively only when each participant attains free, equal opportunity of speech. On the contrary, strategic action takes language (rational discussion) as one of many media which a speaker employs in order to influence the opponent or to bring forth the intended effect and results. Strategic action tends to subordinate the communicative interests to the interests of another medium, such as money and power. Only a communicative model of action presupposes language as a genuine medium of unrestrained communication.

Communicative action attempts to reach consensus on four distinct areas of human validity claims: comprehensibility, truth, rightness, and truthfulness. The criterion of comprehensibility requires a speaker to speak something understandably to hearers. It has to do with the semantic, grammatical, and compositional dimension of a speech act. A speaker is required to construct a speech in a way that is comprehensible to hearers, following the semantical and grammatical rules of a particular language. Secondly, the validity of truth is concerned with the test of the claim on the objective reality. In a speech act, speakers offer *something* to understand for hearers. Communicative action in this domain investigates the factuality of the statement—whether the statement made is true or not to a situation or a reality external to both speakers and hearers. It is essentially descriptive in representing the relevant facts. Thirdly, the validity of right-ness deals with the question of whether the speech act is right with respect to the existing normative context. It is concerned with legitimacy of the norm. Its referent is the social world which is shared by speakers and hearers. Testing the claims on normative sanctions and regulating princi-ples, communicative action in this domain is basically evaluative.

Finally, the validity of truthfulness pertains to the domain of the subjective world of a speaker. It pertains to the question of sincerity or integrity of a speaker as a dialogical partner. By expressing one's inten-tions truthfully, one makes oneself trustworthy to others. Communicative action in this realm inquires the question of whether or not the intention of the speaker is truthfully expressed through conversations.[9]

B. System and Lifeworld

According to Habermas, the late industrial society consists of two parts: system and lifeworld. System refers to the functional-institutional core of modern society, namely the economy and the governmental admin-istrative system. Strategic action and instrumental rationality represents a prevailing type of action and morality here. System function is mediated through money and power. System and lifeworld operate through two dif-ferent modes of integration. Society can neither survive nor progress with-out some structured form of coordination. If society materially reproduces itself through the system, it symbolically reproduces itself through the lifeworld. Through system integration, society controls and regulates physical, biological environments and other social systems, and thus copes with various kinds of threats and challenges. The end of the system is its efficiency and effectiveness, and material growth and productivity.

The lifeworld refers to the totality of shared beliefs, values, and ide-als that society culturally inherits.[10] As such, it forms the horizon or the background for ethical decisions. Habermas identifies symbolic action as a prevailing mode of action in the lifeworld. Symbolic action underlies every aspect of socialization, identity formation, and public discourse. Individuals obtain their particular social identities through participation in the symbolic process of society. The lifeworld has two aspects of sym-bolic integration: normative and communicative. Normative integration is pre-reflective, precritical, customary, taken for granted, and repetition of the assumed normativity and expectation of society. Communicative inte-gration refers to the critical, reflective, argumentative process of reaching integration by bringing the problematic or contested social norms and their applications into public scrutiny. The lifeworld symbolically reproduces itself through communicative action.[11] Through such action, the lifeworld adjusts to a new situation—thus reintegrated—and transmits norms, values, and patterns of cultural tradition to a next generation. The successful function of both system integration and social integration is indispensable for the material survival, prosperity, and stability of society. If anomie, disorder, and anarchy are pathologies of social disintegration, low productivity, poverty, disease, malnutrition, and unemployment are the results of system disintegration. Habermas argues for the cooperation and balance of the two realms. The two functional activities must not interfere with each other but rather support each other.

However, the late industrial society is characterized by the domination of the system over the lifeworld. The social relations and life-process of the lifeworld are increasingly subordinated to the commodifying power of capitalist markets, money, and the impersonal bureaucratic control of the state. He calls this phenomenon the "colonization of the lifeworld" by the system. Habermas insists that these media of power exercised through the state and corporations be subjected to the collective will of the lifeworld. Otherwise, the system itself faces a series of crises, such as motivation crisis, rationality crisis, and legitimation crisis. The system depends on the lifeworld in its function, for the system borrows motivation, support, and legitimacy from the lifeworld.

III. Communicative Ethics

Communicative ethics refers to the aspect of communicative action which is concerned with the possibility of the rational adjudication of norms through discourse. It pertains to a human dialogical procedure seeking mutual understanding and agreement concerning the rightness of the norm. It takes place when the hitherto socially-accepted normativity of moral principles is challenged.

A. Methodology

1. Understanding

Habermas identifies understanding as the immanent goal of communicative human discourse. For him, every human language act, primordially, is oriented toward mutual understanding. Human discourse, although historically situated, is not purely contingent. Language, even in its radical form, does not abrogate the possibility of universal adjudication. Discourse carries in it the possibility of transcending various local traditions and forms of life, and to reach universal common understanding.

And this intrinsic *telos* provides a basis for rational discourse and the resolution of differences and conflicts. It is so because communication implies the cooperative search for consensus on various claims of truth, rightness, and truthfulness.

Discourse has both contingent and universal characteristics. Every claim is raised in a concrete historical situation, yet, once raised, it points its final redemption at the universal community of discourse. Habermas states,

> ...these validity claims have a Janus face: As claims, they transcend any local context; at the same time, they have to be raised here and now and be *de facto* recognized if they are going to bear the agreement of interaction participants that is needed for effective cooperation.[12]

In other words, every validity claim is, in principle, universally accountable and eschatological. The intrinsic *telos* of human speech points to the universal community of communication. This means that although reason does not operate outside a human language community, as a regulative idea of conversation, it has a capacity to go beyond its linguistic boundaries. Even if claims are raised here and now, in a specific historical context, they are, once raised, to be considered as claims of universal implication. They wait for the final redemption of their validities by all members of the human community. This *telos* intrinsic in the language event is the ground for social critique and social coordination, namely solidarity. This provides normative and critical thrusts to communicative ethics.

2. Rationality

Rationality refers to the human endeavor which tries to come to mutual understanding by overcoming differences and conflicts. Rationality is intimately related to the process of justification or the redemption of validity claims. It is an attempt to make something intelligible or sensible to others. When human beings experience discrepancies in their understandings, they try to resolve them through providing valid claims and warrants for their arguments.

Communicative ethics presents an intersubjective model of rationality. For Habermas, rationality is not the function of the faculty of the intuitive, individual subjective consciousness or transcendental epistemological capability. Rationality functions through the intersubjective exchange of argumentation and criticism. That is, rationality is manifested and concretized in history through intersubjective practices of free discourse. In Habermas' view, rationality is inevitably situated in a particular time and space as intersubjective discourse deals with various contingent social issues and concerns.[13] He notes,

> In culturally embodied self-understandings, intuitively present group solidarities, and the competence of socialized individuals that are brought into play as know-how, the reason expressed in communicative action is mediated with the traditions, social practices, and body-centered complexes of experience that coalesce into particular totalities.[14]

In this respect, Habermas' ethics is congruent with the historicist dimension of communitarian philosophy. Yet, his idea of rationality rejects any form of relativism. He believes that the historical grounding of human rationality does not repudiate a universal possibility of mutual understanding and agreement. His idea of rationality is predicated on the universal solidarity presupposed in language. By positing the universal, discursive unity of reason, Habermas tries to save rationality from the hands of defeatists and skeptics. In other words, he rejects a communitarian thesis of the incommensurability of life forms. He claims that "the borders of allegedly incommensurable worlds prove to be penetrable in the empirical medium of mutual understanding."[15] Habermas assumes that human discursive rationality has a capacity to achieve consensus on the universalizable norm by critically reviewing one's particular historical, ethical tradition. Habermas proposes a "weak and transitory unity of reason"—a linguistically embodied, but not defeatist, concept of reason.[16] The unity is not given but must be achieved through the actual participation of people.

Communicative ethics centers on the premise that every moral claim is open to rational evaluation and redemption. According to Habermas, the goal of this method is to encourage all moral agents to become involved and in so doing "to adopt a reflective attitude toward [their] own expressive manifestations," to "see through the irrational limitations" to which they are subject, and to "clarify [their] systematic self-deception."[17] Actual participation, interaction, and mutual exchange of validity claims are critical contours of moral reflection. In this respect, Habermas' theory is distinguished from John Rawls' idea of "the original point" or "the veil of ignorance." Habermas contends that it is not sufficient for one person to test the universalizability of maxim through examination of the consequence and implications of a contested norm upon others. Definition and discernment of moral situation and selection of the pertinent norms are relative to a person. There is no guarantee that every person in the identical situation would come up with the same result. This situation of relativity necessitates a justificatory process for a resolution of conflict. Benhabib is prudent in saying, "To judge rationally is not to judge as if one did not know what one could know (the effect of hanging the 'veil of ignorance'), but to judge in light of all available and relevant information."[18]

The effort to reach understanding inevitably presupposes that other participants are also free, equal beings. Genuine communicative discourse is possible only when speech is not constrained by a consideration other than that of reaching mutual understanding. Validity of argument is determined solely on the basis of cogency of argument, not upon privilege or status, motive, self-interests, coercion, utilitarian considerations or rewards for assent. There is no sacred or privileged area removed from mutual discursive examination. Participants evaluate the claims only on the basis of their validity.

3. Ideal Speech Situation

Communicative action proceeds under the presupposition of an ideal speech situation which indicates the counterfactual, ideal, epistemological condition in which the participants freely, without restraint or consideration of interests and consequences, engage in conversation. Habermas contends that when human beings, although always conditioned and limited by culture, tradition, and histories of community, enter into communication, they do not do so without believing in the possibility of mutual understanding. The attempt to reach mutual understanding presupposes the conditions of ideal communication in which every one has free, equal, and fair opportunities to make claims and counterclaims. Habermas calls this epistemological presupposition of conversation the "ideal speech situation." It is ideal because it exists only counterfactually as a presupposition of conversation and also because it *ideally* anticipates a certain fully emancipated, universal speech community. The ideal speech situation projects a form of life which is characterized by pure intersubjectivity and reciprocity.[19] In other words, the unlimited, free dialogue is posited as the regulative idea of the emancipated life. This regulative idea makes self-reflection and mutual critique possible and potent.

Habermas argues that the ideal speech situation is not an imposition of a particular moral vision. It is rather an unavoidable, constitutive, formal presupposition necessarily implied in the structure of human speech.[20] It idealizes the values that every participant is entitled to equal chances to speak, challenge, propose, and refute any raised questions. Habermas calls this the "general symmetry requirement." This implies that in the long run, no argument is exempt from mutual, critical examination.

As a counterfactual embodiment of a universal community, the ideal speech situation functions as a regulative ideal of immanent social critique and reconstruction. Specifically, understanding presents an empirical ground of normativity and critique for communicative practice. For Habermas, discourse is not a pure system of symbolic exchange. It often functions as a medium of domination, oppression, and manipulation. Human symbolic action and linguistic exchange are never free from nonlinguistic intervention or the influence of the political interests of domination, the material relationship of labor, capital, and constraints on our nature. There is always a possibility for partisan interests and ideology to interpenetrate one's claims of rightness. This awareness requires free, equal and fair speech and co-examination as the necessary aspect of human interaction and communication.

The idea of the "ideal speech situation" implies that there is an inherent connection between intersubjective recognition and justice. Free and undistorted communication and genuine consensus represent an ideal which our daily practice strives to approximate and the source of the true order. For Habermas,

> The anticipation of the ideal speech situation has...the significance of a constitutive illusion which is at the same time the appearance of a form of life. Of course, we cannot know *a priori* whether that appearance is a mere delusion—however unavoidable the suppositions from which it springs—or whether the empirical conditions for the realization of the supposed form of life can practically be brought about. Viewed in this way, the fundamental norms of rational speech built into universal pragmatics contain a practical hypothesis.[21]

As mentioned above, communicative action takes place against the background of the lifeworld when the spontaneity—the taken-for-grantedness of the lifeworld—is interrupted and suspended. Lifeworld names a symbolically shared structure of social intersubjectivity and mutual expectation. The lifeworld constitutes "the totality of socio-cultural facts." According to Habermas, it constitutes "a reservoir of 'taken-for-granteds,' of unshaken convictions that participants in communication draw upon in cooperative process of interpretation."[22] As the base and background of human language and culture, the lifeworld forms a horizon and context for human interaction, making human action and speeches intelligible for each other. It underlies and is present in every form of human action and interaction. The lifeworld is internalized in the individual members through the process of socialization. It takes a certain transcendental stance toward individuals. In turn, the lifeworld is maintained and reproduced through the dialogical praxis of the members. As such, it is the womb of individual identity, the source of socialization.

Communicative action, in this context, indicates a communal, dialogical attempt to repair this disrupted, shared, symbolic universe. The norms and values which have been uncritically accepted so far are brought into mutual test with regard to their validity and plausibility. Through communication, society's conventional beliefs, values, and ideals are brought to public scrutiny to bear mutual criticism. "Suppressed generalizable interests" are excavated into the true common interest of society, and nongeneralizable interests, with the guise of the common good or national interests (such as special interests of the dominant group), are criticized and finally dismissed. "Suppressed generalizable interests" are the kind of interests ultimately benefiting all but those which the system has not allowed so far to come to the surface. Through this process the lifeworld is reconstructed and its norms and values obtain new meanings.

4. The Process of Ethical Reasoning

Communicative ethics is composed of two processes—justification and application. If justification means the discursive selection of adequate maxims for action, then application means the practical employment of the selected moral principle to the case in a most appropriate way. This is according to the most exhaustive studies and analyses of the situation available today. Reciprocal justification is required for both the legislation of universalizable principles and their application to particular concrete cases.

The justification process includes the selection of appropriate maxims for action. Maxims constitute the smallest units regulating social intercourse and action. They represent "a network of operative customs in which the identity and life projects of an individual (or group) are concretized; they regulate the course of daily life, modes of interaction, the ways in which problems are addressed and conflicts resolved, and so forth."[23] The examination of maxims is guided by a series of implicit questions: How do I want to live? Is the maxim good for me? What is the right course of action for me? and Is this maxim right and appropriate in the given situation? This means that in the selection of the maxim, the moral and the ethical are compounded.[24] Each particular tradition may contain sets of norms/principles as distinguished from the good life it envisions. Communicatively achieved morality has a binding power over all persons equally and indiscriminately. Moral norms provide the minimal conditions of social coordination at an institutional and juridical level. They delineate some form of mutual moral expectations through which each person's pursuit of the good is directed in the context of social cooperation.

5. Tasks

The theory of communicative action enacts two political tasks for the lifeworld and the political community: critique and reconstruction. First, communicative ethics institutionalizes reciprocal critique as a constitutive aspect of political life. As communicative action is concerned with the construction of universalizable norms, it inevitably takes into account the cultural and institutional practices and social relationships of society. Habermas notes,

> ...membership in an ideal communication community has the power to burst bonds. The structures of nonalienated social intercourse provoke action orientations that reach beyond established conventions in a different way than universalistic orientations; they are aimed at filling in the spaces for reciprocal self-realization.[25]

The intersubjective process of reaching agreement provides the participants with the opportunity of critical detachment from their particular cultures and traditions. Habermas says that "Universalistic action orientations reach beyond all existing conventions and make it possible to gain some distance from the social roles that shape one's background and character."[26] The capacity of a critical distance embedded in a communicative process is crucial for a democratic politics. The communicative process exercises a prophetic function to challenge and correct the systematically distorted cultural presumptions, practices, and social arrangements which are supported by various strategic and instrumental forms of communication, rules, and conventions of society.

A communicative reasoning is typically called for when a usual current ("know-how") of the public life is disrupted. The disruption ordinarily includes the two characteristic situations: when validity claims do not correspond to the shared normative background of the lifeworld, and when the normative background of the lifeworld itself is questioned. In the former case, the hearer can reject the claim on the basis of the existing normative consensus of the lifeworld. The latter case refers to the situation where the hearer claims that the normative background of the lifeworld itself is systemically distorted and therefore needs to be reformulated. The scope and the magnitude of a normative crisis in this case are not comparable to the former where the social consensus remains intact. The overcoming of this challenge usually requires extensive and enduring social conversations and soul searches. Today the movement in favor of gay and lesbian marriage exemplifies this case. By arguing that heterosexuality is not constitutive of a conjugal relationship, the advocates of the movement challenge the conventional social presumption of marriage itself.

Communicative ethics performs another important service to the lifeworld. The communication process is the process of critical renewal and reconstruction of culture and tradition. It is instrumental for the construction of a new form of social integration and solidarity, and intervenes in the process of forming a personal identity. Communication renews previous cultural commitments and practices as they are constantly reexamined through the diverse groups and the members of a society. Regarding this creative process of communicative ethics for the renewal and reconstruction of the lifeworld, Habermas observes,

> In coming to an understanding with one another about their situation, participants in communication stand in a cultural tradition which they use and at the same time renew; in coordinating their actions via intersubjective recognition of critical validity claim, they rely on memberships in social groups and at the same time reinforce the integration of the latter.[27]

Further, he adds,

> Under the functional aspect of reaching understanding, communicative action serves the transmission and renewal of cultural knowledge; under the aspect of coordinated action, it serves social integration and the establishment of group solidarity; under the aspect of socialization, it serves the formation of personal identities.[28]

Thus, the relationship of communicative ethics to culture and tradition is dialectical—both continuous and discontinuous.

B. Communicative Idea of Morality and Laws

For Habermas, moral norms do not mean the sets of regulatory principles which exist independently of human history and culture, accessible only through intuition or by superior minds or reason. They refer to normative beliefs and principles which are shared by members of society as they live together. Moral norms, intersubjectively constructed, become the precondition for social cooperation. They delineate some form of mutual, moral expectations through which each person's pursuit of the good is directed in the context of social cooperation.

In Habermas' theory, this communicative notion of norms also applies to democratic laws. A modern democratic state is characterized by rule by laws. Laws provide the minimal degree of coordination and cooperation. Habermas says that laws find their "binding force from the alliance between the positivity of law and its claim to legitimacy"[29] Laws combine both compulsory and compelling dimensions, the threat of sanctions and an appeal to the shared convictions of people.[30] Yet, when society no longer has any shared metaphysical or religious basis for morality and law, where do morality and law derive their authority? Habermas finds it in the consent of people and the fair procedure of legislation. Laws are legislated through the democratic process on the basis of the consent of people. This implies that participation and free, unrestrained conversation are indispensable for the whole political process. Laws lose their legitimacy when they are not grounded in the democratic consent of the members.

Moral norms and laws, together, represent the formal, institutional modes of social integration which regulate and coordinate various human behaviors. Their role is indispensable to control social conflicts and maintain the order. Habermas writes,

> Morality and law are specifically tailored to check open conflict in such a way that the basis of communicative action—and with it the social integration of the lifeworld—does not fall part. They secure the next level of consensus to which we can have recourse when the mechanism of reaching understanding fails in the normatively regulated communication of everyday life, that is, when the coordination of actions anticipated in the normal case does not come to pass and the alternative of violent confrontation becomes a reality.[31]

Communicatively achieved moral norms and laws take a symmetrical and impartial nature. Legislated by all concerned members of society, the discursively obtained norms and laws incarnate the generalized interests of society.

C. Communicative Ethics and Democratic Politics

1. Participation

The communicative ethic institutionalizes the participation of all concerned members in public discourses and decision-making processes. Communicative ethics is "an ethics of practical transformation through participation."[32] The question of membership and participation, who are involved and who are excluded in conversation, is a critical question for ethics. Injustice, in its primal form, is often associated with a willful exclusion of a particular group of people (race, ethnicity, gender, and class) from public policy-making processes. That is, the absence of communicative participation of the members of society is either the indication of their own malaise regarding the public life or the evidence of their oppression and marginalization by others.

2. Freedom of Speech

By positing a free and equal dialogue as a constitutive procedure of ethical methodology, communicative ethics contributes to the democratization of a society. A just society presupposes the free, equal participation and self-determination of people. Through conversation, authoritarian and patriarchal cultural norms and practices—together with other systemically distorted forms of public discourses—are brought to mutual examination and critique for the reconstruction of a social life.

3. Solidarity

The communicative process, through its emphasis on participation and free and equal speech, serves as the process of "democratic will formation." The democratic will refers to a generalized will of people. Communicative action combines actions of separate individuals into a coordinated plan of action. It emerges when actions of separate individuals are combined into a coordinated plan of action. That is, through a public discourse, private or individual morality is transformed, via the communicative process, into general moral concern, and narrow self-interests are transformed into the common interests. The process of reaching consensus is simultaneously the process of exploring possible connections and potential commonalities across the different forms of goods, as well as adjudicating the differences and consequently bringing solidarity.[33]

By inviting every member to the process of a public discourse, communicative ethics ties the democratization process with the cultural renewal of society. The communicative process is crucial for the cultural renewal because through their participation, diverse social groups inevitably bring and share their diverse and rich cultural insights, perspectives, and traditions on the public life with others. Communicative ethics ensures that democracy is not isolated from culture and tradition. At the same time, it continuously receives new stimuli and motivations from the latter. In this respect, communicative ethics preserves a critical, democratic, and inclusive thrust which is improbable in any monological or foundational form of ethics.

Habermas' theory of communicative ethics offers a new perspective on the nature of social integration in a postindustrial society. There is no *a priori* theory of solidarity. Solidarity is not given either in nature or in a metaphysical principle, nor is it derived from any singular, predetermined form of the good. Rather, it arises through the process of discursive exchange of validity claims. Solidarity is achieved by means of actual political engagement and struggle. Solidarity is continuously renewed through a communal reflective process.[34] Every social arrangement is determined by the members through public discourses in the context of actual social needs and cultural conditions. The legitimacy of a political system is measured by the criterion of whether social institutions and their arrangements are congruent with the general will of all those affected by them.

D. Moral Agency: Post-Conventional Self

Habermas rejects the liberal idea of the unencumbered self. A human being is a social and relational being. Personal identity is formed and achieved only through social interaction and socialization. The fact that a human being is social is most distinctively demonstrated by his or her dependence on language and communication for social survival and cooperation. The use of language and communication grants human beings the unique possibility of raising and challenging the claims presented by others, that is, to be critical and reflective, and to adjudicate and coordinate differences for the sake of common interests.

This critical reflexive capacity of the agent is especially important in a pluralistic society, for it enables the agent to take a post-conventional attitude toward one's tradition and community. That is, the agent no longer coordinates his or her action solely by appealing to the good of his or her own community. The agent is able to modify and correct his or her claims through the process of communication. Habermas refers to this reflective nature of the agent as post-conventional. His view is based on the observation that social differentiation in a pluralistic society has resulted in the overburdening of the self, being divided by conflicting claims of values which can lead to the disintegration of the conventional self.

Yet this disintegration is not necessarily detrimental. It is rather an ambivalent process. The process of disembedding could be emancipatory by liberating individuals from the shackles and bondage of traditional forms of social hierarchy, conventions, and the systematically distorted form of communication. It could also lead to the destructive abyss of fragmentation and anomie. Through the process of intersubjective critique, the agent may overcome the danger of fragmentation and be led to the re-integration of the self on a more flexible and reflective basis.

A post-conventional self takes a critical and reconstructive attitude toward one's tradition, history, and narrative. It is highly aware of the fact that human interpretation of needs and wants is always culturally mediated and socially conditioned. "Needs and wants are interpreted in the light of cultural values. Since cultural values are always components of intersubjectively shared traditions, the revision of the values used to interpret needs and wants cannot be a matter for individuals to handle monologically."[35] However, this post-conventional idea of the self does not imply the complete desertion of one's tradition and history. As Habermas puts it, "If the actors do not bring with them, and into their discourse, their individual life-histories, their identities, their needs and wants, their traditions, memberships, and so forth, practical discourse would at once be robbed of all content."[36] The idea of a post-conventional self rather speaks of the possibility of reconstructive possibility of selfhood and identity through social interaction.

E. The Right and the Good

Communicative ethics does not regard the relationship of the right and the good as irreconcilable. It brings the two into a constructive tension and critical harmony through intersubjective rationality.
Communicative method refuses to subordinate particular theological convictions and beliefs to the preconceived universal moral principles.
The latter are constructed through mutual argumentation, discernment, and deliberations among people with different religious perspectives and moral understandings. In other words, communicative ethics puts the relationship of the right and the good in a constant, dialectical tension and balance. The right is illuminated and enlightened by the good for the con-

creteness/empiricity of its stipulation, whereas the good maintains its
moral legitimacy through its capacity to accommodate the right which is
intersubjectively achieved.

The relationship of the right and the good is most systemically discussed in Habermas' explication of social morality. According to Habermas, the rise of social morality has to do with the protection of the vulnerability of individuals and solidarity. Social morality postulates two things:
equal respect for each individual and the protection of the well-being of
society within which individuals engage each other. In other words, as a
social mechanism to protect vulnerable individuals from abuses and violence, morality is grounded in the inviolability of the individual (which
postulates equal respect for the individual) and in the well-being of society
(which postulates social solidarity) at the same time. Habermas says,
"[Morality] cannot protect the rights of the individual without also protecting the well-being of the community to which he belongs."[37]

He identifies social interaction as the source of individual vulnerability as well as of morality. These two aspects, vulnerability and solidarity, are converged in discourse as the primary form of human social
interaction. As discourse is a primary social mechanism which mediates
individuals and society, it is attentive to both particularity of the individuals and the solidarity of society. Individuals are individuated (thus become
individuals) through the socialization process, specifically through linguistically mediated interaction. As they are socially individualized, they become vulnerable in their increasingly extensive exposure to others. The
more they are exposed to this process, the more they are vulnerable to others.[38] The need for morality emerges in this process for the protection of
the vulnerable individuals. That is, they are in need of moral consideration
by others, and morality fulfills this function.

As such, Habermas proposes an inextricable link between justice
and solidarity, duty and the good. Habermas notes, "Justice concerns the
equal freedom of unique and self-determining individuals, while solidarity
concerns the welfare of consociates who are ultimately linked in an intersubjectively shared form of life."[39] The relationship between justice and
solidarity is not antithetical but complementary. For both duty and the
good, justice and solidarity share one and the same root: the vulnerability
of the individuals and their protection in social life.[40]

Hence, in communicative ethics, individual freedom and social solidarity are not antithetical, but internally connected by virtue of the intersubjective nature of human discourse and social life. In other words, the
ideas of freedom and solidarity are mutually implicated in the intersubjec-

tive nature of human existence. Here freedom does not mean neutrality or abstraction from particularity, but an equal and symmetrical opportunity to speak and engage reciprocally. In communicative ethics, freedom, constituted in sociality and language, is not private, but public in nature. Nor does solidarity mean uncritical loyalty to a particular idea of the good; it is what emerges out of the continuous social interaction of intersubjective critique and agreement. Solidarity means the achieved social agreement which gives human actions predictability and structure. Respect for individual freedom is indispensable for the formation of solidarity. For individual freedom and social solidarity are internally connected through intersubjectivity of human discourse. He notes,

> The agreement made possible by discourse depends on two things: the individual's inalienable right to say yes or no and his overcoming of his egocentric viewpoint. Without the individual's uninfringeable freedom to respond with a "yes" or "no" to criticize validity claims, consent is merely factual rather than truly universal. Conversely, without the empathetic sensitivity by each person to everyone else, no solution deserving universal consent will result from the deliberation. These two aspects--the autonomy of inalienable individuals and their embeddedness in an intersubjectively shared web of relations--are internally connected, and it is this link that the procedure of discursive decision-making takes into account.[41]

Thus, the discursively achieved solidarity "encompasses both a concern for a (thin) common good (or group/lifeworld integrity) and a concern for the individual's good."[42]

F. Communicative Ethics and Civil Society

Habermas divides political power into two types: communicative and administrative. If communicative power operates in the lifeworld, administrative power has its primary place in the system function. Although in their function, communicative power and administrative power are complementary for social well-being, administrative power must be checked and guided by communicative power. Otherwise, the colonization of the lifeworld is unavoidable. Administrative power of institutions has its origin in communicative power. That is, formal institutions draw their energy and stimulus from people's communicative participation. The unilateral domination of administrative power is detrimental to the body politic and ultimately threatens the basis of democracy itself. The state under rule of law (*Rechtsstaat*) and its institutions must be bound by and responsible to communicative power and protected from the domination of administrative power.[43] In short, formal institutions do not live through administrative power, but through the communicative recognition of people.[44]

Communicative power is produced through mutual recognition and bestowal of legitimacy by people. Communicative power, as the source of the communicative consent of people, becomes the basis of popular sovereignty. However, the popular sovereignty here does not mean the sovereignty of autonomous individuals. Popular sovereignty is formed and exercised in various intermediary institutions where the non-expert culture abounds through everyday discursive interactions and opinion formations. He notes,

> In the *Rechtsstaat* as conceived by discourse theory, popular sovereignty is no longer embodied in an identifiable assembly of autonomous citizens. It draws back into the so to speak subjectless communication circuits of forums and associations. Only in this anonymous form can its communicatively fluid power bind the administrative power of the state apparatus to the will of the citizens.[45]

Habermas envisions a dynamic complementary relationship between formal institutions and the informal, non-institutionalized communicative processes of opinion formation and circulation. That is, democratic politics cannot function properly or survive either by a formal legal guarantee for private autonomy alone or by administrative social engineering alone. The ongoing flow of informal communication and the sharing of public opinions are the lifeblood of democracy and the basis of its institutions. Habermas recognizes the significance of the informal structures of dialogue, mutual recognition, and opinion formation for democracy. Spontaneity cannot be compelled by law; it is to be regenerated out of traditions of freedom, and it preserves itself in the associative relations of a democratic political culture.[46] The proper function of democracy requires a certain ethical disposition and undergirding within the lifeworld. Democracy thrives upon communicative power, and communicative power itself depends on particular traditions of the lifeworld which encourage freedom, equality, and participation.

The public sphere is where democracy takes place and is operative. The public sphere is "a network for the communication of contents and the expression of attitudes, i.e., of opinions, in which the flows of communication are filtered and synthesized in such a way that they condense into public opinions clustered according to themes."[47] Therefore, the relationship of formal institutions and the informal communication process of the public sphere is complementary. Democratic politics is dependent on the public participation of people. Formal institutions and laws are best understood as the configuration of the cluster of consensus achieved through democratic process on various themes, issues, wants, and needs.

Habermas refuses to introduce or endorse any one particular type of religious tradition or the good to achieve this goal. He does not believe that the problem can be solved through the reintroduction of a particular form of the good, for our society has outgrown religion, he says, and a radical form of plurality does not allow this option. A proper function of democracy, in his view, demands a critical distance from one's own religious tradition. However, as will be discussed in the next section, the rejection of religious traditions is not the only political option available today. Rather, I shall argue that the function of democracy requires the support and empowerment of religious traditions. Democracy and the *Rechtsstaat* cannot sustain themselves without the undergirding tradition. I shall show how his pragmatic methodology could provide insights for the adjudication of various forms of the good. One may say, among various traditions available in our society, some traditions may be more effective in the generation of communicative power, while others may not. And some forms of religious life may be more congenial to the spirit of communicative ethics.

IV. Critique of Habermas: Habermas and Religion

A. Contribution
Habermas' communicative ethics effectively addresses the political and moral concerns raised by globalization and pluralism. Habermas' ethics suggests an alternative to the two extreme responses to postmodernity, deconstructionism and neo-Aristotelian communitarianism. He seeks to retain the rational, emancipatory ethical impulses of modernity on a non-foundational philosophical ground. He turns to the discursive, intersubjective form of rationality as the alternative to the Kantian transcendental subject. He shows that the adjudication of truth and justice is possible while respecting the plurality of moral visions and stories. As a conversation continues, one could not deny the possibility that "overlapping consensus," or the fusion of horizon arises among different groups, despite

their differences on the nature of the ultimate good. His method also responds to liberationist concerns. The idea of intersubjective rationality provides the formal-procedural ground to exercise a critique of ideology and of instrumental rationality reigning in a global society, namely a technological control, scientism, and commercialism. By identifying this intersubjective rationality as the core of ethical methodology of critique and adjudication, Habermas contributes profoundly to the possibility of public discourse in a postmodern, global society.

B. Critique

By proposing a more adequate methodology of ethics dealing with pluralism, Habermas' communicative ethics suggests a reconstructive possibility of liberal projects in a postmodern society. Also, Habermas' methodology provides methodological insights to overcome the limits and difficulties both liberalism and communitarianism. Habermas points out that the neo-Aristotelian critique of modernity is very limited and flawed because it fails to cope with a more complex version of liberalism. Habermas' critique of Alasdair MacIntyre is relevant on this point:

> MacIntyre makes things too easy for himself from a critical perspective by selecting in Alan Gewirth an untypical and rather easily criticizable example of a universalistic position instead of dealing with Rawls or Dworkin or Apel. Second, his appeal to the Aristotelian concept of praxis gets him into trouble as soon as he tries to extract a universal core from the pluralism of equally legitimate forms of life that is unavoidable in modernity. Where can he find an equivalent for what Aristotle could still fall back on--I mean a substitute for the metaphysical preeminence of the *polis* as the exemplary form of life in which people (all those, that is, who do not remain barbarians) could realize the goal of a good life?[48]

Habermas' ethics is helpful in pointing out the elements which are indispensable for the construction of a legitimate, democratic form of social order in a pluralistic society. Furthermore, by constituting universal participation with free, equal, intersubjective critique at the center of ethical methodology, Habermas' ethics has an effect of rejecting domination and hegemony which are increasingly prevalent as globalization expands and intensifies. However, Habermas' view faces several difficulties in evaluating the role and function of religion in a global society. His view of religion is biased with a modernist prejudice.

1. Habermas and Religion

Habermas regards every form of religion, either mythic or traditional metaphysical, as the obsolete form of social morality. He believes that modern society has come of age, and individuals have outgrown religion. Habermas' modernist prejudice is found especially in his evolutionary view of social morality. Expanding Max Weber's theory of rationalization, he contends that social morality has evolved from mythic forms of primitive religions to metaphysical forms of traditional religions, and finally to a public, discursive and rational form which is exclusive of/beyond religion. The rise and expansion of the rational and universal form of morality are inversely related to the gradual recession, or "linguistification" in Habermas' term, of the religious form of morality. In a secularized modern society, the bonds of a traditional, "sacrally protected normative context" has given way to a discursive form of legislative morality.[49] He believes that today the integrating and legitimizing power of religion has been replaced by the uncoerced "binding/bonding force" of discursively obtained public consensus.

This modernist, evolutionary view is not only unfair but it also runs the risk of ignoring the significant roles that religion plays in contemporary society. His view does not respect any positive role which religious groups play in the public realm. Surely, this is a great disservice to public discourse because today religions constitute the most prominent and resilient undercurrent of the lifeworld. Far from being obsolete or irrelevant, religions are resurgent in almost every corner of the world as significant political and social players, as cultural and moral forces today. Rather than completely secularized and disenchanted, our society, on a certain level, is experiencing the process of reenchantment and desecularization.[50] The increased role and the expanding appeal of religious beliefs are strongly felt in a global society. The public role of religions, whether positive or negative, is impressive, as shown in the Civil Rights Movements in the United States of America, the Islamic Revolution in Iran, and religiously inspired liberationist movements in the Third World countries. As global society is witnessing the eruptions of religious conflicts, the exclusion of religious groups from public discourse is not only impractical, but also unproductive for the cause of peace and social justice.

Habermas contends that religious beliefs are hierarchical and predetermined, thus incommensurable with a public discourse. Contrary to his claim, religious beliefs are hardly monolithic or predetermined. Nor is every religion necessarily theocratic or authoritarian. Some religions, especially monotheistic-prophetic religions such as Judeo-Christianity, as

Max Weber analyzed, have played a critical role in the process of the de-sacralization (disenchantment) of Western society. Furthermore, religious discourse is analogous to rational discourse. Religious discourse takes a rational form in seeking mutual understanding and agreement. Members of religious communities make strenuous efforts to arrive at consensus on significant moral issues or doctrinal matters. As the history of Christianity demonstrates, through various councils and movements, religions often allow their traditional creeds and conventional practices to be "problematized" or thematized to achieve a new form of understanding and consensus in responding to changing environments.

If it is the premise of communicative ethics that the agreement regarding common moral principles is possible through critical conversation despite different conceptions of the good, no conceptions of the good life, such as religious ones, should be excluded from the process of public discourse. Religious notions, ideas, and languages cannot be permanently bracketed from public discourse because the latter constantly borrows its ideals, values, and notions from the former. The narrow identification of public discourse with rational, non-religious discourse will not only truncate the richness of the human speech act, but also unfairly marginalize religious groups and their members from the public realm whose lives are formed around religious symbols and metaphors. This intellectual stance has the effect of reducing the richness and complexity of human discourse into a narrowly rational one. As sociologist Robert Wuthnow contends, the exclusion may be tantamount to another enthronement of instrumental reason over the lifeworld.[51]

2. Social Spheres

Habermas' bias against religion is also disclosed in his discussion of the integration of social spheres. Habermas recognizes the need for a balance among various social spheres. In the midst of a highly functional differentiation and the subsequent narrow, specialized definition of expertise, society is losing its sense of wholeness and coordination. The unbalanced and incoherent progression of differentiation of the social spheres results in the fragmentation of social life and the increasing domination of instrumental rationality over communicative rationality. His theory of the colonization of the lifeworld is concerned with the dilemma which a post-industrial society faces in balancing and harmonizing various independent social spheres. He contends that the overgrowth of the system (through its uncoupling from the lifeworld) eventually led to the colonization of the lifeworld by administrative and economic spheres. Colonization indicates the breakdown of balance, harmony, and integration as the bureaucratic-administrative system and market economy intrude into the realms of other spheres, such as family, culture, arts, etc.

He strongly feels that some sense of harmony and balance must be restored without violating the specialized functional autonomy and inner logic of each sphere. His understanding is based on the observation that each sphere is "incomplete in itself." Various spheres are interdependent as they constantly interact with each other and require one another to function properly and to fulfill their tasks. For example, as Habermas aptly analyzes in *Legitimation Crisis*, the function of the administrative and economic spheres requires the lifeworld's support in securing political legitimacy and in equipping members with adequate motivations to participate and pursue goals in those spheres.[52]

However, Habermas refuses to ascribe this balancing and integrative function to religion even to its most limited degree. Instead, as the source of balance and harmony, he appeals to "intuitive knowledge of unity" which we "always already" implicitly utilize and employ in our daily discursive activities.[53] Elsewhere, he argues that radical forms of differentiation and extreme specialization need to be mitigated by "an equilibrated interplay of the cognitive with the moral and the aesthetic-expressive."[54]

Habermas' approach poses a question: If the spheres of the lifeworld need to be invigorated against the colonizing intrusion of the system, and if some degree of integration is indispensable for a proper coordinating functioning of society, to what extent can this invigoration and integration be achieved through a mere reliance upon intuitive knowledge alone? If the lifeworld itself is severely impaired, or *colonized* to use Habermas' term, where can one find the resources for rejuvenation and restoration? It should be noted that historically those insights or the intuitive knowledge, which Habermas identifies as the basis of social integration, have been originated from religious traditions. As Michael Wazer's theory of 'sphere justice' suggests, the contemporary western notion of sphere is religiously informed, specifically by Judeo-Christianity. Religion indicates a world perspective which encompasses all three spheres of validity (cognitive, moral, and expressive) in an integrated way. Today the resistance and struggle against the domination of cognitive-instrumental rationality (and the colonization of the lifeworld) is most strenuously and effectively enacted by religious groups in terms of advocacy of their family values, civic virtues, religiously informed ecological and liberation movements, etc.

3. Communitarian Virtues and Communication

Habermas' communicative ethics presumes the commitment of speech participants to the value of benevolence. That is, when a person enters a public discourse, he or she does so with the expectation that he or she will be treated fairly. As we have seen, this expectation is embodied in his idea of the "ideal speech situation." This implies that communication, to function properly, relies upon at least some minimum form of trust and commitment, available in the lifeworld. As Habermas himself acknowledges, "The equal rights of individuals and the equal respect for the personal dignity of each depend upon a network of interpersonal relations and a system of mutual recognition."[55]

Religious languages and practices contribute to the enhancement of the affective, empathetic, and compassionate dimensions of human relationships. As religion is significantly involved in the process of socialization and identity formation, it can assist public discourse by forming and strengthening rudimentary and embryonic forms of trust and commitment in the lifeworld. Religion presents probably the most resilient and distinctive basis of identity and dedicated affection.

Specifically, this implies that a certain religious tradition, such as covenantalism, may provide much needed resources to nurture empathetic and compassionate attitudes, if that religious tradition is supportive for the communicative ethical values of equal respect, mutual recognition, and empathy through its religious beliefs and practice. If a strong habit and ethos of respecting freedom, equality, and fairness are inculcated and supported by a religious tradition, it will greatly empower and facilitate the enterprise of communicative public discourse. Furthermore, without the continuous support and contribution of a viable religious tradition to the revitalization of the lifeworld, communicative ethics will increasingly deplete the reservoirs of social trust and benevolence, in the face of the colonizing forces of money and technocratic power

Habermas' theory has been criticized for its abstractness, formality, and universalism. Specifically, the idea of "ideal speech situation" has been the focus of criticism. Critics of Habermas doubt that the counterfactual idea of the ideal speech situation alone can secure the condition of unrestrained communication among participants against the recalcitrant forces of self-interest, greed, and ambitions to dominate. They point out that in human history the reality of human sin and egoism is often stronger than the ideals of mutual respect. According to the critics, Habermas' communicative ethics, in the final analysis, cannot but rely upon a particular historical-cultural tradition for its effective function. For example,

Gadamer argues that every critique is historically situated; there is no Archimedean point of critique in history. Hence, the very ideas of "ideal speech situation" and of "ideology critique" are illusory; they present a particular form of moral history and tradition. Gadamer contends that unless some truth of solidarity of the ethical spirit and some community of ethical tradition are already present and operative, ideology critique is hardly possible, not to mention the improbability of any positive impact it might have on social change.[56]

Similarly, Paul Ricoeur, joining Gadamer, contends that ideology critique is a tradition. As such, it is possible only within the tradition of emancipation. He says that ideology critique, in order not to be empty and ineffectual, needs a concrete form of life and tradition which attends to the moral concerns of emancipation. He notes,

> Distortion can be criticized only in the name of a consensus which we cannot anticipate merely emptily, in the manner of a regulative idea, unless that idea is exemplified; and one of the very places of exemplification of the ideal of communication is precisely our capacity to overcome cultural distance in the interpretation of works received from the past. He who is unable to reinterpret his past may also be incapable of projecting concretely his interest in emancipation.[57]

Yet, Ricoeur is more specific than Gadamer in pointing out that in western history the Christian theological tradition of Exodus and Resurrection has been the historical source of social critique. He says that only the creative renewal of cultural heritage such as the Exodus tradition and the Resurrection would concretely support communicative action. He says, "Perhaps there would be no more interest in emancipation, no more anticipation of freedom, if the Exodus and the Resurrection were effaced from the memory of mankind [sic]..."[58]

If Ricouer's critique of Habermas is correct, then the linkage between Habermasian ethics and Christianity becomes much closer than one may imagine. For emancipation and reconciliation represent the core values of Christian moral tradition. As discussed later, the Christian idea of covenant presents a religious tradition which is able to attend to the moral concerns of both emancipation and reconciliation which Habermas' theory implicitly promotes.

4. Rationality and Religious Discourse

Habermas delimits the possibility of discursive redemption of validity claims narrowly to non-religious speech acts. Habermas contends that religious speeches are beyond public adjudication. They are either too narrow or too general to give an action orientation to people in the public realm. Habermas believes that the questions of religious truth claim must remain in the realm of a personal subjective expression. By isolating all non-rational forms of speech, such as aesthetic, poetic, or metaphoric ones, from the normal, problem-solving function of rational language, Habermas relegates the former to a subordinate, supplementary status.[59] It is based on his observation that religious discourses can hardly be thematized in terms of truth, rightness, and sincerity. Specifically, metaphoric languages are removed from a problem-solving function of speech act because they are not communicative, bracketing the operation of illocutionary force. Habermas says that metaphoric, poetic languages are self-referential as their utterances are directed to the linguistic medium itself.[60] However, his assertion, contrary to our common experience, presents a very narrow understanding of metaphors, symbols, and religious discourses.

According to Sallie McFague, symbolic or metaphorical thinking constitutes the foundation of human thinking and languages.[61] Our ordinary thinking and speech rely upon symbols and metaphors for the construal of their meanings and contents. Metaphors and symbols are the way we understand the world. Reality cannot be described without them. From our infancy, we construct our world through symbols and metaphors. All concepts, ideas, and rational speech are metaphoric or symbolic in nature to the extent that they indirectly interpret reality. Hence, analogy is essential to a symbolic, metaphoric thinking.

Symbols and metaphors point to the reality which is beyond literal description. They are not nominal. They have objective referential values. However, symbols and metaphors do not exhaust the mystery of reality. Symbols and metaphors are especially fit to explicate the reality which is beyond any literal description. They are capable of disclosing complex, unknown reality (with its numerous meanings and dimensions) in multiple, varied ways. Symbols and metaphors enable us to see reality in an unusual and innovative way. Sallie McFague says,

> Far from being an esoteric or ornamental rhetorical device superimposed on ordinary language, metaphor *is* ordinary language. It is the *way* we think. We often make distinctions between ordinary and poetic language, assuming that the first is direct and the sec-

ond indirect, but actually both are indirect, for we always think by indirection. The difference between the two kinds of language is only that we have grown accustomed to the indirections of ordinary language; they have become conventional. Likewise, conceptual or abstract language is metaphorical in the sense that the ability to generalize depends upon seeing similarity within dissimilarity; a concept is an abstraction of the similar from a sea of dissimilars.[62]

The distinction between symbolic or metaphoric language and rational language is far from being as absolute as Habermas suggests. Symbols and rational concepts are not antithetical; i.e. they are symbiotic. Religious metaphors and symbols feed and enrich rational discourse and rational discourse disciplines and generalizes metaphors.[63]

Symbolic and metaphorical languages possess fertility. Fertility indicates how effectively and comprehensively a symbol or metaphor communicates the diverse dimensions and elements of the invisible reality in response to various human situations.[64] That is, a fertile symbol retains the capacity for diverse sacramental expressions and conceptualizations in response to the different needs and problems of various people. Metaphors and symbols are critical for our analogical thinking. For analogy is an art of enlarged thinking.[65] The fertility of symbols and the elasticity of narrative work together to enable the intensification and enlargement of our moral perception and analogical imagination beyond conventional understanding.

Symbols and metaphors are central to a religious language. Every religious language is an indirect, symbolic speech of the divine or ultimate reality. One comes to the knowledge of the divine reality through religious symbols and ideas. Symbolic, metaphoric languages have a world-disclosing, revelatory power. They illuminate and clarify the meanings, goals, and values shared in the lifeworld which often are hidden to or poorly seen by the public. They help us to construct or alter the ways that we perceive and respond to the world. Far from being subordinate or supplementary, symbolic or metaphoric languages, when properly articulated, can play a prominent role in public discourse by inspiring people to desired moral actions. Martin Luther King, Jr.'s speeches and sermons during the Civil Rights Movement are prime examples of this.

5. Religious Validity Claims
The validity redemption of a religious speech is not entirely impos-

sible. It should be noted that a religious community constantly engages in the process of validity redemption to differentiate the authentic forms of doctrines, speeches and worship from the inauthentic ones. Symbolic, metaphoric languages may perform some problem-solving function in their own terms, namely by generating adequate and appropriate meaning for a speaker and a hearer, and integrating various human experiences into a plausible, coherent perspective which otherwise would be fragmented and segregated. Redemption of a religious speech may be possible in each of the three validity spheres as participants thematize and examine relevant claims. It is possible, first, because religious discourses include, implicitly or explicitly, all the three areas of validity claims—cognitive (or objective), moral (interactive), and affective (subjective). In actual speeches, they exist in an intermingled, undifferentiated form, thus being able to speak of highly encompassing and complex reality of human existence in a comprehensive and integral manner. Yet this does not necessarily mean that thematization of a particular dimension of validity claim is impossible (Cf. natural science and theology dialogue in the area of cognitive truth claims). For example, the redemption of rightness of religious discourse is possible through the discovery of the overlapping moral consensus among religious beliefs. In other words, religious groups may come to mutual agreement on important moral principles despite their substantial differences in metaphysical and theological frameworks.

Religion is a comprehensive interpretive framework through which the believers understand meanings and purposes of their lives. A religious model thematizes the world as a whole and single unit of the good. It heuristically thematizes the world as an integral moral, metaphysical entity. That is, religious speeches can be assessed in each of the three domains of validity claim (truth, justice, and sincerity) in terms of their comprehensiveness, coherence, adequacy, appropriateness, and relevance. They can be evaluated in terms of their capacity to effectively conceptualize a plausible reality of the good which encompasses all three domains of reality (objective, intersubjective, and subjective).

Religious speeches can be tested if we understand religion as a plausibility model of the good, or coherent scheme of meaning. For this task, the idea of model is crucial as it is widely discussed today among philosophers of science and theologians. The latter contend that one has access to the invisible reality by relying on a constructive model. A model obtains a referential, cognitive value through the plausibility it conveys. A model indicates a conceptual framework where diverse symbols or metaphors are coherently or systemically arranged for a plausible understanding of the reality. A competent and plausible model is the one which coherently and meaningfully organizes seemingly disconnected, discrete information and data for a better, intelligent explanation of the reality. A model provides us with a way to think about the invisible or unknown in terms of the visible or known. A model is a mixture of metaphors and rational, theoretical concepts.[66] When symbols and metaphors are organized with concepts in a systematic and coherent way, they develop into a model. Theoretical concepts interpret and clarify symbols or metaphors by providing cognitive perspective and understanding of invisible, complex reality. A model is a major way of structuring and ordering our experiences. A rich model with many supportive and associated metaphors and symbols has wider appeal to and enduring moral power for people. A model is a dominant metaphor.[67] A model is not a mirror of the reality, but the best human conjecture (best abduction) of it. It discloses the features of reality.

A religious model has plausibility in illuminating the way the self is related to the divine reality and the world. If religion indicates a way of explaining the reality of the divine, a good religion has certain plausibility. That is, it may retain a problem-solving, explanatory power for human existence by effectively illuminating the nature of human predicaments and also by providing some solutions and remedies for them. The idea of model shows that religious language is neither purely objective nor arbitrary. Human knowledge in model is hypothetical and provisional.[68] This tentativeness makes continuous theological reflection, mutual examination and revision indispensable.

V. Summary

Habermas' ethics provides a viable philosophical, practical resource for reinstituting liberal democracy in a postmodern context. Postulating free, equal, and unrestrained discourse as the necessary conditions of moral adjudication and reaching agreement, Habermas proposes a pragmatic basis upon which various religious communities engage each other. The question is how a particular religion can accept this practical basis. If the communicative ethics does not take the good and the right to be antithetical, and if it puts the relationship of moral principles and particular traditions in a constant dialogic and dialectical tension, this implies that it does not have to suppress or subordinate particular theological convictions. Rather, theological convictions and traditions should be brought into conversation, through argumentation and cross-examination, for the construction or reinterpretation of moral principles. In this symbiotic tension of the good and right, moral principles are illuminated by theological perspectives, and theological perspectives achieve their practical relevance and moral authority as they are able to discursively redeem moral principles into new forms and meanings. This, in turn, implies that a solution to religious, cultural conflicts will be found not by relegating religious communities to a private realm, but by navigating how a particular religion can adopt and incorporate a formal-pragmatic methodology of communicative ethics into its own religious framework.

On the basis of the above observation and criticism, in the next chapter, I will show how Habermas' reconstructive project of communicative ethics could make a profound contribution to a constructive method of Christian ethics. I shall do this by showing a striking resonance and commensurability between his idea of intersubjective rationality and the Reformed Christian idea of covenant.

But first, let us briefly examine the historical, constructive relationship between a covenantal theology and the liberal political institutions of America, and its implication to our task of constructing a new methodology of Christian ethics upon a communicative rationality.

Notes

1. The meaning of this term will be explored more fully as this chapter unfolds.

2. Jürgen Habermas, *Moral Consciousness and Communicative Action* (Cambridge, MA.: M.I.T. Press, 1990), 100ff.

3. Jürgen Habermas, "Struggle for Recognition in the Democratic Constitutional State," in *Multiculturalism: Examining the Politics of Recognition*, ed. Amy Gutmann (Princeton: Princeton University Press, 1994), 130-131.

4. Habermas, *Erläuterungen zur Diskursethik*, Frankfurt: Suhrkamp, 1991, 208, quoted in William Rehg, *Insight & Solidarity: The Discourse Ethics of Jürgen Habermas* (Berkeley: University of California Press, 1994), n26. 77.

5. Jürgen Habermas, *The Theory of Communicative Action*, vol. 2. (Boston: Beacon Press, 1988), 397-398.

6. Seyla Benhabib, *Situating the Self: Gender, Community, and Postmodernism in Contemporary Ethics* (New York: Routledge, 1992), 49.

7. Habermas, *Moral Consciousness and Communicative Action*, 106.

8. Ibid., 58.

9. Jürgen Habermas, *The Theory of Communicative Action*, vol. 1. (Boston: Beacon Press, 1984), 99.

10. Jürgen Habermas, *The Philosophical Discourse of Modernity* (Cambridge, MA.: M.I.T. Press, 1987), 326.

11. Habermas, *The Theory of Communicative Action*, vol. 2, 137.

12. Habermas, *The Philosophical Discourse of Modernity*, 322.

13. Jürgen Habermas, *Postmetaphysical Thinking: Philosophical Essays* (Cambridge, MA.: M.I.T. Press, 1992), 116.

14. Habermas, *The Philosophical Discourse of Modernity*, 326.

15. Habermas, *Postmetaphysical Thinking: Philosophical Essays*, 116.

16. Ibid., 142.

17. Habermas, *The Theory of Communicative Action*, vol.1, 21.

18. Benhabib, *Situating the Self*, 169.

19. Thomas McCarthy, *The Critical Theory of Jürgen Habermas* (Cambridge: M.I.T. Press, 1978), 325.

20. Jürgen Habermas, "Toward a Theory of Communicative Competence," *Inquiry* 13 (1970): 372.

21. Habermas, "Wahrheitstheorien," in *Vorstudien und Ergänzungen zur Theorie des kommnunikativen Handelns*, 2nd ed. (Frankfurt: Suhrkamp, 1986), 258-259; quoted in Thomas McCarthy, *The Critical Theory of Jürgen Habermas*, 310.

22. Habermas, *The Theory of Communicative Action*, vol.2, 124.

23. Jürgen Habermas, *Justification and Application: Remarks on Discourse Ethics* (Cambridge, MA.: M.I.T. Press, 1993), 7.

24. Habermas says, "Maxims are the plane in which ethics and morality intersect because they can be judged alternately from ethical and moral points of view." (Ibid.)

25. Habermas, *The Theory of Communicative Action*, vol.2, 97.

26. Ibid.

27. Habermas, *The Theory of Communicative Action*, vol.1, 137.

28. Ibid.

29. Habermas, *Faktizität und Geltung: Beiträge zur Diskurstheorie des Rechts und des demokratischen Rechtsstaats*, (Frankfurt: Suhrkamp, 1992), 58; quoted in William Outhwaite, *Habermas: A Critical Introduction* (Stanford: Stanford University Press, 1994), 140.

30. Outhwaite, *Habermas: A Critical Introduction*, 140.

31. Habermas, *The Theory of Communicative Action*, vol.2, 173-174.

32. Seyla Benhabib, *Critique, Norm, and Utopia: A Study of the Foundations of Critical Theory* (New York: Columbia University Press, 1986), 312.

33. William Rehg, *Insight & Solidarity: The Discourse Ethics of Jürgen Habermas* (Berkeley, Los Angeles, London: The University of California Press, 1994), 95.

34. Hypothetically, solidarity extends to the whole of humanity because conversation takes place under the presumption of the ideal speech community. The unity of the human species in discourse regulates and conditions rationality as the ground and the ultimate context of rational justification and redemption.

35. Ibid., 67-68.

36. John Thomson and David Held, *Habermas:Critical Debates* (Cambridge, MA.: M.I.T. Press, 1982), 255.

37. Habermas, *Moral Consciousness and Communicative Action*, 200.

38. Ibid., 199.

39. Habermas, *Justice and Solidarity* 47; Benhabib, *Situating the Self,* 192.

40. Habermas, *Moral Consciousness and Communicative Action,* 200.

41. Ibid., 202.

42. Rehg, *Insight & Solidarity,* 108.

43. Outhwaite, *Habermas: A Critical Introduction,* 142.

44. Habermas, *Politik, Kunst, Religion* (Stuttgart: Reclam, 1978), 117, quoted in Tony Smith, *The Role of Ethics in Social Theory: Essays from a Habermasian Perspective* (Albany: State University of New York, 1991), 182.

45. Habermas, *Faktizität under Geltung,* 170; quoted in Outhwaite, *Habermas: A Critical Introduction,* 143.

46. Ibid.

47. Ibid., 436; quoted in Outhwaite, *Habermas: A Critical Introduction,* 147.

48. Habermas, *Justification and Application,* 150.

49. Habermas, *The Theory of Communicative Action,* vol.2, 77.

50. Cf. Peter L. Berger, ed., *Desecularization of the World* (Grand Rapids: William B. Eerdmans Publishing Co., 2000).

51. Furthermore, if Habermas acknowledges the world-disclosing power of aesthetics, then he must do the same for religion. For both aesthetics and religion rely heavily on symbolic metaphoric languages and images, and they both have world-disclosing powers. As aesthetics cannot be identified with the narrow realm of the subjective world, religion cannot be dismissed as obsolete.

52. Jürgen Habermas, *Legitimation Crisis* (Boston: Beacon Press, 1975).

53. White, *Recent Works,* 136.

54. Habermas, *The Theory of Communicative Action,* vol.1, 73-74; quoted in White, *Recent Works,* 135.

55. Habermas, *Moral Consciousness and Communicative Action,* 202-203.

56. Hans-Georg Gadamer, *Philosophical Hermeneutics*, ed. David E. Linge, (Berkeley, Los Angeles, London: University of California Press, 1976), 26-36.

57. Paul Ricoeur, *Hermeneutics & the Human Sciences: Essays on Language, Action and Interpretation*, ed. John B. Thompson, (Cambridge, New York, Port Chester, Melbourne, Sydney: Cambridge University Press; Paris: Editions de la Maison des Sciences de l'Homme, 1981), 97.

58. Ibid., 99-100. Similarly, Charles Taylor charges that the ideal moral order Habermas proposes is "an order which is inseparably indexed to a personal vision" (Charles Taylor, *Sources of the Self: The Making of the Modern Identity* (Cambridge, MA.: Harvard University Press, 1989), 510). According to Taylor, only the moral order which has a strong personal resonance and meaning can survive and exercise its binding upon people. He suggests Judeo-Christian theism, with "its central promise of a divine affirmation of the human," as the historical example which embodies such a moral order.

59. Habermas, *The Philosophical Discourse of Modernity*, 208-209.

60. Ibid., 200.

61. Sallie McFague, *Metaphorical Theology: Models of God in Religious Language* (Philadelphia: Fortress Press, 1982), 15.

62. Ibid., 16.; italics are original.

63. Ibid., 26.

64. One example of a fertile symbol may be the Christian symbol of the Kingdom of God. It presents seemingly opposite dimensions simultaneously, such as personal/impersonal, present/future, institutional/noninstitutional, this worldly/heavenly.

65. Benhabib, *Situating the Self,* 9.

66. Sallie McFague, *Metaphorical Theology,* 117.

67. Ibid., 23.

68. Wentzel van Huyssteen, *Theology and the Justification of Faith: Constructing Theories in Systematic Theology* (Grand Rapids: W. B. Eerdmans Publishing Co., 1989), 142.

CHAPTER 2

COVENANTAL THEOLOGY AND COMMUNICATIVE ETHICS

In chapter one, we discussed the tenets and significance of Habermas' communicative ethics as a methodology of adjudication and political change in a postmodern society. Habermas reconstitutes the significant elements of modernity and liberal political institutions on a formal-pragmatic basis, instead of a foundational one. I call these elements communicative requisites of human social interaction which are crucial for a fair and just construction of the common morality. These elements emphasize the more explicit and positive acknowledgements of individual creativity, freedom, equality, and universal participation. These communicative requisites are necessary for protecting the minimal common ground of human existence, basic freedom, and the rights of individuals which are now accepted as moral values of global consensus. These elements are concretely embodied in the ideas of *an equal and fair process of adjudication, the universal participation of all concerned,* and *intersubjective dialogue as a constitutive process in constructing a common morality.* Attention to these aspects is necessary to construct a common order of symbiosis in a pluralistic society on the basis of dialogue rather than violence.

In this chapter, I shall show how this communicative methodology can be incorporated into Reformed covenantal theology without seriously sacrificing or impairing theological convictions and beliefs of the latter, and, how it provides a relevant and adequate methodology of Christian moral reasoning by overcoming the difficulties and limits of covenantal theology, such as hierarchicalism and exclusivism. My contention is that Habermas' formal-pragmatic methodology of communicative ethics, when appropriated into a covenantal theological framework, presents a constructive methodology of Christian ethics which attends to both public relevance and theological particularities of Christian communities. The incorporation is possible because communicative ethics implicitly envisions and prioritizes a certain form of life which is commensurate with the Christian ideal of the trinitarian Kingdom of God. It is also possible because Habermas' formal-pragmatic methodology of practical reasoning exhibits dynamics and mechanisms which are strikingly similar to a covenanting process.

First, let us now turn to a brief overview of the historical connection between liberal political institutions and covenantal theology.

I. Covenantal Theology

A. An Overview

The understanding of covenant in a Reformed theology is pluralistic. That is to say, a Reformed theology presents diverse and complex strands of ideas and beliefs rather than a monolithic tradition. Hence, my discussion of covenantal theology in this chapter will primarily focus on the Free Church Calvinist tradition.[1] The Free Church Calvinistic tradition has developed explicit covenantal theories of church, politics, and social institutions with emphasis on individual responsibility and voluntary participation. According to Max L. Stackhouse, the basic ethical motif of this tradition was "freedom under the moral law."[2] The Free Church Calvinists believed that individuals are free by God-given rights, to organize self-governing associations, and to determine their own destinies under the divine law.

The Free Church tradition—especially in its Dutch Reformed, English and American Puritan traditions—understood covenant as the universal governing and organizing principle of God. The covenant was understood as the constitutive principle of social organization, political construction, and religious formation. It identified covenant as the method which God has consistently relied upon in dealing with humanity. "As soon as God had Created man, he plighted a Covenant with him."[3] The Free Church tradition understands human beings as covenantal beings, and the whole of human history as a covenantal history—first in terms of the covenant of works, then later in the covenant of grace.[4]

According to the Free Church Calvinists, the covenant of works was established between God and Adam before the Fall. Adam was conceived as the federal head and representative of all humanity. He could act for all his descendants under the condition of perfect obedience. In return for his obedience, by remaining faithful to the covenant, Adam was promised eternal life and bliss. The covenant of works was understood in purely legal terms. It relied on the law of nature. The covenant of works was believed to provide a common, objective, moral foundation for all human beings. Since the fall of Adam, his sin and death were passed on to all his descendants. Free Church Calvinists found the proof of the existence of the covenant of works in three areas: in human conscience which enables a person to discern good from evil; in human will which seeks and aspires the good and the eternal life; and finally in all the benefits granted by God to humanity. The covenant of works remains valid as a testimony to God's sovereignty even after the advent of the covenant of grace. The former is not abolished but fulfilled by the latter. This implies that the covenant of works is universally valid and effective between God and non-believers through the operation of divine laws and conscience. The covenant of works was believed to provide the universal basis "for moral, civil, and religious obligations binding upon all men [sic], elect or non-elect, regenerate or unregenerate, professedly Christian or pagan."[5]

When the covenant of works was broken by a human being, a special covenant, the covenant of grace was introduced to restore a broken relationship between God and humanity. The covenant of grace was made between God and believers on the condition of faith in Christ. The covenant of grace requires faith in Christ as its condition of redemption, whereas the covenant of works requires perfect obedience to law. Free Church Calvinists' understanding of covenant of grace was somewhat different from that of Calvin. It was understood in a more reciprocal and conditional way rather than in unilateral and unconditional terms, thus allowing human will to play a significant role in bargaining with God. It had the effect of mitigating and leveling a fatalistic aspect of predestinationism.

Free Church Calvinists did not understand covenant of works and covenant of grace as the two antithetical pacts. Rather they believed the two covenants were the different dispensational aspects of the one and the same reality of the divine providence (Cf. Westminster Confession of 1647). This made the political-institutional generalization of covenant possible. For them, God was the Creator of the universe, and the source of order and morality as well the redeemer. God's power and rule reach every corner of the universe, and every realm of human life. They are not confined to the church. God is involved directly in every aspect of human activity and in the historical development in achieving God's purpose. Later this idea was developed into a belief that all authorities and all realms of human life are covenantally accountable to God.

B. Meaning of Covenant

The Free Church Calvinist tradition understood covenant as a pact which a community of persons voluntarily reached through a common perception and dedication to divine law.[6] The term *covenant* refers either to the act of covenanting or to the relationship created as the result of covenanting. Covenant is voluntary from the human perspective, but it is distinguished from mere contract by virtue of its ground in divine law. Every form of human covenant, such as marriage, is limited and conditioned by the divine law. Conversely, every human covenant must embody and fulfill the divine law and its purpose.

Covenant has two dimensions: moral (reflection and choice) and religious. If a moral dimension refers to the free, voluntary aspect of covenant in coming to the agreement of the wills between the different parties, a religious dimension refers to a transcendental ground of that moral agreement by inviting the deity as a third, overseeing party of covenant. The religious dimension alerts us that human covenantal agreement is ultimately constrained by a transcendental moral structure. That is, human moral consensus may change but the foundational moral purpose of God remains constant.[7] This last point is significant because it distinguishes covenantalists from liberal contractarians such as Hobbes and Rousseau. Covenantal relationship is more than an expedient temporary bargaining or negotiation in which participants are simply responsible by the terms of agreement to contractual partners.[8]

C. Covenant and the Church

The Free Church Calvinists retrieved the Christian biblical principle of covenant as its primary religious and political organizational principle for the church, the state, and family.[9] Yet the original impulse was religious. The rediscovery of the true apostolic church and its reorganization in a covenantal, congregational form was their primary concern prior to its application to political or conjugal relationship. The idea of covenant was expressed through two auxiliary practical principles determining the nature of the "free church."

1. The Independence of the Church

In his book, *The Kingdom of God in America*, H. R. Niebuhr identifies independence as the tenet of Puritan ecclesiology. It was the belief of New England Puritans that the church should be independent from any intervention and control of any external authority. Yet, this principle does not advocate independence as the absolute principle in itself. Rather, it is ultimately dependent upon and derived from the sovereignty of God. The church is independent of any human political power and institutions by virtue of its dependence on God. The principle of independence constitutes the other side of the sovereignty of God. Niebuhr says, "The converse of dependence on God is independence of everything less than God."[10]

The principle of independence was necessary to protect the freedom of worship and the purity of the church. Niebuhr says, "[U]nder the sovereignty of the living God, man's [sic] first concern was the building of the church, not as an institution but as the social expression of the movement of life toward its true goal."[11] The Calvinists did not absolutize the church; nor did they give up the ideal of purity and sanctification, conformity to the ideal of Kingdom through the church. The independence of the church means "the church's right to determine its own conditions of communion and to discipline its members always by reference to the will of God."[12] The independence of the church was intended to protect the purity of the church. The purity of the church was the underlying rationale for the separation of church and state. The church can be church when its institutional autonomy is protected by law. The state has no right to appoint church officers or interfere with its internal administration. The Church was viewed as divinely ordained, and directly responsible to God. The churches were not merely voluntary associations, no matter how similar they were to other institutions. This laid the ground for the idea of religious freedom.

2. The Limitation of Power

The Free Church movement was concerned with the limitation of power in its ecclesial life. Puritans had a high awareness of the destructive power of unchecked authority. That means that Free Church Calvinists, in some important aspects of their theology, continued the Augustinian political realism that the state was a consequence of the fall, arising from the necessity to check and curb destructive human lust, greed, and violence. They believed that every human power has a tendency to exalt and absolutize itself. For them, hence, the sovereignty of God functioned as a regulative principle over the elevation of any human power. This principle was also equally applied to the church's organization. The congregational and associational types of church organization were an historical expression of this principle of limitation. The strict and rigid application of the limitation of power of the church and the state may have led to moral inertia and mediocrity. Yet, this realism did not develop into cynicism or fatalism, or individualistic pietism because it was countered by covenantal voluntarism.

3. Church and Covenantal Principle

The Free Church Calvinists conceived of the church as a covenantal community of the saints. The church presented itself as the covenantal model for social order. Free Church Calvinism experimented with the alchemy of order and justice through their local congregations. Concretely the covenantal idea was expressed through the voluntary model of organization. The church was not a natural community, but an intentional association, built upon the basis of free, equal participation and voluntary commitments and consent of members. Individuals were free to participate and leave the group which resulted from the belief that only the voluntary type of organization could enlist the maximum motivation of people.

We have seen that Calvinists were eager to transform every aspect of society in conformity to the divine purpose and will revealed in Scripture and the divine law. In actualizing this ideal, they found its concrete and empirical model in the Free Church. In other words, the church provided an organizational insight and vision for the renewal of society. It presented an alternative model of social association to traditional paternalistic, authoritarian institutions. Specifically, a covenantal idea of the church has played a formative role for the emergence of modern types of institutions. In modern history, according to Stackhouse, the secular associations—the university, corporation, guild, and political party—attained "theological legitimacy based on the analogy of a free church."[13] Stackhouse says, "The basic, primordial freedom of the church to order its own life is taken as the basis for the organization of political, economic, educational, familial, and other aspects of life. Political authority does not grant "concessions"; it does not have the authority to allow or disallow these groups to be formed, or to give or to withdraw permission—quite the contrary."[14] Inspired by the free church, individuals were free to organize various associations under God's universal moral law. It created new public habits, set the new pattern of the public discourse, and shaped the public behavior. It precipitated the emergence of modern form of professional civil, political, economic, and cultural institutions. Stackhouse observes,

> The churches prepared the way, demanding a guaranteed autonomy from exterior control. The autonomy was, at first, to ensure the freedom of worship and the congregation's right to govern its own affairs. But as the implications of the message and the polity were translated into habit and public behavior, the pattern inevita-

bly spilled over into the reform of professional, political, economical, and familial institutions.[15]

Hence,

> The covenants of the independent Free Churches became, in the Anglo-American traditions, the paradigms of political parties for shaping governments, of corporations for shaping market, of unions for influencing corporations, of lawyers for shaping jurisprudence, of doctors for shaping the practice of medicine, and of scholars for shaping sciences. Even the family was transformed, for it was to become the 'little congregation'. . . . In the nineteenth and twentieth centuries, this same pluralistic, covenantal model became the basis of mass movements for abolition of slavery, reform of women's status, prohibition of alcohol abuse, control of child labor, defense of consumer rights, and dozens of other movements.[16]

The Free Church tradition expanded beyond specific religious boundaries, and created a distinct arena for human freedom and community organization. The Free Church movement generated the public, democratic ethos and impulse for society, paving the way for the advent of a pluralistic model of democratic public space.

D. Human Rights

Stackhouse contends that this organizational nature of the Free Church tradition had made a profound contribution to the development of modern theory of human rights. Through its political struggle, the Free Church Calvinists gained the rights to be free and independent from the interference of the state. Participation in those groups signified the beginning of democratic politics in its truly modern sense. He claims, "Ecclesiology, rooted in covenant, is the mother of democracy; the church is the model for family, political regime, and the common wealth."[17] The right to freely organize the church was the prototype of modern human rights. For Free Church Calvinists, the centerpiece of human rights was the freedom and entitlement to form an independent church.[18]

The rights of the church over the state and other institutions were rooted in the fundamental theological conviction that God is the ultimate authority over the earthly form of authorities, and the church is to serve God, not human authority. As the principles of freedom, equality, and reciprocity of communication constitute the moral basis of a genuinely free community, the Free Church first ensured the freedoms of speech and proclamation within community. Individual rights, freedom, and equality were sustained, empowered, and activated through the communities of believers. Other forms of rights were implied or ensued.

> It is precisely such groups which articulate the source and norm of human dignity, practically empower persons to care for the neighbor, and act to defend the rights of individuals when they are thought to be compromised by governmental or corporate or ethnic discriminations--claiming that they are "members" with equal standing in a more universal community.[19]

E. The State

The Free Church Calvinists understood the government in covenantal terms. They believed that government was constituted by a covenant between the rulers and the people. On the basis of the theory of covenant, they were able to attack the very theological foundations of the divine right of the king, and thus protect the freedom of the church and individuals against the intrusive powers of the monarchy. The subordination of the individuals to the state was justified only by their voluntary consent.

Like the liberals, the Calvinists required the government to represent the collective will of the people. Yet, the Free Church Calvinists' understanding of the state differed from that of liberal philosophy by its belief in God as the ultimate foundation and source of sovereignty. Any form of government was to be judged and evaluated by the eternal and objective decree of God, which was revealed in Scripture. In their view, the governmental actions and laws must be consistent with God's decree and ordinances. The true knowledge of God, worship, and the practice of piety were necessary elements for peace, harmony and justice in society. They were also the bases for the benevolent and rightful exercise of the government. This means that the Free Church Calvinists firmly believed that any moral and effective governing and symbiosis of society required both piety and justice.[20] In the Calvinist understanding, piety cultivates social harmony and peace by providing the transcendental moral basis for public order and trust. Piety enhances and underwrites politics. Hence, the magistrates were as much responsible for the promotion and enhancement of morality and holiness as were the ministers. The civil liberty alone cannot subsist. It must be buttressed by the public morality. The civil liberty must emulate the model of Christian liberty. The political covenant of law must reflect and correspond to the religious covenant of the church. Liberty does not indicate permission of sin but the path to holiness.

However, the significance of piety for the public morality does not condone the direct control or intervention of the ecclesiastical authority over other secular realms of society. The Calvinists did not expect the church to exclusively mediate God's law and grace—representing God for the whole society. Conversely, ecclesial institutions should not submit to the control of the political body. The Calvinists did not accept the total neutrality of state or other institutions from the requirements of the divine covenant and order. Free Church Calvinists rejected both ecclesiastical domination and political totalitarianism. Neither political power nor ecclesial power may exercise a direct, total control over each other. The state should be free from ecclesial control not in order that it may be completely secular and self-sufficient, but in order to develop its unique vocation, namely public justice, in conformity with God.

This differentiation was critical in providing a theological basis for the separation of society. If the church is directly obligated and guided by the covenant of grace, civil society and the government are rooted in and bound by the covenant of works. The meaning and the significance of political community are not primarily defined by its relationship to an ecclesiastical institution, but rather by God's covenant with creation. That is to say, even if political institutions are not obliged to directly serve or follow an ecclesiastical institution, they are nonetheless responsible to God's covenant given in creation. God's ruling and ordering grace for God's creation are publicly available to all humanity and to all kinds of communities.[21] This implies that human beings are made, from the beginning, to associate in political communities according to God's laws by forming political symbiosis and working for a just social relationship.

God maintains the order of the state through human authorities, the magistrates who were conceived as the guardians of communal ideals and purposes. People elect and give power to the ruler. God works through the medium of people in granting the ruler God's right and mandate. God is the ultimate authority behind any political authorities. Even if the magistrate is functionally elected to the office by the people's free consent, its power ultimately is accountable to God. In other words, the sovereignty of people is qualified by the sovereignty of God. This was practically reflected in the idea of office. The office of the government, not a person, was conceived to be divinely appointed. It assigns some permanent status to the government and its function. The Free Church Calvinists separated the person of the magistrate and the office itself. Although the magistrates are elected to office, thus impeachable and dispensable, the office itself is not; it is divine. By separating the persons of the magistracy from the office, they tried to prevent the abuse and corruption of power, yet, without endangering the stability of order and system.

The magistrates were required to carry out God's commission. The power of the magistrate is subjected to the word of God and the divine law, and conducted in conformity with them. They must obey God's will in all political decisions. The magistrates needed to draw the rational inferences from the covenant of God for practical purposes and moral discretion. The use of logic and reason, within the confines of revelation, was highly encouraged. If the activities of the magistrate were consistent with the word of God and the law, then their judgment must be respected and obeyed as if they were God's judgments. Whenever the ruler breaks the covenant made with the people, all divine authorization is deprived. Thus, the magistrate is responsible to both God and the people.

Specifically, the magistrate is limited by the "covenant of people" as well as by the "covenant of works." Spykman notes, "First it [the power of the ruler] is dependent upon the divine law. Second, the ruler is accountable to the people through covenant. The powers of the state are limited, third, by other associations, and finally by its own internal law and regulation."[22] The magistrate exists as a public servant. To govern is to serve and care for the benefit of others. The governing action, the imperium, is guided by the goal and the end of society. Since the rulers exist to serve the people, they should not do anything contrary to the common good of society.

Free Church Calvinists redefined the meaning of political sovereignty in covenantal terms. They challenged the theory of the divine right of kings. Sovereignty does not belong to the ruler but to the people. The people elect and give power to the ruler. Sovereignty is synonymous with the common will of people. Sovereignty does not belong to isolated individuals but to the solidarity of these consociated people. Covenant forms the communal will for a governmental purpose.

> The right of the realm, or right of sovereignty, does not belong to individual members, but to all members joined together and to the entire associated body of the realm. For as universal association can be constituted not only by one member but by all the members together, so that right is said to be the property not of individual members, but of the members jointly. Therefore, what is owed to the whole (*universitas*) is not owed to individuals, and what the

whole owes individuals do not owe.[23]

The communal will is vested in the constitution which takes a form of covenant. This constitution is established via the consent of the people. It refers to a fundamental principle of association which regulates and conserves the mutual relationship of the ruler and people. Any serious violation of the terms by the ruler is equivalent to the annulment of covenant, thus justifying the right of the people to resist them. Constitution provides a built-in procedure and order which checks, prevents, and corrects the possible abuse or misuse of the power as well as disorder of society. Constitution emboldens and buttresses the strong rule by controlling haphazard, individualistic, arbitrary, disorderly rebellion and resistance. Constitution provides a protection against any threat of tyranny. Constitution delineates the concrete guidelines, procedures, and responsibilities of both the ruler and the people. Sovereignty is delegated and exercised by various forms of associations and different bodies of government. The sovereignty of each association and individual must be protected and respected under the guidance of divine sovereignty. This idea helped, to a great extent, to prevent the rise of statism. The covenantal understanding of sovereignty is not only relevant to democratic society, but effective to deal with the problems arising from an increasingly interdependent, and pluralistic, global society such as institutional needs for international bodies and their arrangements with traditional forms of national institutions (Cf. World Trade Organization, the United Nations, the European Union, etc.).

F. Covenantal Theology and Liberalism
Reformed Christianity and liberalism have closely interacted for the formation and development of democracy and human rights in Western society. Elazar observes,

> The road to modern democracy began with the Protestant Reformation in the sixteenth century, particularly among those exponents of Reformed Protestantism . . . who developed a theology and politics that set the Western world back on the road to popular self-government, emphasizing liberty and equality.[24]

Covenantal theology shares several important political insights and ideas with liberalism: constitutionalism, democracy, the separation of powers, the ideas of voluntary association, government by consent, the preservation of the individual's rights, the belief in due political process, and the rule by law. Both Free Church Calvinists and liberals believed that the public life, the state and institutions, must be governed by the self-evident truths disclosed in natural laws. However, there were profound and substantial differences in their perspectives because of the theological orientation of the Free Church Calvinism. Let us examine some of them closely.

Liberals and the Free Church Calvinists both believed in the universal existence of moral laws and their ordering and regulating authority for society and individuals. Moral laws provided a secure basis of social morality and order. However, the liberal and Calvinist understanding of moral laws were not identical. If Calvinists believed in moral laws as the divinely instituted rule of the universe, then the liberals regarded them as something reason alone could legislate, thus requiring no particular religious experience or membership. For the liberals, moral laws have almost independent status from religion, and the knowledge of these moral laws was universally accessible to human reason.

Free Church Calvinists and liberals shared the view that the political powers must be limited by the law. They shared the similar political concern, "What political design would satisfactorily prevent the abuse and misuse of the power?" The rule by law was understood as a practical means to realize the idea of the limitation of power. Law must be given relative autonomy from political authority. Yet for the Calvinists, it was God, not reason, who was the source, ground, and the goal of the law. Although Calvinists did not invalidate reason or intellect, they maintained that independently the two were insufficient. Reason and conscience, although necessary for the moral ordering of society, must be guided by revelation.

Like liberalism, the covenantal idea emphasized the inviolability of human dignity, individual rights, and freedom. Yet, covenantal ideas were significantly different from those of liberalism by virtue of their theonomous characteristics. The idea of freedom in covenantal theology was neither a self-sufficient nor purely individualistic concept. Human freedom was not the starting point for the Calvinists. Rather, it was derived from and based on human beings' covenantal relationship with God which was squarely opposed to the liberal assumption of self-autonomy—freedom as the absolute ideal in itself. Conversion was the precondition for freedom, and freedom must be perfected into holiness through discipline. By virtue of the covenantal premise, individuals are never prior to community, or absolute in themselves. Rather, individuals are social in their nature. Individuals cannot be totally free from the demand and obligations arising from their covenantal relationship with God. Freedom and responsibility go hand in hand. Therefore, the idea of freedom in Free Church Calvinism is different from that of liberalism. Individual rights and freedom are not absolute. Freedom is always a freedom under the divine rule. Freedom is a divine gift. Individuals are free but bounded by God's grace and moral law. Individuals are free from any form of human control and intervention because they are primarily accountable to God. Dependence on God is the source of their freedom and independence.

A Reformed idea of freedom was always checked and balanced by the idea of holiness. As the grammar of Christian life, freedom and holiness are not contradictory but complementary. The ideal of the holy community was a constant moral theme among Puritans, despite their theological, political, and ideological variations. Woodhouse defines Puritanism as "a determined and varied effort to erect the holy community and to meet, with different degrees of compromise and adjustment, the problem of its conflict with the world."[25] Holiness calls for righteousness, justice, and love in obedience to God. It is also a calling to participate in the formation and ordering of public life with responsibility. Various realms of society were understood as the spheres where their individual and communal callings were to be realized. The idea of vocation or calling was the social expression of sanctification. Sanctification pertains not only to individual holiness and moral perfection, but also to the transformation and sanctification of social relationships and institutions in harmony with the divine law and purpose. Through its balanced understanding of freedom and holiness, Calvinism could maintain a creative tension between criticism and stability, at the same time. Synthesis of freedom and holiness provides the reconstructive as well as critical perspective on social relationship.

Also, in comparison to liberalism, Free Church Calvinists had a different view of the sovereignty of people. It would appear that the idea of the sovereignty of people is incompatible with the Calvinist's idea of the sovereignty of God. Yet for the Free Church Calvinists, the sovereignty of people was derived from the God-given freedom of humanity. Furthermore, the Calvinist idea of divine sovereignty provides an important qualification against the danger of anarchy and the government of fools. They were as suspicious of the sovereignty of people as they were of the sovereignty of the kings. The form of democracy advocated by the Calvinists was different from that of liberalism. It was democracy subjected to and empowered by the sovereignty of God. Because of their reliance on covenant, the Calvinists refused to render the state and its politics to total control in the secular hands independent of Christian faith.

Both Free Church Calvinists and liberals relied on the idea of the pact (interpreted as covenant or contract) as the foundational principle of society. The idea of covenant institutionalizes the idea of freedom, yet without losing perspective on obligation and responsibility. It makes a good contrast to the liberal understanding of society. For liberals such as Hobbes, Rousseau and Locke, the covenant of government was derived from a prior covenant of society. Society was self-consciously organized on the basis of the rational choice and agreement among individuals. The government represented a derivative institutional mechanism grounded in the consensus of the individuals to protect their interests (e.g. liberty, life, property) from various threats, such as anarchy, disorder, and lawlessness.

On the contrary, for the Free Church Calvinists, the covenant of society was not conceived as the archetype of all covenants. It was one of many secondary covenants derived from a divine covenant. The covenant of society was grounded in the covenant of works, or the covenant of nature (*foedus naturae*), which God had made with humanity. The covenant of works existed prior to any pact of government or society. According to the Calvinists, at the moment of the Creation, God endowed human beings with rational capacity to perceive the requirement of the divine justice, and to form a collective life on its basis. Thus, society cannot be purely contractual or utilitarian. The difference between covenant and contract is clear here. Contract does not make any objective reference to the law of God which, for Calvinists, constitutes the source of every human moral existence. Liberal contractual theory forfeited the existence of some sort of primordial freedom prior to any society and government.

G. Covenantal Theology and Pluralism: Social Spheres and Institutions

From the beginning of its movement, Free Church Calvinism has been appreciative of a pluralistic nature of human social formation. Calvinists believed that the differentiation of spheres is a part of creational order for the benefit of society and its members. Yet, it did not understand pluralism in purely secular terms. The Free Church Calvinists accepted institutional and spheral pluralism on the basis of theological principles of covenant and common grace. By virtue of these doctrines of covenant and common grace, Calvinists could avoid both the purely contractual idea of society espoused by liberalism and the organic hierarchical view of society espoused by the medieval Roman Catholics, and their ensuing dangers of, respectively, individualism and authoritarianism.

The Free Church Calvinists understood pluralism as a part of God's ordinances in creation. Social differentiation has a theological ground. Each sphere of society and association is sovereign in its own sphere, and thus must be protected from interference or intrusion by the state and other spheres. God's ordinance is specifically designed for each and every particular sphere. In other words, God's ordinance is not blind or indiscriminate, but specified and discriminate. Every social sphere has its unique social mission, duty, function to fulfill as ordained by God. Society needs a wide array of independent spheres for the fulfillment of God's providence and its corollary of human vocations. Society and history are understood as the theater of God's action. God's covenant in creation constitutes the environment of human orderly existence and fulfillment.

Abraham Kuyper was a modern covenantal theologian who grasped the significance of this theological insight regarding a complex differentiated institutional life. According to Kuyper, the pluriformity of life was God's original creational design. As the story of Genesis tells, God's creation was not monolithic, but a rich variety of life forms and species. Nature is inhabited by pluriformity of creatures—plants, fish, animals, and birds. Similarly, in the area of human culture, God intended plurality. Each sphere has its unique domain of goal, meaning, and action for society as prescribed by God. Marked by and animated with its own identity, each sphere is required to express and fulfill the demand of God's creational order in its organization and activities. That is, state, church, university, science, business, and arts have their own internal spheral mandates and purposes bestowed upon them by God at the moment of creation. God is the author of spheres. As such, each sphere is directly, and covenantally, responsible to God.

Kuyper believes that because of the existence of multiple spheres and their interactions, human social life is "neither simple nor uniform but constitutes an infinitely complex organism."[26] A rich, multifaceted, infinitely complex, organic form of life arises through interaction and engagement of various spheres in covenant. The idea of sphere sovereignty provides openness and freedom and social protection for distinctive sets/patterns of human activities (family, education, work, worship, arts, science), thus facilitating human creativity, productivity, stability and predictability. The idea of sphere sovereignty implies that any one social institution (state, or corporation, or church) cannot claim any subsuming authority over others. It communicates that society should be arranged in such a way to prevent any absolute, totalitarian claim of one sphere. The boundaries and parameters of spheres are set and protected by the faith-fulness of God's economy.[27]

A political community and social associations may maintain their relative autonomies and freedom from a religious community by establish-ing their own realm of jurisdiction through the stipulation of proper posi-tive laws. There was nothing wrong with those plural expressions of the life force. However, this does not condone the *laissez-faire* view of soci-ety. In this respect, the Calvinist view of the formation of society substan-tially differed from a liberal contractarian view of society. Every sphere of society is under the sovereign rule of God. Therefore, its exercise and practice must conform to God's covenantal purpose. For example, the economy must be free from ecclesial or governmental control, not so that it can become exploitative and greedy, but so that it may develop eco-nomic goods, resources, and technologies to the full extent. Without ex-plicit public acknowledgment and the social-moral basis of God's cove-nantal order, society will ultimately disintegrate and dissolve into the end-less state of war, one against each other. In other words, the ideas of insti-tutional autonomy and differentiation were accepted and practiced within the bounds of the Christian covenantal understanding of God and society.

This theological thinking was also possible because of the Calvinist doctrine of common grace: God's grace is not confined to the institutional churches and Christians alone. Rather, God's grace is ubiquitous. God's common grace is working universally to restrain the power of sin and de-struction, to preserve necessary minimal order and good for all people. Although social spheres and institutions are free from the direct control of institutional churches, they cannot be separated from God's creation and ordinances because God's common grace permeates every aspect of hu-man life. No person, group, society is completely exempt from God's gov-erning grace. And it was believed to be indispensable to prevent human society from degenerating into complete chaos and anarchy. The faithful God cannot abandon God's creation. God's common grace allows a basic good and order to be possible in every realm of society. Human society—its spheres, associations, and members—is afflicted and distorted by sin. Yet, disobedience, sin, and rebellion are not left unchecked. They are con-fronted by God's common governing grace. Without this integrating power, social spheres become contested areas between the power of sin and common grace under given periods of God's providence. Thus, the gap between the church and the body politic was bridged by the ideas of the covenant of works and the doctrine of common grace.

With the same covenantal principle, the Calvinists rejected the

Catholic corporate view of society which maintained that God's grace is mediated by the divinely appointed persons or institutions such as the king or the bishops. Society cannot be ruled by a single authority or sphere, neither ecclesially, nor politically, nor economically. Nor should it be left to the invisible hands of natural harmony and regulation. For Calvinists, hierarchical or a purely individualistic model of society was considered incongruent with the essential tenets of God's ordinances. If the former leads to authoritarianism or a totalitarian iron cage, choking the creativity, initiative, and voluntary participation of people, the latter leads to chaos and anarchy by dispensing the fundamental source of order and authority.

The covenantal principle enabled Calvinists to maintain the necessary degree of social order without suppressing the diversity of associations and individuals. Free Church Calvinism understood various social institutions (such as family, church, guilds, commercial institutions, provinces, and government) and their mutual relationship in covenantal terms. That is, each institution was created through covenant among members, and related to other institutions also through covenant.

> In sum, a covenant-based politics looks toward political arrangements established or, more appropriately, compounded, through the linking of separate entities in such as way that each preserves its respective integrity while creating a common and continuing association to serve those purposes, broad or limited, for which it was called into being. These purposes range from keeping the peace through a permanent but very limited alliance of independent entities to the forging of a new polity through the union of previously separate entities to create a new whole.[28]

The Calvinist view of covenant and pluralism provides an important perspective and insight into the nature of modern civil society. A civil society is constituted by a covenant (i.e., federalization) in which a number of political communities enter into mutual arrangements to work out solutions making communal decisions on communal problems. Through covenant, a unitary political community is differentiated into a federally organized whole. Covenantal relation is not fixed but is open to further revision and change.[29]

II. Critique of Covenantal Theology

1) Covenantal theology faces some philosophical and practical difficulties in a postmodern society. Closely identified with racial, national,

and ethnic distinctions, covenant was used as a means of domination and oppression toward outsiders and minorities, suppressing diversity and criticism and inculcating a parochial form of social solidarity. It justified the powers and privileges of one covenantal group over others. There are some theological grounds for these mistakes. First, when it was interpreted under a narrow notion of election, the idea of covenant tended to create a caste-like social relationship between "the chosen" and the others (Cf. South Africa under *apartheid*). The idea of covenantal election drew a strict boundary between social groups and set the criterion of membership. Although it may have provided a distinctive sense of identity to a covenantal group, it separated the insiders from the outsiders. Secondly, often appealing to the inequality given between God and humanity, many Christians used covenant to justify a hierarchical form of social relationships between ruler and people, husband and wife, parents and children, and priest and laity. That is ruler, husband, parents, and priest justified their dominion by claiming the divine sanction modeling on the inequality of the divine-human relationship.

These dangers of domination and exclusion still remain if covenantal membership is confined to a particular social group, or covenantalism is practiced only within the homogeneous social context— society sharing the same core values and moral standards.[30] The challenge for covenant today is how it can overcome these hierarchical and exclusivistic tendencies of covenantalism. As I shall discuss, such dangers can be corrected by incorporating Habermas' methodology. A communicative reconstruction of covenant helps to overcome the evils of exclusivism and hierarchy by placing covenant in a consistently democratic framework of freedom, equality and mutuality.

2) A classical covenantal theology, in its moral understanding, shows some tension between the living, free God, and divine law. It begs the question: What is the primary object of Christian commitment? If we apply the Reformed idea of the sovereignty of God more consistently, the primary object of Christian loyalty is not the divine law, but the will of the living God. For Christians, the living God, not the moral law, is the ultimate universal reality and the object of obedience. The divine will cannot be boxed into a formula as its final form, for God is not confined, but continuously intervenes in the historical process as a free and living God.

The solution to this difficulty requires a more thoroughly historical and particularistic theological understanding of God.[31] In Chapter 3, I will show that a consistent trinitarian understanding of God will help to overcome this problem. Trinitarian thinking provides a much more dynamic,

historical, and concrete view of God's activity in history and a more consistent understanding of covenant than a classical covenantal theology. As
such, it provides a more propitious theological framework to incorporate
Habermas' methodology.

3) Covenantalists relied on the foundationalistic ontology of divine
law and the epistemology of conscience. They believed that divine law
exists universally and it is immediately accessible to the human conscience
in a self-evident way. Yet this foundational stance is hard to be maintained
in a postmodern society. There has been unresolvable disagreement on the
nature and content of the divine law and on its application to a particular
situation. For example, it would be hard to contend that the structure of
social institution is given with immutable form in natural laws or natural
order. Human civilization shows that spheres are not fixed but evolve and
further differentiate through technological and scientific advances. They
are constantly reconfigured in history through human creativity and the
ordering and structuring work of the Logos and the Spirit. This dynamic
and contingent aspect needs to be understood in a new, different theological framework than static creational order or ordinances.

In addition, a postmodern society dismisses the Christian idea of
God and faith as a particular claim of meaning. The major challenge for
the covenantal ethics is how to keep the covenant, democracy, and human
rights theonomous in a society that no longer culturally confesses the same
God. The Free Church Calvinists struggled hard to keep covenant from
degenerating to contract, democracy to pure human sovereignty, human
rights to human self-sufficiency, and majority rule to majority dictator-
ship. In a society where Christianity no longer constitutes the common
cultural language and symbol of society, the task for Christian community
is much more complex and difficult. This raises the question of how we
should understand the nature of covenant and its universal basis in postmodern society. How should we understand covenant today? How is it
possible, and on what basis? The incorporation of a more thoroughly fal-
libilistic and intersubjective methodology of practical reasoning, such as
communicative ethics, would help to overcome the foundational fallacy of
covenantal theology.

III. Nature and Characteristics of Covenant

From the theological and political beliefs of the Free Church Calvinist tradition, one could infer the following social and moral characteristics of covenant:

1) The idea of covenant espouses the belief that human beings are

essentially social. Although their origin and destiny may transcend history, they are always situated in, thus conditioned by, the particular circumstances and needs of society. However, a covenantal community is different from a purely natural community by virtue of its emphasis on human critical willfulness and the existence of divine law. A covenantal community is partially artificial and partially natural. That is, a human being is a creature whose life is fundamentally dependent on God, and interdependent with other human beings and creatures. The social nature of humanity implies that human beings are naturally inclined toward one another, thus some form of social cooperation, such as nurture, love, and companionship, and assistance, is indispensable for survival and fulfillment. This idea is adequately captured and expressed by Johannes Althusius' idea of symbiosis.

For Althusius, human beings are essentially symbiotic beings. "Symbiosis" means, literally (from the Greek word, *symbioticus*), "living together." That is, human life is symbiosis, which is possible in society by means of various forms and patterns of social uniting. Symbiosis encompasses both social (as stated by *"sym-"*) and natural (*"-biotius"*) dimensions. Althusius says, "[M]an [sic] by nature is a gregarious animal born for cultivating society with other men [sic], but not by nature living alone as wild beasts do, nor wandering about as birds."[32] For Althusius, the term *symbiosis* is interchangeable with that of covenant; covenant refers to a basic political-moral mechanism used to form and unite various individuals and institutions. For Althusius, the term *social* is synonymous to covenantal or associational.

By virtue of their covenantal origins, according to Althusius, human beings are not isolated individuals but symbiotic social beings. Although human beings are conditioned and subjected to the natural, biological necessities and processes, they are more fundamentally bound by a moral relationship to God and other human beings. The necessity is always mediated, interpreted through human history and culture. In other words, necessity is always understood as a socialized necessity and human moral volition is always influenced by particular needs and concerns of life. Human social life deals with both needs (and utilities) arising from natural, biological contingency, and morality demanded by God's law. Covenant includes these two aspects in a dynamic and organic way. Althusius' theology is distinguished from that of the naturalists and contractarians by means of his belief in God and God's order in the universe. Human life is more than mere natural, biological existence by virtue of its essential social nature. Symbiotic life is possible because of the divine moral order that is infused in every aspect of human life.

2) Covenant transforms natural human beings to conscious, discursive moral agents, and natural or private relationships to moral and public ones. It brings forth the formation of a new social solidarity on a free purposive volition of moral agents. Moral agency is inconceivable and meaningless without acknowledging human capacity for freedom and decision. Human obedience to God is morally imperfect unless it is motivated and done by free will. Although human beings are morally imperfect and easily tempted and swayed, God rendered this capacity possible to human beings. Power to choose and freedom to decide are the gifts of God which make human beings moral agents thus obeying God's laws freely in cooperation with God.

3) Covenant indicates a cooperative, willful human endeavor to achieve a common ground of action under the guidance of the divine law. Covenant, in the Reformed Christian tradition, is concerned with the question of order. Covenant is a primal mechanism of creating a moral community under God. In covenantal thinking, a community is not conceived as a homogeneous group of a narrow, protective wall (*munis*) among the likeminded (*com-*) or kin or tribe. Rather its boundary is identified with the whole of God's creation, including both human and non-human members. The idea of covenant was rediscovered in the sixteenth and seventeenth centuries when a traditional society was in disarray, its social relationships were under strain, and the structure of society was undergoing radical institutional and material changes. For Calvinists, the social order was not something naturally given, once and for all, but was something purposive and artificial which was to be achieved by a willful struggle and decision of the agent.[33] They believed that genuine order was based on freedom. Coercive order still falls short of perfect order. As such, it was intimately related to the will of the agent, such as God and human beings. Specifically, order is achieved only when a human being freely obeys God; perfect order resides in the consent of humanity to God, as inspired by grace.

For Free Church Calvinists, covenant provided a new theological and political principle to secure the foundation of social order upon human free consent. Covenant recognizes the dimension of free will in individuals. It represents government by consent. It works on the premise that only a shared moral understanding provides a legitimate basis for order. Conversely, social order, once disrupted, can be restored only by human consent.[34] By emphasizing "consensus" as the basis of social morality, covenant harmonizes the demands of freedom and order. In covenantal relationship, freedom is neither anarchic nor orderless, yet order does not suffocate individual freedom and creativity.[35] By harmonizing these seemingly conflicting ideas of freedom and order, covenant achieves the optimum social conditions for individual freedom and social order. It presents a political mechanism that renders a maximally constructive and minimally destructive social arrangement.[36]

This political design was derived from profound theological insights into human nature. Free Church Calvinists understood a human being as a creature of inalienable worth made in the image of God. This constituted the fundamental basis of human dignity and thus human rights. Every human being is vested with the rights to life, freedom, and self-decision. Every human being is equal before God, and to each other. On the other hand, they understood a human being as a sinner who is tempted by the destructive desires and goals of domination, greed, and indulgence. Thus, a human being needs an adequate form of control, regulation, and restraint. These two contrasting anthropological insights gave structure and shape to the Reformed understanding of politics. Polity should be that which protects human dignity, freedom, and equality before God, yet at the same time, with proper means and institutional legal arrangements, that which helps to prevent and restrain destructive human desires. Political powers must be arranged in a way to ensure the protection of the basic human dignity, freedom, and justice. Hence, it is no surprise that Reformed Christian churches, equipped with these anthropological insights, have contributed significantly to the formation and development of modern ideas of human rights, separation of power, and democracy. For the Free Church Calvinists, covenant presented the most feasible theological and political idea, which best embraces and harmonizes these anthropological insights.

Doctrinally, this issue was adequately discussed and expressed in the Puritan dispute with Arminians and Antinomians. The dispute focused the relation of the divine election and the human free action, i.e., the divine agency and human agency.[37] Specifically, the doctrine of predestination was a focal issue. The Puritans responded to this theological challenge by means of covenant. Arminians challenged Calvinists on the latter's deficiency in moral sanction. They argued that if everything depends on the decree of the divine election, that is to say, if it is in God's hand to elect and reject, regardless of our achievements or character, what is the nature and meaning of human responsibility? If I am not elect, why should I try at all?[38] By pivoting the idea of rational choice, Arminianism asserted that human beings were naturally good, intelligent, and capable to ascertain the right from the wrong. By inference, it denied original sin, proclaimed the competence of human reason, and allowed the autonomous individual a self-interest prior to all other moral concerns.[39] On the other hand, antinomianism charged that Calvin did not give enough attention to the sufficiency of grace and the assurance of salvation. If Arminius proposed a kind of ethical rationalism, displacing the divine initiative, Antinomians failed to suggest any method of moral struggle or achievement, and any significance of human response and participation in the divine initiative. Licentiousness and moral indolence seemed to be their logical conclusion.

The idea of covenant effectively resolved the problems and difficulties posed by the Arminians and Antinomians. Puritans prevented the doctrine of grace from mistakenly sliding into moral laxity, inertia, passivity and indolence. The Puritans needed to discover the explicit theological ground for the good works without compromising the absoluteness of the divine sovereignty in election. Puritans needed to rebut Arminians by re-emphasizing the absolute sovereignty of God over humanity, while at the same time, rejecting Antinomians by pointing to the assurance of salvation, yet without sacrificing human imperfection to holiness, on the other hand. Covenant was the theological idea they utilized to solve these difficulties. Perry Miller's comment is relevant here:

> Antinomians expected God's grace to do all, [while] Arminians attributed everything to our consent. The covenant theology held to both the grace and the consent, to the decree of God and the full responsibility of man, to assurance in spite of sin and morality in spite of assurance.[40]

4) In the Free Church tradition, covenant has a bilateral, reciprocal character. Covenant is created through the exchange of mutual entrustment. In covenant, one entrusts oneself to the other party, correspondingly accepting the entrustment of the latter.[41] By giving and taking entrustment, the relationship becomes a commitment to each other. This bilateral, reciprocal character stretches to include the divine-human relationships, such as in the covenant of grace. Although a covenant between God and humanity is an asymmetrical one, it does not impair human responsibility. The God-human relationship in covenantal thinking, however much God's sovereignty is emphasized, does not abolish human participation and responsibility. Elazar supports this self-determining volitional nature of covenant by pointing out that Biblical Hebrew has no word for "obey." Rather "hearken" is the correct description for human response to God's

covenantal initiation. He comments, "The act of hearkening is an act of hearing, considering, agreeing, and then acting. It is a sign of human freedom, of free will, whereby in order to act human we must consciously decide to do so, even in response to God."[42]

How then did the covenantal theologians reconcile the idea of God's sovereignty with that of a bilateral covenant? According to covenantal theologians, bilateral, reciprocal relationships are possible through God's own self-limitation and accommodation to humanity. God, through *kenosis*, made room for human participation and free consent. This view protects human participation and God's sovereignty, at the same time. The sovereign God is obliged only by God's own free will. Perry Miller notes that covenant "made possible a voluntary relation of man to God, even though man's will was considered impotent and God's grace irresistible."[43] It is "an agreement of the unequal upon just and equal terms."[44]

The idea of covenant helped Reformed theology overcome the tension between grace and human responsibility. It responded to soteriological and moral questions simultaneously. In covenantal theology, human beings became free, willful agents, without impairing assurances of their salvation, and also without denying their permanent moral imperfection.

5) Rational discourse has a critical place in covenantal theology. First, rational discourse is necessary in the covenanting process because the concrete demands of divine law are not directly discernable in nature. The divine truth and demands required rational discourse. No one may claim a privileged possession or full, complete knowledge of God's demands. Yet, no one is exempt from at least some participation in it. Therefore, the knowledge and discernment of the divine will require participation and cooperation of all members for its maximum result. Secondly, rational discourse is necessary in order to screen disguised partial interests, to overcome limitations of any human knowledge, and to bring mutual edification. Human understanding and application of morality are always limited, and vulnerable to manipulation, distortion, and ideological deception.[45] Some form of the hermeneutics of suspicion can be noted operating here.[46] That is, the Free Church Calvinism institutionalized criticism as an integral aspect of its institutional life. Its profound understanding of human depravity and sin, as mentioned above, made criticism an indispensable aspect of the political process. Calvinism challenged abuses and pretensions at every level and every point of society. No human authority, religious or secular, was exempt from mutual examination and scrutiny. As such, criticism contributed to the protection of individual freedom and the institutional integrity of society. Faith in the sovereignty

of God was behind the impulse to challenge pretentious authority and power. Calvinists believed that every human being is free and responsible before God through his or her conscience, which is accepted as the universal source and ground of moral authority.

This critical orientation was conducive to social change. Free Church Calvinism was infused with the impulse toward social reform. The zeal for positive social reform and the passion for religious freedom were necessarily correlated. The Free Church Calvinists attempted to carry out the practical implications of religious beliefs, such as the sovereignty of God and holiness, in the non-religious realm, such as family, the church, kingship, law, parliament, and economy.

> The zeal for positive reform is one of the most constant and indisputable notes of Puritanism. Reform the universities . . . Reform the cities . . . the countries, . . . the Sabbath . . . the ordinances, the worship of God . . . Every plant which my heavenly Father hath not planted should be rooted up.[47]

6) Covenant is a mechanism of binding different individuals or social groups under God. Covenant has an effect of reconstituting diversity and differences into a newly ordered social relationship. Transcending previous forms of loyalties and tribal divisions, covenant tends to generate a new form of social solidarity which is more public than previous ones.[48] A covenantal approach acknowledges legitimate differences among diverse groups. Solidarity is understood neither as something given in nature nor as something imposed from above. It is rather understood to emerge through a pact between the different parties. In a covenantal thinking, diversity is constitutive aspect of human social relationship. God created the universe in pluriform. Diversity presents, on the one hand, the potentiality of a higher fulfillment, and on the other hand, the threat of anarchy. It respects the individual freedom and agency of each party. Reflection and choice are involved from the beginning in the process of reaching agreement. As such, it helps to preserve their respective integrities and identities in binding each other in pursuit of a common purpose.[49] A covenanting process, which is communicative in nature as I will discuss later, presents a methodology of adjudication of different moral claims among various groups.

7) Covenant is adaptive and responsive to the changes and vicissitudes of society. It allows a constant revision of the rules of polity in response to the changing needs and concerns of society. This implies that

social structure and polities are neither absolutely fixed (in nature or rationality) nor entirely arbitrary; instead, they tentatively and provisionally formed and arranged through mutual agreement in light of divine laws.

8) Covenant establishes social relationship upon the obligation of mutual accountability and fidelity. Behind the obligation is the authority of God. God is the overseer of a covenant. Covenant obliges us to God as the highest source and ground of our existence. "Covenant involves an acknowledgment of what we did not create that has made us what we are."[50] Obligation is usually specified in laws, but not exhausted by them. Covenantal obligation is larger than the letters of laws. Covenantal obligation points us beyond the immediate goals and individual interests. These obligations include the responsibilities toward people wider than the immediate partners of a particular transaction. Covenant connects us to the vulnerable others who may not be the immediate partners of our transaction, but along the way will be affected by our decisions. This presence of others, "which we cannot fully fathom or control, calls to us, requires our recognition, and obliges our response, even before we place ourselves under obligation or decide to assume responsibility for this other."[51] Covenant enables us to realize the interdependent nature of our existence as the members of God's creation. Obligation is not confined to the immediate partners of transaction. Every transaction must be examined in light of the solidarity of creation in God. Something universal is represented in covenant. Every human-human covenant must be reminded of its gift character. It is possible through the gift of God. It is indebted to the invaluable natural resources and human resources of the past. It should be situated and assessed in light of the ultimate covenant of God with God's creation in Jesus Christ. The poor, the oppressed have a new moral status in this covenantal context. They are the invisible partners of covenant. God listens and defends their causes. Law is not identical to covenant, yet it specifies the minimal requirement of obligation. Covenantal obligation is larger than law.

One may say that covenantal obligation is the obligation toward the common good, which specifies God's concern for the well-being of all members of creation. The Christian idea of the common good is based on the fundamental interconnectedness and interdependence of human and non-human existence in God. Because of its universal obligatory nature, covenant is intimately related to the common good. As covenantal obligation extends universally to every living creature, the common good fleshes out the aim and context of covenantal obligation. Covenantal obligation could be properly figured out in light of and in the context of the common good. Every human transaction, to be covenant, must be consistent with and contributive to the common good. The common good helps to spell out the scope and nature of covenantal obligation. It points out our often forgotten obligations to the invisible, vulnerable others.

The obligatory nature of covenant becomes clearer when compared to contract. Covenant is different from contract in terms of its scope of unlimited commitment and obligation.[52] Contract implies limited commitment. In covenantal thinking, the responsibility is not confined to immediate covenantal partners. Covenant presupposes the moral community of persons which is universal and inclusive in God. Hence, the sense of responsibility in covenant goes beyond all limited causes, loyalties, and ethical boundaries. In the final analysis, the scope of covenantal virtue is co-extensive with the universal community of creation.

Love is the true, germane, underlying ethos of covenant. According to Coccejus, covenant is "nothing other than a divine declaration of the method of perceiving the love and God and of obtaining union and communion with Him."[53] Love is always more than formal procedure and rules. As Paul Tillich aptly analyzed, love does not exclude the demands of justice but fulfills them. Love requires the appropriate forms or structures of mutual interaction. As a structuring mechanism, covenant is an important means to achieve the principles of justice. In covenant the concerns of both love and justice are adequately addressed. Covenant embraces both symbolic-organic and rational-discursive aspects in its framework. Guided and inspired by love, covenant is not allowed to degenerate into contract.

IV. Covenant in a Global Society

A covenantal polity and moral thinking is especially suitable and appropriate for a global, pluralistic society. As a strict independence of the nation-state recedes and many states are now linked into new constitutional bonds, a global society experiences the enormous need for an elaborate and diversified system of cooperation among different national, political, cultural, economic groups to deal with common problems. At the same time, many groups continue to insist on maintaining their identities, uniqueness, and traditions. As the world becomes more and more interdependent and compressed toward each other, as we observed in the introduction, covenant has become a viable paradigm of polity. Covenant helps to meet these conflicting demands for the cooperative order (shared rule) as well as independence and self-rule of each group. Covenant presents a moral mechanism to produce some shared moral principles among different groups. This indicates the existence of a significant theoretical elective affinity between covenant and pluralism. This point is also proved by the historical study of the emergence of covenantal polity in the West, especially in the United States of America and in Switzerland.

According to Jewish political scientist Daniel Elazar, the genesis of covenantal society is closely associated with certain geographical or temporal characteristics, such as a new frontier, borderland, or a transitive epoch. Switzerland and the USA are a couple of historical examples for these characteristics. Many people fled from autocratic rules to wildlands, to form themselves into civil communities with minimum interference.[54] A frontier society is characterized by the inflow of new people and the vacuum of any established social order. A frontier society does not have any established structure or patterns of polity, thus it is in need of a structure which inculcates and guides cooperative efforts among new settlers. Often previous experience of the evil of collectivism further encourages the experiment of a new political polity such as covenantalism. In a formative period, settlers often remain in isolation from the previous country or culture in order to maintain higher moral standard and purity.

The encounter between different peoples and cultures in borderlands (e.g. the Romano-Germanic borderland from the Alps to the North Sea, the Celtic-Norse borderland northward to the Arctic) also shows the rise of a new form of moral order for mutual regulation. The encounter, if it does not lead to war, tends to unsettle and negate a previous political pattern of one people or culture, anticipating the invention of a new form of polity through deliberate mutual reflection and choice between different peoples.[55]

All these sociological and political features of borderlands and frontiers show that the possibility and necessity of covenanting increase to the extent that people are detached from their previous forms of life and traditions.[56] There are strong incentives for cooperative partnership such as the necessity to solve the problems together rather than individually. In these situations, the polity tends to be the product of a new conscious design rather than a customary repetition of authoritative convention and tradition.

One can easily see that free trade and incessant flows of people, information, and goods in a global society create social and existential situations equivalent to frontiers and borderlands. As peoples of different religious and ethnic/cultural backgrounds are migrating to and settling in the same place, the idea of covenant becomes extraordinarily relevant to cope with the challenges of order, peace and justice ensuing from the situation of pluralism. As evidence of this trend, a global society also witnesses the rise of many covenantal or quasi-covenantal forms (federate, confederate) of political economic bodies and constitutional structures in global, regional, state, and local levels (e.g. WTO, UN, EU, ASEAN, etc.).

V. Communicative Ethics and Covenant: Critical Comparison

This section explores the possibility of synthesis between covenantal theology and communicative ethics. I contend that there exists a striking similarity between the two in terms of mechanisms and dynamics for forming agreement. I will undertake this task first by comparing the idea of covenant in covenantal theology with the concept of communication in Habermas' communicative ethics. I shall show that this synthesis helps covenantal theology not only to preserve its essential theological and ethical insights, but also to reformulate them on a more pluralistic, historical, and post-foundational basis by overcoming its own inherent difficulties in these areas.

A. Similarities

Covenant displays political and sociological premises that are analogous to those of communicative ethics. In fact, the idea of covenant has the following distinctive affinities with communicative ethics:

1) The similarity between covenant and communicative ethics is found in their methodological reliance on a performative nature of human utterance. Habermas, borrowing from J. L. Austin and J. R. Searle, defines utterance as the most elementary unit of human communication. An utterance has two components: performative statement and propositional statement. As every utterance is made in a society, in the matrix of relationality, a performative statement situates a propositional statement in a particular social situation regarding the three realms of validity claims. According to Habermas, a performative force means the capacity of the speech act to move and persuade the hearer as desired by the speaker. That is, a performative speech is the one which incurs actions by saying something. Some examples of performative statements are "I (hereby) promise you . . . ," "I (hereby) command you . . . ," "I (hereby) assert to you . . . ," etc. In a performative action, the speaker proposes a specific engagement into which the hearer is invited to respond.

In a performative speech, a speaker intends to generate an interpersonal relationship with the listener. In a performative speech, the speaker and the hearer raise validity claims by inviting the recognition of each other's claims. And when the validity of a particular claim is accepted, an obligatory relationship is formed. The performative power of an utterance consists in its capacity to move a hearer. With a performative speech, a speaker makes an offer that can be either accepted or rejected. Habermas notes,

> An utterance can "count" as a promise, assertion, request or question if and only if the speaker makes an offer which, insofar as the hearer accepts it, he is ready to "to make good"—the speaker has to engage himself, that is to indicate that in certain situations he will draw the consequences for action. The kind of obligation constitutes the content of the engagement . . . hereafter I shall take speaker-engagement to include both a specific content and the sincerity with which the speaker is willing to enter into the engagement.[57]

A new reciprocal relationship may arise when the hearer accepts an offer of the speaker. If the hearer believes the validity of a claim, the hearer enters into the indicated relationship, accepting accompanying obligations and consequences. Habermas argues that a reciprocal bond engendered by a performative action is not purely subjective or constructive. It has a rational basis. He says, "In the final analysis, the speaker can have an illocutionary effect on the hearer (and vice versa) because the speech-act-typical obligations are tied to cognitively testable validity claims, that is, because the reciprocal bonds have a rational basis. The engaged speaker normally connects the specific sense in which he wants to take up an interpersonal relation with a thematically stressed validity claim."[58] Then, where does a performative force come from? When a speech act takes place in the context of institutionalized social relationship, the performative force is borrowed from the binding authority of existing norms. In the case that any established social relationship is not in place, the speaker develops this force by soliciting the recognition of the hearer through the cogency of his or her claims.

A covenanting process is essentially performative. It consists of the exchanges of entrustment around a promissory engagement that is performative. In a covenant, a speaker, in making a suggestion or proposal, solicits the hearer to the intended relationship. Yet covenant is different from communicative ethics by its inclusion of a non-verbal, symbolic dimension. Covenant usually consists of not only performative exchanges of verbal promise (oaths, vows) but also non-verbal symbolic gestures or actions (e.g. shaking hands, exchange of gifts, eating together). However, this non-verbal, symbolic action also has a performative force. A performative symbolic action, like performative speeches, contributes to the establishment of relationship between the parties of covenant. Regarding a performative nature of symbolic actions in the covenanting process, Donald Evans says,

> Sometimes an institutional act can be performed not only verbally but also non-verbally. I acknowledge status by bowing or saluting; I welcome by shaking hands; I bless by laying on of hands; I marry by mingling blood; I command by pointing; or I mourn by rending garments. Each action, like a performative utterance, has a performative force.[59]

Another similarity between covenant and communicative ethics is found in their emphasis of trustworthiness as the immanent basis of dialogic engagement. For their success, covenant and communicative processes rely upon the sincerity of the parties to keep the promises and agreements. Habermas says,

> In the expressive use of language the speaker also enters into a speech-act-immanent obligation, namely the obligation to prove trustworthy, to show in the consequence of his action that he has expressed just that intention which actually guides his behavior. In case the immediate assurance expressing what is evident to the speaker himself cannot dispel ad hoc doubts, the truthfulness of the utterance can only be checked against the consistency of his subsequent behavior.[60]

This implies that all three dimensions of validity claims (truth, rightness and sincerity) are inextricably related to each other. For example, in entering moral agreement around redeemed validity claims, moral agents are expected to prove their sincerity through their subsequent actions following the agreement.

2) The idea of covenant implicitly proposes an intersubjective form of human interaction and sociality over against an individualistic or collectivistic one. Although covenant does not specify intersubjective discourse as the necessary process of covenanting, it strongly implies it. The covenant-making process is essentially reciprocal and bilateral, thus communicative, in its nature.[61] It inevitably includes the exchanges of promise, validity claim, argumentation, and mutual criticism. This charac-

teristic is disclosed in every kind of covenantal relationship including the God/human relationship, as mentioned above. Covenant does not abolish human participation and responsibility, however much God's sovereignty and absoluteness are emphasized.

Covenant postulates that each individual has a right of equal access in the decision-making process. Like communicative ethics, its premise is that community, and consequently any human polity which undergirds it, is incomplete or flawed when one party is unjustly excluded or is endowed with unequal opportunity. This implies that participation in the covenanting process and membership in the covenantal community are essential aspects of human life as a social being, and indispensable for the protection and affirmation of one's dignity. Exclusion or marginalization is an inexorable violation and offense against the humanity of the other. This implies that every human being is theoretically a member of the universal communicative community in Habermasian terms, or members of the divine Kingdom, in covenantal terms.

3) Both communicative ethics and covenant, in their discursive process, have the effect of bringing a new form of solidarity that constrains fragmenting plurality and heterogeneity among people. Covenant brings once-separated entities into a new harmony without sacrificing their respective freedom, integrity, and identity.[62] It elevates the participants to a new level of social relationship. Participants in covenant assume a new moral responsibility toward each other. In its political dimension, covenant tends to transform individual voluntary participation and the subsequent intersubjective reasoning process into "a democratic will formation." Elazar is valid in saying, "a covenant establishes a partnership linking diverse entities into a purposeful union of unlimited duration, but one in which the partners maintain their respective integrities throughout."[63]

Both communicative ethics and covenant claim that a common morality is a historically situated one. This is so because the discursive process to reach agreement takes place always in a concrete historical situation. For Habermas, the communicative action takes place in response to particular social problems which threaten the community. Similarly, a covenant is made in a concrete historical context. Every social covenant is a situated covenant. It responds to human necessity and utility under the guidance of the divine law. As such, they attend to historical contingency as well as the normativity of social life.

Communicative ethics and covenantal theology suggest that the institutional structure and order of society are not absolutely fixed, but provisional and penultimate, always open to further revision and reformation.

As the environment and the nature of relationship change, the content of agreement must change accordingly. They attend to both the provisional-historical as well as the enduring structural aspects of the human relationship. They respond to the demands of change and creativity as well as stability and continuity. This reformulation is a vital process in maintaining the continuity and stability for social life with an openness to change.

Covenant renews social relationship on a newly constituted moral basis. Concretely, covenant redefines the terms of mutual interaction among people around things, services and rights.[64] It stipulates a new pattern of social interaction and engagement for people. It sets the parameters of future social expectations by bringing predictability, reliability, and structure to previously disarrayed, confused, and disordered relationships.

4) Covenant and communicative ethics show a critical awareness of the limitation and fallibility of every human moral endeavor. Theologically speaking, covenant takes seriously the sinfulness and fallibility of human nature. Habermas and covenantalists are deeply aware of the limited ability of human beings to do good and be just, and of the fallibility of social systems and institutions that often manifest this sinfulness in an extreme form. Every power must be limited, divided, and shared among the separate bodies. Society needs a constitution and a mechanism to check the human tendency toward the domination and exploitation of others. This awareness leads both covenantalists and Habermas to emphasize critique as a necessary aspect of the social process, and to endorse democracy, pluralism, and human rights as the core polity and values of society.

5) Like communicative ethics, covenant has the effect of correcting or modifying a previously unequal power relationship into a more equal and symmetrical one by redistributing status, authorities, and privileges. Covenant rejects any predetermined permanent rank, grade, status, or privilege among human beings. It implies equal access to membership, goods, and information, and equal opportunity to speak, criticize, and to address in the covenanting process. Elazar indicates that a covenant-based politics is not simply a symbolic matter; it has to do with very concrete demands for power-sharing and the development of institutionalized forms, and the process for doing so.[65]

6) Covenant and communicative ethics share the idea that moral adjudication is not possible on a purely conventional or artificial basis. It needs a certain universal basis, whether it is ontological or epistemological. In this respect, both covenant and communicative ethics are distinguished from the idea of contract, which is, by and large, based on the expediency of the situation and the political interests between people.

I contend that this universal moral basis is expressed in Habermas and the Free Church tradition in terms of the idea of "the transcendental community", that is, in the "ideal speech situation" (or the universal community of communication) for Habermas, and the divine law for covenantal theology. As noted, there is a specific reason why Habermas tries so vigorously to retain some element of universalism in his ethics. Some form of universal basis is indispensable for the critique of ideology, and the adjudication and resolution of differences. Otherwise, criticism itself loses its edge and basis.

This idea of "transcendental community" is nothing new to Reformed Christian theology. For Christians, the ideal community has been identified primarily as the Kingdom of God, and the church as the manifestation and realization of the Kingdom. The idea of "transcendental community" has a practical implication for the church and society in the Free Church tradition. As expressed in the ideas of "the invisible and visible church" and "the church within the church," the church understood its identity and mission in terms of its relationship to the Kingdom of God. Also, this theological understanding had enormous political implications for the development of democracy, human rights, and institutional-associational pluralism in modern society. As the earthly manifestation of the Kingdom, the church understood itself as the ideal moral community of holiness and freedom for society. Therefore, society must emulate the Free Church. Furthermore, they believed in "the possibility of the realization of the Holy Community on earth by the efforts of the elect."[66]

7) Habermas views sincerity or faithfulness as being indispensable for genuine human communication. Unless the participants are sincere and truthful to their intentions, motives, and goals, discourse will be either misled or frustrated despite its free, equal, and uncoercive nature. On the other hand, for Habermas faithfulness refers to the enduring commitment to the content of consent drawn by each participant. Covenant, not only in the process of consenting but also after consent is reached, requires faithfulness of the covenanting partners. Each party is obligated to the other to keep the content of agreement. Durability or faithfulness is a necessary virtue of covenant. It is a moral quality which discriminates covenant from contract. Durability of human covenant has its basis in the durability and faithfulness of God who is faithful to the creation and Godself. Sincerity and faithfulness obtains much more lasting and sustaining character and power by virtue of God's covenantal love and commitment.

B. Differences

1) Although covenantal theology appreciates the role of human will in moral decision, this does not mean that covenant purely relies on human voluntarism. God's grace is what enables the believers to volunteer for God's service. God initiates the covenant; human beings respond to it. Baptism was the sign of this free, active interaction between God and human beings. In other words, human consent to God's action is not the consequence of pure self-autonomy on the part of humanity. Rather, voluntary action was viewed as the sign of election. Walzer's observation is very relevant on this point. He comments,

> The covenant was a way of activating men and not of controlling God. Nor was that consent a matter of free choice for grace sought out the saints and no man earned salvation by volunteering for it. What the covenant did was to suggest a disciplined and methodical response to grace, a new, active and willing obedience to command--these were the major themes of Puritan "practical" theology during the seventeenth century.[67]

2) Like communicative ethics, covenantal theology implicitly promulgates the ideals of freedom, equality, and reciprocity among covenantal partners. However, covenant and communicative ethics, despite their striking similarities, have substantial differences in their understandings of those concepts. For covenantalists these ideals are not counterfactual epistemological values embedded in a communication process. Rather, they are based on the recognition of all human beings as the children of God— as free, equal, worthy members of the Kingdom of God. Specifically, freedom, equality, and fairness arise from the dignity of every human being.

3) Covenant respects the value of individuality and freedom. In covenantal thinking, individuality refers to the infinite, irreplaceable value of each human being. However, in Christian context, especially in a Reformed theological context, individuality is understood in the context of the agent's relationship with God. Human beings are social animals, but by virtue of their primordial covenantal relationship with God, they are not simply products of a particular society.

Affirmation of individuality is critical for the task of social criticism. Liberalism espoused individual ability to transcend their surroundings, communities, traditions, and their own life history. Habermas proposed an intersubjective notion of neutrality, detachment, and critical transcendence. His idea of the "ideal speech situation" proposes a kind of committed universalism, freedom, and criticism. Constructive criticism is possible through its presuppositional commitment to the universal community of communication as the precondition for free, reciprocal, unrestrained dialogue. Yet, in covenantal thinking, the critical ability resides not in any intrinsic human moral or epistemological capacity, but in humanity's primordial covenantal relationship with God.[68] As *imago dei* (the image of God), human beings are made to be free to the "other" by virtue of their relation to God. Yet, this freedom and self-transcendence is not individualistic or monological, but essentially dialogical and relational.

Self-transcendence takes place in a relational, dialogical way. God is the most important other in the process of critical reflection. The capacity of dialogical self-transcendence is critical for covenantal method (as it is for communicative ethics) for renewing and restructuring community, because it indicates the ability of the agent to distance one from one's interests, preferences, and goods and one's community and to reach out to the others in common search for truth and justice.

4) Habermas states that an undistorted communication is possible only with the full recognition of the other as one's dialogical partner. Like communicative ethics, covenant is based on the presupposition that recognizes others as free, equal partners of life. Recognition of the other as the equal, worthy partner carries an enormous moral implication in it. Equality is a critical element of covenanting process. Covenant envisions and promotes the equality of human beings. However, covenant theory is different from Habermas in its theological orientation; the equality of human beings is rooted in and sustained by the fact that human beings are created in the *imago dei*. And God affirms the worth of every human being as God's covenant partner in Jesus Christ. To accept the other as a covenant partner or as a communicative partner means that one affirms the fundamental human dignity of the other as the creature of God and as a member of God's community. Covenant requires the recognition of others as *others*—their dignity, freedom, equality, rights to be different, to address their concerns, and to challenge any of the others.

The theological basis of the human dignity attains methodological significance in covenantal ethics. The membership of humanity in God's creation is the basis of intersubjective acceptance and role exchange. To accept the other as a covenantal partner means that his or her fundamental human dignity as the child of God is affirmed. Conversely, this implies that participation in the covenanting process and membership in the covenantal community are indispensable for the protection and affirmation of one's dignity. Exclusion or marginalization means the violation of and offense against this fundamental God-given-dignity. A just society is possible only with the full recognition of others as one's equal covenantal partner.

5) By emphasizing the theistic ground of human relationality and sociality, covenantism goes beyond the limitation of Habermas' formalism. The Christian idea of covenant clarifies and specifies the relational ground of human freedom, equality, and reciprocity. As mentioned earlier, covenantalism presumes that all humanity is interrelated and interdependent in God. It acknowledges the irreducible sanctity of each person as the latter is created in the image of God. The idea of a personal God provides a concrete basis of relationality for moral beliefs and endeavors. As feminist social theorists correctly point out, Habermas suppresses a concrete relational ground of human moral actions. Covenant gives a sense of concreteness, a sense of relatedness to commitment, for commitment arises out of the nexus of relationship. Relationship to God defines and specifies the scope, boundary, and direction of human freedom and responsibility.

VI. Summary

The idea of covenant has shown a great degree of formal-procedural affinity with Habermas' communicative ethics. The Reformed theological idea of covenant, because of its communicative structure, does not face any difficulty in incorporating the intersubjective rationality of Habermas. Covenant fuses several critical religious ethical thrusts such as prophetic criticism, protection of human dignity, recognition and respect for others, freedom, and sensibility to order and change. It maintains creative tensions between freedom and order, diversity and unity, criticism and structure, individuality and solidarity, change and continuity. Covenantal theology suggests an alternative to tyranny and anarchy, authoritarianism and liberal individualism. As such, it is able to embrace viable aspects of liberal political values, institutions, and politics. Here I suggest the idea of covenant not only as an organizational principle of social associations and politics, but also as an intersubjective methodology of practical reasoning in making covenant. One may refer to communicative action as a concrete methodology for making covenant. Furthermore, Habermas' theory may help covenantal ethics to overcome the exclusivistic or chauvinistic tendency and practices of covenant, thus possibly helping to make the notion of covenant genuinely open, inclusive, and universal. Habermas helps to connect the Christian idea of covenant to the democratic politics of public discourse, justice, and peace in a postmodern society.

If communication is a significant moral category for a free, fair human interaction, how is it related to the divine –human relationship? What interactive form does God use in relating to human beings? Covenantal theologians argue that covenant is the form that God uses to relate to humanity. Then, what is the implication of our discussion of covenant and communicative ethics for the God-human relationship? What does communicative action mean for God? Does God also use communicative action to communicate with us? How is God's communication different from ours? What does this difference mean for our project in this volume? The discussion of these questions makes us revisit the doctrine of God. I believe that our discussion has a profound implication for a more adequate and constructive understanding of God and God's economy. A new understanding of the being and action of God has implications for our moral reasoning because the latter, unlike secular philosophical ones, is shaped in response to God who was revealed in Jesus Christ. With these questions, we turn to the next chapter to discuss the relationship of the doctrine of the Trinity and communicative ethics.

Notes

1. Max L. Stackhouse, *Creeds, Society and the Human Rights: Studies in Three Cultures* (Grand Rapids: W. B. Eerdmans, 1984), 57ff. Stackhouse divides the Reformed tradition into three branches: Evangelical Calvinism, Imperial Calvinism, and Free Church Calvinism. Free Church Calvinism was the belief of England and New England Puritans, and Scottish Presbyterians. Despite some historical variations, Free Church Calvinism is characterized by a congregationalist, covenantal church constitution. It proposed a republican conception of the polity, and affirmed a consistent separation of church and state. According to Stackhouse, Free Church Calvinism was deeply influenced by Swiss (especially Zwinglian and Bullingerian federalism) and Dutch Calvinist theology.

2. Ibid., 57.

3. Unidentified source, quoted in Perry Miller, *The New England Mind: The Seventeenth Century* (Boston: Beacon Press, 1961), 377.

4. William Klempa, "The Concept of Covenant in Sixteenth- and Seventeenth-Century Continental and British Reformed Theology," in *Major Themes in a Reformed Tradition*, ed. D. K. McKim (Grand Rapids: W. B. Eerdmans, 1992), 94.

5. Leonard J. Trinterud, "The Origins of Puritanism," *Church History* 20 (1951): 48. As such, the notion of a covenant of works has later provided a theological basis for the political theory of social contracts, natural law, and natural rights.

6. Stackhouse, *Creeds, Society, and Human Rights*, 60-61.

7. Daniel J. Elazar, *Covenant & Constitutionalism*, The Covenant Tradition in Politics, vol.3, (New Brunswick, N.J.: Transaction Publishers, 1998), 43.

8. Joseph L. Allen, *Love and Conflict: A Covenantal Model of Christian Ethics* (Lanham, New York, London: University Press of America, 1995), 17.

9. Cf. Stackhouse, *Creeds, Society, and Human Rights*, 57.

10. Ibid., 69.

11. Ibid.

12. Ibid., 70.

13. Stackhouse, *Creeds, Society, and Human Rights*, 64.

14. Ibid., 57.

15. Ibid., 51-52.

16. Ibid., 64.

17. Max L. Stackhouse, "Moral Meanings of Covenant," *The Annual of the Society of Christian Ethics* (1996): 258.

18. Stackhouse, *Creeds, Society, and Human Rights*, 52; see also John Witte, Jr., "The Church's Legal Challenges in the Twenty First Century," in *Moral Values: The Challenge of the Twenty-First Century*, ed. W. Lawson Taitte (Dallas: University of Texas, 1996), 130ff.

19. Ibid.

20. Calvinists found the unity of piety and justice, faith and holiness in the Decalogue. If the first table is concerned with the piety, the second is with justice.

21. James W. Skillen, "From Covenant of Grace to Equitable Public Pluralism: The Dutch Calvinist Contribution," *Calvin Theological Journal* 31 (1996): 76.

22. Gordon J. Spykman, "Pluralism: Our Last Best Hope," *Christian Scholar's Review* 10 (1981): 107.

23. Johannes Althusius, *The Politics of Johannes Althusius*, abridg. & trans. by Frederick S. Carney, 3d ed. (Boston: Beacon Press, 1964), 65.

24. Daniel J. Elazar, *Covenant and Commonwealth*, The Covenant Tradition in Politics, vol.2, (New Brunswick, N.J.: Transaction Publishers, 1996), 312.

25. A.S.P. Woodhouse, "Introduction" in *Puritanism and Liberty: Being the Army Debates (1647-9) from the Clarke Manuscripts with Supplementary Documents*, A.S.P. Woodhouse (ed.) (London: J.M. Dent and Sons Limited, 1938), 37.

26. Abraham Kuyper, "Sphere Sovereignty," in *Abraham Kuyper: A Centennial Reader*, ed. James D. Bratt (Grand Rapids: W. B. Eerdmans Publishing Co., 1998), 467.

27. Kuyper's idea of sphere sovereignty finds its striking resonance in Michael Walzer's idea of sphere justice.

28. Daniel J. Elazar, *Covenant & Polity in Biblical Israel*, The Covenant Tradition in Politics. vol.1. (New Brunswick, N.J.: Transaction Publishers, 1995), 44.

29. Cf. Carl Friedrich, *Trends of Federalism in Theory and Practice* (New York: Frederick A. Praeger, 1968).

30. Eric Mount, Jr. also points out the hierarchal and exclusivistic tendency of covenantalism when it is too closely identified with the bonds of community. ("The Currency of Covenant," *The Annual of the Society of Christian Ethics* (1996): 306)

31. Cf. H. R. Niebuhr, *The Responsible Self: An Essay in Christian Moral Philosophy* (New York, Hagerstown, San Francisco, London: Harper & Row Publishers, 1963).

32. Althusius, *The Politics of Johannes Althusius*, 17.

33. Michael Walzer, *The Revolution of the Saints: A Study in the Origins of*

Radical Politics (New York: Atheneum, 1970), 161. Calvinists tried to find the source of order and morality on a non-metaphysical basis. They rejected the traditional, medieval hierarchical understanding of the social system and morality which was based on the idea of a chain of being, a natural inevitability of hierarchy, hereditary loyalty, and organic connection. According to Walzer, the Calvinist idea of covenant has changed "the chains of being" to the chains of command and office, and social relationships from status to mutual agreement (Ibid., 166).

34. Elazar, *Covenant & Polity in Biblical Israel*, 3.

35. Covenantal theology provided correctives to rigid Calvinistic determinism and to the dangers of both Antinomianism and Arminianism.

36. Elazar, *Covenant & Polity in Biblical Israel*, 75.

37. Cf. Miller, *The New England Mind*, especially chapter 13.

38. Calvin says,

> When man [sic] has been taught that no good thing remains in his power, and that he is hedged about on all sides by most miserable necessity, in spite of this he should nevertheless be instructed to aspire to a good of which he is empty, to a freedom of which he has been deprived (*Institutes of Christian Religion*, ed. John T. McNeil, 2 vols. Philadelphia: Westminster Press, 255).

39. Miller, *The New England Mind*, 415-416.

40. Ibid., 389.

41. Cf. Joseph Allen, *Love and Conflict*, 32.

42. Elazar, *Covenant & Polity in Biblical Israel*, 70-71.

43. Miller, *The New England Mind*, 382.

44. Ibid., 376.

45. Elazar says, "The conditions of covenant require communication with both sides participating, in which the radical inequality is modified or suspended at least for purposes of the communication." (*Covenant & Polity in Biblical Is-*

rael, 44)

46. Even faith cannot be understood as esoteric or idiosyncratic; it is to be reasonable. Thus, it cannot contradict the essential findings or accumulated wisdom and knowledge of common human rationality. It criticizes any claim of faith which is nonsensical or absurd (Stackhouse, *Creeds, Society, and the Human Rights*, 62). This is an important distinction made between faith and fanaticism. Christian faith is a "faith seeking understanding."

47. Woodhouse, "Introduction," in *Puritanism and Liberty: Being the Army Debates (1647-9) from the Clarke Manuscripts with Supplementary Documents*, 43.

48. Daniel J. Elazar, *Covenant and Civil Society*, The Covenant Tradition in Politics, vol. 4, (New Brunswick and London: Transaction Book Publishers, 1998), 308.

49. Covenant does not repudiate the particular identities of covenantal parties but reconstitutes them. In Scripture, the covenanting process usually begins with a preamble that discloses the identities and the relationship of the parties. (Cf. Exodus 20:2; Stackhouse, "Moral Meanings of Covenant," 253.)

50. Eric Mount, Jr., *Covenant, Community and the Common Good: An Interpretation of Christian Ethics* (Cleveland: The Pilgrim Press, 1999), 158.

51. Ibid.

52. H. R. Niebuhr, "The Idea of Covenant and American Democracy," *Church History* 23 (1954): 134.

53. Coccejus, *Summa doctrinae de foedere et testamento Dei*, 1648; quoted in William Klempa, "The Concept of Love," 101.

54. Elazar, *Covenant & Constitutionalism*, 42.

55. Ibid., 247.

56. Ibid., 24.

57. Jürgen Habermas, *Communication and the Evolution of Society*, trans. Thomas McCarthy (Boston: Beacon Press, 1979), 61.

58. Ibid, 63.

59. Donald Evans, *The Logic of Self-Involvement*, (New York: Herder & Herder, 1969), 75.

60. Habermas, *Communication and the Evolution of Society*, 64.

61. Joseph L. Allen notes that covenantal relationship is not simply a biological one, but that which comes about through interactions of mutually entrusting relationship (*Love and Conflict*, 32).

62. Elazar notes that the Hebrew idea of covenant accurately expresses this clarifying and institutionalizing function of covenant. In his view, the Hebrew word *brit* (covenant) means "to bind together or fetter." Its verb form, *lichrot brit*, cutting or making a covenant, is derived from a religious ceremony which first cut a sacrificial animal in half and then bound the two parts together after the participants of the covenant had passed through them (Ibid., 65).

63. Elazar, *Covenant & Polity In Biblical Israel*, 70. This formative organizational efficacy of covenant is well-captured by Althusius' idea of association (Cf. Althusius, *The Politics of Johannes Althusius*). According to Althusius, covenant characterizes the nature of social institutions and their interrelationship.

64. Althusius, *The Politics of Johannes Althusius*, 29-32.

65. Elazar, *Covenant & Polity in Biblical Israel*, 44.

66. Christopher Dawson, "Religious Origins of European Disunity," *Dublin Review* (Oct. 1940); cited in Stackhouse, *Creeds, Society, and the Human Rights*, 65. In recent American history, Martin Luther King Jr.'s idea of "the beloved community" and his civil rights movement show a similar political-religious dynamic. He employed and utilized the implicit idea of the universal covenant of the U.S. Constitution and Scripture as the criteria for his prophetic criticism of segregation, racism, and economic injustice. One may view the civil rights movement as the religiously motivated and democratically enacted communicative-covenantal action.

67. Michael Walzer, *The Revolution of the Saints*, 167.

68. As will be discussed in Chapter 4, in a classical covenantal theology, individuality and critical ability were understood in terms of conscience. For Calvin, conscience was the source of this freedom and transcendence with an implication to be critical of traditional practices, hierarchy and status of society

and religious institutions.

CHAPTER 3

THE TRINITY AND COMMUNICATIVE ETHICS

The goal of this chapter is to explore a trinitarian theological basis for covenantal-communicative ethics. I want to show that the idea of communication is not an alien philosophical idea, but an intrinsic component of Christian doctrines. Specifically I contend that the doctrine, especially a social doctrine, of the Trinity, places communicative interaction at the very center of Christian understanding of God—God's being and action. A social doctrine of the Trinity is not only compatible with the ethical vision and values that communicative ethics presents, but also helps to deepen and expand the theological insights of covenantal theology in a pluralistic social context. It locates covenantal-communicative ethics in a rich, comprehensive, and deep theological horizon and context.

The idea of the Trinity has several merits for a Christian incorporation of covenantal-communicative ethics. First, the doctrine of the Trinity provides a theological framework for the implementation of covenantal-communicative ethics in Christian communities. It is a valuable insight of Hauerwas that the effective implementation of a formal ethics, such as communicative ethics, requires a rich, deep communal underpinning and convictional ground. The formal proceduralism of communicative ethics needs to be undergirded and empowered by a particular religious tradition and moral vision in a way to bolster a communicative procedure; otherwise, communicative proceduralism will wither like cut flowers. Only when it is rooted in a rich religious tradition is communicative ethics prevented from deteriorating into expedient contractualism.

Secondly, intimately related to the first point, the idea of the Trinity provides a comprehensive and dialectic theological framework in which the diverse aspects of Christian experiences, such as the mystical, the sacramental, and the prophetic, are harmonized in a meaningful and coherent way. The Trinity is a religious symbol *par excellence* which integrates the complex and highly differentiated aspects of the divine in a coherent, intelligent, and effective way. That is, the formal and procedural dimension which embodies the prophetic thrust is balanced and empowered by the mystical and the sacramental dimensions. To speak more concretely, the idea of the Trinity embraces and balances what Paul Tillich calls the polarity of ontological elements, namely participation and individualization, dynamics and form, freedom and destiny. According to Paul Tillich, the Trinity is a theological mechanism which resolves a tension experienced between the universal and the historical, the personal and the impersonal, the transcendental and the immanent, the hidden and the manifested.[1] This balance and creative tension is found in the symbols of the three trinitarian persons.

In a trinitarian framework, the mystical and the prophetic are in a creative tension, balancing each other in harmony. If the sacramental refers to the visible, concrete aspect of the divine experience, and the mystical to its ineffable, intimate aspect, the ethical indicates the objective, universal moral demands of the divine. In a trinitarian framework, the infinite mystery of God does not degenerate into ahistoricism, nor is the divine revelation reduced to a theological moral rationalism or ethicalism.[2] The idea of the Trinity helps to relate intimate, subjective religious experiences to objective ethical principles without exhausting the mystery of divine transcendence.

The idea of the Trinity constructively responds to the complex religious-moral situations of a global, pluralistic society which are impinged upon by the diverse religious needs and experiences of people. That is, communicative ethics obtains a comprehensive moral framework for appropriating and translating the rich insights and experiences of a Christian scripture and tradition into a specific moral principle with the universal import. The symbol of the Trinity makes possible the multiple interpretive appropriations of the divine reality in diverse contingent moral situations. The idea of the Trinity helps us to relate the dynamic, complex, highly differentiated divine life to diverse aspects and situations of contemporary human life. Expanding Christian vision and horizon onto the whole realm of divine creation, the idea of the Trinity grants Christians a dynamic openness in engaging with other religious and cultural groups. The doctrine of the Trinity enables Christianity to embrace pluralism without compromising its uniqueness and identity.

However, it must be noted that the discussion of a social doctrine of the Trinity does not indicate the imposition of a Christian master narrative or a grand religious paradigm for a global society under a new guise.

Rather it intends an internal Christian theological justification of covenantal-communicative ethics. That is, the idea of the Trinity provides a plausible theological foundation and warrant for the Christian acceptance of
covenantal-communicative ethics. It locates communicative ethics in a
comprehensive theological-cosmological narrative framework without
preventing the former from being a methodology of moral adjudication for
the common morality. Through its congruence with communicative values, the social doctrine of the Trinity suggests a comprehensive form of
the good for Christians.

I. The Trinity: Social Doctrine of the Trinity

The doctrine of the Trinity has a unique status in Christian theology. It constitutes the essence of Christian theological understanding of
God and God's relationship to the world. The doctrine of the Trinity is
experiencing a renaissance today, and at the center of this renaissance is
the social understanding of the Trinity, which presents a communal and
relational understanding of God's inner Trinitarian life and God's relationship with humankind. This relational and intersubjective turn of the
doctrine of the Trinity has a profound implication for Christian theology
and ethics in a postmodern, global society. It challenges us to reexamine
the monarchical notion of God, the individualistic doctrine of the *imago
dei*, the hierarchical model of the church, and ethics.

The social doctrine of the Trinity implies the movement away from
essentialist metaphysics to a relational ontology, identifying the unity of
the three persons not in the sameness in essence, but in personal communion in love. The idea of "person" is at the center of this theological sea
change. The Latin (Western) idea of the divine person emphasized the
unity of the three persons, contending that God's agency resides in the
indivisible substance. The primary analogy was the individual mental act
of self-consciousness. This tradition provided a theological undercurrent
for the Western philosophy of individual subjectivity, or self-
consciousness.

The social doctrine of the Trinity discovers the relationship and
communion at the heart of a trinitarian theology.[3] It holds that the essence
of God is not an isolated, self-enclosed being in itself, which is unable to
relate to others, but a being in relation. God's inner life is social. The
unity of God exists in fellowship. "God exists as diverse persons united in
a communion of freedom, love, knowledge."[4] God is not a single subject,
but the union of the three persons. The unity of the triune God is not undifferentiated or unstructured unity, but dynamic, differentiated, and re-

ciprocal. The divine persons—Father, Son, and the Holy Spirit—are co-equal persons, united by love. Therefore, the Kingdom of God, in this perspective, is not a kingdom of the solitary subject, but the kingdom of the triune God in love, reciprocity, and fellowship. The trinitarian Kingdom of God posits an open, inclusive form of life with a free, equal, reciprocal form of social relationship. This relational personhood provides a critical point of contact between Christian theology and Habermas.

A. Perichoresis

Perichoresis is a theological concept that explains the nature of inner trinitarian relationship. It describes the way the three trinitarian persons are interrelated and interact with each other in an intra-trinitarian relationship as well as their relation to creation. In other words, perichoresis refers to the divine *modus vivendi*. The trinitarian persons, in perichoretic relationship, are mutually inhering to one another, inter-dwelling, drawing life from one another, thus creating the perfect state of communion. The trinitarian persons cooperate in their mutual service and glorification. God's economy means the historical manifestation of this perichoretic fellowship of the triune God in love and justice. That is, God's economy is, in its historical expression, communicative as well as cooperative. Trinitarian persons are acting together in the world to bring the reconciliation and liberation of the world. Trinitarian persons become, mutually, the subject as well as the object of their respective actions. The Spirit glorifies the Son and the Father, and unifies them. The Spirit was sent by the Father through the Son. The Son, in his ministry, is commissioned by the Father and empowered by the Spirit. Jesus preached and acted in the power of the Spirit. The Father was known through the work of the Son and the Spirit. Jesus was raised from the dead through the power of the Spirit.

Perichoresis is a key notion to unlock the economy of God, and thus the being of God. Perichoresis indicates the structure and pattern of divine economy. It refers to a relational, dynamic, animating reality of God who is open to others. The openness of the triune God is inferred from God's economy. The Father, the Logos, and the Spirit perichoretically penetrate every reality imparting particularity as well as order in their relationship with others. Perichoresis denotes the way the triune God creates, orders, and renews the world. Perichoresis also implies that the divine reality is complex and multifaceted. It includes both static and dynamic, transcendent and immanent, unified and diverse dimensions simultaneously. Yet by virtue of the perichoretic nature of divine economy, these distinctive attributes do not collide or impede one another. As to perichoresis, Gunton notes,

> [Perichoresis] is a concept heavy with spatial and temporal con-
> ceptuality, involving movement, recurrence and interpenetration;
> and second that it is an implication of the unity-in-variety of the
> divine economic involvement in the world. Because the one God
> is economically involved in the world in those various ways, it
> cannot be supposed other than that the action of Father, Son and
> Spirit is a mutually involved personal dynamic. It would appear to
> follow that in eternity Father, Son, and Spirit share a dynamic
> mutual reciprocity, interpenetration, and interanimation.[5]

Perichoresis embodies the ideals of inclusiveness, love, and freedom. Intersubjective in nature, it respects both differentiated individuality
of the Trinitarian persons and their inseparable solidarity. The goal of the
cooperative action of the Trinity is the redemption of creation in the triune
God, so that God may be all in all. The Trinity opens its intra-personal
fellowship "for the reception and unification of the whole salvation."[6] The
perichoretic fellowship of the triune God is the basis of and promise for
our communion with God and other creatures. The reign of God is the
reign of this inclusiveness, freedom, and community of love as epitomized
and manifested in Jesus' earthly ministry and the early Christian ecclesial
life. This perichoretic reign of love and mutuality is not confined to the
church. It is open to all humanity. Christians are co-workers of God, who
invites them to become God's universal covenant partners in Jesus Christ.
Therefore the trinitarian union has soteriological meaning. Moltmann
says, "The union of the divine Trinity is open for the uniting of the whole
creation with itself and in itself."[7] History is an open history of the triune
God in fellowship. In other words, the salvation history is "the trinitarian
history of God in the concurrent and joint workings of the three subjects,
Father, Son, and Spirit."[8] There are no two sets of communion, one for the
divine persons, and the other for human beings. The one perichoresis of
God includes God and humanity in one communion as beloved partners of
the divine choreography.[9] Jesus' High Priestly prayer says "that they may
all be one. As you, Father, are in me and I in You, may they also be in
us..." (John 17:21). The trinitarian persons, on the basis of their eternal
perichoretic fellowship, work together to achieve redemption of (i.e., reconciliation with) the rebellious fallen creation.

The social doctrine of the Trinity implies the covenantal nature of

God. God is covenantally with us and for us in Jesus Christ. This doctrine demonstrates that God is essentially relational—free and loving—to engage covenantally with humanity. From eternity, through God's election, humanity is made a covenantal partner of God. God and human beings are not only covenantal partners but also co-workers in anticipation of the trinitarian Kingdom. Trinitarian history is the history of covenant: its formation, renewal, preservation, and fulfillment. The love and unity among the trinitarian persons, and their perichoretic communion are the source, basis, and *telos* of Christian social witness. Moltmann states, "In the community of Christ it is love that corresponds to the perichoretic unity of the triune God as it is manifested and experienced in the history of salvation; in human society, it is solidarity that provides this correspondence."[10] The human struggle for justice, peace, and reconciliation has a firm foundation in the covenant of creation and redemption wrought by the trinitarian persons of God.

The triune God invites us to God's perichoretic fellowship and communication. Jesus Christ, through his death, elevated us as the covenantal partners of God. It is in Jesus Christ that we call God the Father. We are "heirs of God and joint heirs with Christ" in the fellowship of the Son. St. Paul said that we are the co-workers of God. God listens to the requests and supplications of God's children. Our communicative action with God takes the form of prayer, supplication, and intercession. The sending of the Son and the descent of the Holy Spirit indicate the opening of the trinitarian fellowship to us.

B. Father, Son, and the Spirit

The Father, the Son, and the Spirit are the symbols that speak of the three different dimensions of God's economy as experienced by human beings. Although every divine attribute is shared mutually by the three trinitarian persons, a certain attribute is ascribed to a particular person of the Trinity. For example, the attribute of transcendence, although shared by the Son and the Spirit, is ascribed primarily to the Father. The Father is understood as the unbegotten, infinite, inexhaustible source of life and power. As the creator and progenitor of all, the Father is above all...and also among all and in all (Ephesians 4:6). A sense of awe and majesty arises when one encounters the Father.

The Son is understood as the sacrament of the invisible Father through whom one has an access to the mystery of transcendence. The Son is the symbol of the divine logos, divine revelation.[11] As the rational principle of Wisdom, he functions as the criterion to discern the immanence of the Holy. By giving a meaning and direction to people, the Logos unlocks the divine mystery. Without the Logos, the Godhead is indistinguishable from darkness and chaos. The attribute of immanence is ascribed to the Spirit. The Spirit bears the divine presence. Two distinctive attributes of God, fascination and judgment, attraction and terror of the holy (*mysterium fascinans et tremendum* in Otto's terminology) are represented through the unifying power of the Holy Spirit. "Through the Spirit the divine fullness is posited in the divine life as something definite, and at the same time it is reunited in the divine ground."[12] The Spirit brings a sense of intelligibility and understanding, a deeper knowledge of the reality, a sense of wholeness and illumination.

II. Communicative Economy of the Spirit and the Logos

The economy of the triune God in history takes a communicative form. The trinitarian persons work together to restore the Kingdom on earth. The Spirit and the Logos work in unity to bring the glory to the Father. That is, God as the all in all is the final goal of the trinitarian economy. When God is the all in all, all creatures are also restored to their particularities to the fullest potentials and extent. And then there will be a full revelation of the glory of the Father. Toward this end, the particularizing force of the Spirit and the universalizing power of the Logos work toward the common *telos* of restoration and unify the creation with the Creator. The Holy Spirit offers every person the possibility of understanding the Logos. This witness of the Holy Spirit is not delimited to Christian communities. The Spirit witnesses to the Logos, Jesus Christ. Jesus said to the disciples, "[The Spirit] will teach you all things" (John 14: 25). The Spirit does not teach new truths, or new revelations, but gives new and deeper articulations, expressions, and applications to what Jesus taught. This is what Gavin D'Costa calls "a non-identical repetition of the revelation which is given."[13] The Spirit exegetes the Logos in a particular situation. The Spirit proclaims the Word ever anew to people in various situations. The Spirit illuminates the hearts of human beings with the Logos. The Spirit confesses and bears witness to Christ. "Now the Lord is the Spirit, and where the Spirit of the Lord is, there is freedom" (2 Corinthians 3:17). Through the communicative action of the Spirit—witnessing, awakening, illuminating, affirming the Logos, human beings turn to Jesus Christ. The Spirit and Jesus Christ are not intelligible apart from each other. The Spirit neither creates a new revelation (apart from or against Jesus Christ), nor mechanically repeats the past dogmas and beliefs. The Spirit recalls and recreates the ministry of Jesus in a particular time and space.

The Spirit enables the ministry of Jesus Christ to be reincarnated through the church today.[14] Communicative action of the Spirit takes place in several dimensions. The Spirit speaks to our spirits. As we will discuss later, conscience is the locus where a communicative action of the Spirit takes place. The communicative action of the Spirit also takes place in the public realm as Christians engage with others for the liberation of the oppressed and the promotion of the common good. Yet for Christians it occurs most explicitly in the Christian community.

The Spirit and the Logos are in their perichoretic collaboration to bring the audience of the gospel to the understanding of the divine will and intention. The communicative action of the Spirit intends to enable people to reach the understanding of the divine will in a particular situation. The distance between the text and one's situation is bridged by the present communicative action of the Spirit. The Spirit communicates the Logos to us in our particular situations. Through the communicative action of the Spirit, the Logos is newly incarnate in each of our particular situations. The Spirit, in his communicative action, illuminates the meaning of the scriptural text for a particular time and place. The Spirit speaks to us in our particular situations through the appropriation of the scripture. Through proclamation, the Spirit addresses us in order to bring the truthful meaning of the Scripture, which is the witness to the incarnate Logos, to the heart. The performative action of the Spirit for the Logos takes several forms, according to 2 Timothy: teaching, reproving, correcting, and instructing (2 Timothy 3:16). Using the biblical texts, the Spirit engages in a communicative action, inviting people in understanding to respond to the divine promises and blessings available in Jesus Christ.

Through a performative, persuasive work of the Spirit, the heteronomy of laws is overcome. Laws are no longer experienced as an alien or estranged entity, but gladly and voluntarily accepted into one's hearts as the guidance and directives of life. It is different from a blinded, fearful form of submission to law where no human voluntary consent is involved. The observation of law becomes theonomous through the communicative work of the Spirit. St. Paul's statement that "real circumcision is a matter of the heart" (Romans 2:29) emphasizes this communicative and transforming aspect of the Spirit's work. One may say that "circumcision of the heart" takes place when a person accepts the teaching, guidance, and admonitions of the Spirit with full assent, and righteousness—entering a right relationship with God and others—is its result.

The communicative action of the Spirit is not independent of the original intention of the text. The Spirit uses and exploits the symbols and metaphors–their fertile and laden, even multilayered, meanings—of the text to communicate the divine will to a person or a community in a particular situation. The Spirit bridges the reality upon which the text was created with a situation today, thus representing the texts in a meaningful way. The author of the biblical texts does not completely bind up the Spirit's action. The Spirit, the inspirational source of the texts, stretches and reappropriates the meaning of the text relevant to the situation without contradicting the original meaning of the texts. The Spirit's action is not the violation of the copyright of the authors, so to speak. Rather, the biblical texts point toward the triune reality of God upon which basis the very texts were created. One's claim to the possession of the divine will (or "God told me last night") must be redeemed in Christian community in conversation with other members, historical tradition, and all concerned public.

The church constitutes the interpretive-communicative community in discerning the will of God in the Spirit. Members first engage with one another, with the rich and enduring history of interpretive traditions, and also with their forebears as the imaginative communicative partners in search of truth and justice. Ecclesiastical authoritarianism or fundamentalism tends to confuse the first hand, self-communication of God with its past interpretation by religious institutions. The Bible and all other ecclesiastic documents (councils and papal) and confessions are not inerrant in this respect. They are not divine speech per se. God uses human beings as the media to communicate God's will in history. This implies that any experience of God's communication is historically limited. The cultural forms and patterns they take limit all these media, human and nonhuman. They should be presented to the public scrutiny of Christian communities.

III. The Trinity and Person: The *Imago Dei*

What implication does this social understanding of the Trinity have for anthropology? What kind of theological anthropology does it present? The social doctrine of the Trinity emphasizes the relational nature of hum an personhood over the individualistic personhood of liberalism.

Specifically, a relational nature of human identity and particularity finds its prototype (strong resemblance) in the trinitarian persons. As indicated above, the trinitarian perichoresis is the basis of human sociality. The trinitarian persons of the Father, the Son, and the Spirit disclose this communicative nature of the subject or agency. The Father is the Father in relation to the Son, and *vice versa*. Similarly, the Spirit is the Spirit in relation to the two other persons of the Trinity. Each trinitarian person obtains his or her particularity only in relation to others. Individuality and relationality are not antithetical. Relationality is that which renders a particularity to individuality. Freedom and relation are two polar aspects of trinitarian persons. In the trinitarian perichoretic relationship, otherness or distinctiveness neither vanishes nor collides. The Nicene Creed of the fully God and fully human, not separate, not mixed, recognizes this reality. Particularity, in a trinitarian understanding, is not derived from the sameness of essence. Particularity is grounded in and constituted in relationship. It is constant and insoluble in relationship. The relationship of Father and Son is constant and insoluble. The Father and the Son are not exchangeable. Relationship defines one's particularity. The Father is the Father in relation to the Son and the Spirit. Persons give and receive their particular identity from one another.

In relationship, there is an otherness of each person from each other. Without the basic particularity of individuals, relationship is not possible.

The respect for freedom in reciprocity, and the reciprocity in freedom, is a constitutive norm of social trinitarian theology. In social trinitarian thinking, freedom is inseparable from love. Freedom has its place and fulfillment in love and fellowship. Moltmann notes that freedom, with the same etymology as "friendly," is the cognate of hospitality, friendship, and community, as a contemporary German word *gastfrei* ("guest-free") indicates. He says,

> [F]reedom does not mean lordship. It means friendship. This freedom consists of the mutual and common participation in life, and a communication in which there is neither lordship nor servitude. In their reciprocal participation in life, people become free beyond the limitation of their own individuality.[15]

A trinitarian understanding of personhood challenges the Enlightenment notion of individuality. In reaction to a hierarchical traditionalism of the Middle Ages, modernity bifurcated person and relationship. This bifurcation of person and relationship, or being and value, created ample problems for ethics. The bifurcation resulted in the reduction of being to essence or substance. It resulted in the separation of essence and existence, soul and body, idea and power, the spiritual and the material. A trinitarian understanding of a person restores the integrity of a person as body, soul, and mind. Personhood is constituted in relationship. No person can be conceived as autonomous, apart from other persons. The communion of persons is the context of personhood.[16] Human freedom is achieved and finds meaning in relationship. Freedom is always freedom toward one another. The exercise of freedom requires a plurality of persons.[17] An isolated, solitary person is not free. Relationality is the matrix of one's identity and freedom. Individual identity implies one's difference from others in relationship. Relationship presupposes a person, and *vice versa*. Relationship and personhood are mutually implicated. A person cannot be identified with an isolated being.

Despite its relational characteristic, a trinitarian notion of agency is different from the post-structuralist or deconstructionist idea of the agency where the subject is continuously deferred to relationship. The subject has its distinctive space, center of agency, in social interaction, although always situated in the latter. That is to say, the mystery is an abiding aspect of a person. Relationship, even intimacy, does not exhaust the mystery of each person. God is the origin of all personhood. Made in the image of God, a person retains a quality of mystery. LaCugna says that a person, divine and human, is by definition all ineffable.[18] Mystery is different from mysteriousness. Divine mystery does not mean that God perplexes our minds to prevent understanding. Mystery is involved in every relationship.

This implies that while a personal identity arises in relationship, relationship does not banish a personhood. A person or a being is not dissolved in relationship. If so, relationship itself vanishes. For relationship presupposes the encounter of a being with another being. A person is actualized and embodied in various relationships but is not completely reduced to one relationship.

The person and work of the Spirit has a theological significance to understand a relational and a particularistic nature of a moral agency. The Spirit is the one who gives rise to other differences. The Spirit respects and strengthens the particularity of each person. At the same time, the Spirit coordinates and harmonizes the difference of persons, their talents and gifts, for the promotion of the common good. The limitations of both individualism (its inability to create solidarity) and collectivism (its suppression of particularity) are finally overcome in the particularizing and the unifying work of the Spirit. The particularizing work of the Spirit is different from liberalism in terms of its relational nature. The essence of political liberalism was its defense of freedom against hierarchalism and totalitarianism. Yet, its deficiency was to abstract individual freedom as the absolute moral value without recognizing any due consideration of relationality and contingency.

The Spirit is the bond of love which simultaneously unites and distinguishes the Father and the Son. In mediating the relationship between the Father and the Son, the Spirit procures the distinctive identity of each trinitarian person. The Spirit works to bring reconciliation and communion. In and through the Spirit, a person experiences a true identity and relationship with God and other persons. The Spirit helps to restore God and humanity to their proper places and a moral relationship, namely the Creator and creature.

In the church, the Spirit plays a similar unifying as well as a particularizing role for the members of the church. The existence of various gifts of the Spirit in the church attests the particularizing power of the Spirit. Spiritual gifts are the results of the particularizing work of the Spirit who is attentive to the potential and talent of each person. The Spirit gives the respect and articulation to differing talents and capacities of the individuals. God liberates us into relationship, rather than to isolation. If baptism signifies the freedom from the power of sin and death into a new life in community, the Pentecost indicates God's charge to and empowerment of us with various gifts to serve the common good. The Eucharist offers the opportunity for the continuous nurturing of our moral agency by the Spirit in community for the further spiritual and moral growth and maturity in the fullness of Christ. The church is the community of freedom, care, and service in Jesus Christ.

Communion between God and humanity is made possible through the unifying and other-respecting work of the Spirit. Communion presupposes differences and individual identity. Just as the triune communion is the communion of the differentiated trinitarian persons, so the communion of God with humanity is also a communion that respects differences. The Spirit is the power who actualizes the communion in historical contingencies without abolishing differences and individual identity. Communion means the state where unity is created without sacrificing the particularity of each person. Communion does not exhaust a personhood or its freedom. In communion, both individuality and sociality are fulfilled and sublimated in love. Communion realizes openness and intimacy at the same time. Particularity is the source of personal identity and freedom as well as the presupposition for relationality. The loss of particularity is tantamount to the deprivation of freedom and the reduction of humanity into mechanical uniformity and homogeneity. In this sense, every person is to some degree transcendental. There is an inherent resistance to subjugation and oppression, just as G. W. Hegel's analysis of the master-slave relationship proves this point.

The Spirit intervenes and mediates the communication of various individuals and groups toward reconciliation and communion. The particularizing power of the Spirit resists the homogenizing, totalizing and commodifying power of globalization. The Spirit sets us free to be ourselves. "Now the Lord is the Spirit, and where the Spirit of the Lord is, there is freedom" (2 Corinthians 3:17). The Spirit is the giver of freedom in the Lord who liberates us from the power of sin and evil. The Spirit liberates and restores us to be ourselves in our particularity and uniqueness as intended by God for the service and realization of God's Kingdom.

A social notion of the Trinity helps to reconstruct the *imago dei* in trinitarian, relational terms. The *imago dei* is more accurately the *imago trinitas*, the image of the triune God. The *imago dei* has a communicative-covenantal structure. In traditional covenantal theology, a human being is understood as the *imago dei*, endowed with a rational capacity. From a trinitarian perspective, this rational capacity is not individualistic but intersubjective and relational. It is intersubjective in relation to the triune God and to one's fellow rational human beings. That is to say, a human being is not an isolated individual but a relational being in its essence. A human being was created as a free, reciprocal partner of God's covenant. As God is relational, a human being, created in the image of God, is relational in his or her disposition. This characteristic gives human beings a strong desire for communion. This fundamental desire for communion is often expressed in a destructive, even demonic form--controlling, dominating, and subjugating others. Yet, as much as there is a wrongful manifestation of this desire, there is also a strong yearning for true relationship, for coming to mutual understanding and reconciliation. In other words, the *imago dei* does not designate the image of a solitary, isolated God, but that of a relational, other-caring God. LaCugna contends,

> A relational ontology understands both God and the creature to exist and meet as persons in communion. The economy of creation, salvation, and consummation is the place of encounter in which God and the creature exist together in one mystery of communion and interdependence. The meaning of "to be" is "to-be-a-person-in-communion."[19]

A true personhood in a trinitarian understanding is neither autonomous nor heteronomous but theonomous.[20] A theonomous person is intersubjective in disposition. And intersubjective human interaction requires freedom as its precondition. Human freedom is anchored in human relationship to God, as God created human beings as God's covenantal partner. In addition, created in the image of God, a person deserves and de-

mands respect from others. The *imago dei* claims that the sanctity of
every human being must be protected at any price because every human
being has a divine origin.

The trinitarian understanding of a person overcomes the deficiencies
of individualistic and collectivist views of a person. In light of perichoresis, one finds that God's intention for humanity is neither separation nor
subordination but rather mutual participation and sharing in freedom and
love. Compared to Hollenbach and Hauerwas, communicative ethics provides
a more explicit and concrete theological ground of human personhood and
relationality. A Christian acceptance of a relational personhood is not simply
to accommodate a postmodern cultural fad. Communicative ethics finds the
deepest foundation of personhood and sociality in the very being of God,
namely perichoresis.

IV. The Trinity, Covenant, and Communicative Action

What is the implication of the social doctrine of the Trinity—
trinitarian personhood and perichoretic divine economy—for our discussion of communicative ethics? How can the insights of social Trinity be
appropriated into communicative ethics? Conversely, what contribution
does communicative ethics make for the Christian understanding of the
Trinity and the triune economy? A trinitarian notion of personhood offers
a profound implication for ethics. By predicating freedom, equality, and
reciprocity, perichoresis specifies the fundamental structure of relationality, namely communication. Communication is the process through which
one's individuality (identity) is formed and realized. And a perichoretic
understanding of personhood does not bypass or relegate the community
to the secondary. Communication is a way of transcendence. The capacity
for self-transcendence, freedom to others, is a necessary condition for the
development and realization of the selfhood, and communion with others.

A social model of the Trinity shows that freedom, equality, and reciprocity, which Habermas calls a necessary and universal formal presupposition of communication, has its constitutive basis in a person of a triune God; it corresponds to the perichoretic sociality and structure of a
trinitarian life. It also points to the original covenantal relationship of God
and humanity which was broken because of human sin. God respects our
freedom and decisions. God expects us to respond to God's love. God invites us to be co-workers in God's Kingdom.

The notion of communication (as associated with *communio*) opens a
new horizon in understanding the nature of divine being and action. Communicative ethics helps to illuminate the structure and nature of divine as well as

human praxis and interaction. As such, it clarifies and refines the categories and concepts of Christian theology and ethics.

A. The Trinity and Communication

Scripture describes God as a self-communicating God. The Father speaks and discloses Himself through the Logos and the Spirit. The incarnation and crucifixion are communicative actions of the Father. Even among the three trinitarian persons of God, there is relationship and communication. The Logos is the self-communication of God and image of the Father. The Father is never without His word. Scriptural designation of the Son as the Logos or the Word is not by accident. The very Christian designation of Jesus Christ as the Logos (rational, intelligible Principle of the creation) is based on their experience of God's self-communication in Jesus Christ. The Logos is the word, image, radiance and self-expression of the Father. The first chapter of the Gospel of John says that the Word is eternally with God, meaning that the Father eternally speaks and communicates, and expresses Godself. Thus, in this vein, one may say, in the beginning there was a communication (Cf. John 1:1). Self-expression of God is not unilateral from the Father to the Son. The trinitarian persons speak and communicate with one another. This intertrinitarian communication is disclosed vividly in the economy of redemption (Matthew 11:25-27). For example, the Spirit cries out to the Father on behalf of us. Jesus prayed and cried out to the Father, as the Father spoke to Son through the Spirit at the moment of baptism. The Spirit groans within us.

Communication indicates the way the trinitarian persons relate to each in enacting their economy in history. God is performing God's economy through communication among the three persons. This does not imply dissent or conflict within the trinitarian relationship. There is communication, but no dissent or disruption of unity among the three persons. Rather, communication is instrumental to overcome the pains and harms caused by the Fall. Human sins have systemically distorted the communication between God and creatures. As the Son was enfleshed, the trinitarian communication began to take place in a historical realm. This communication expands to history through the invitation of human beings into this process. The divine action in history is primarily covenantal and communicative in nature. When the triune God engages in human history, God's action takes the form of communication and covenant. In relating to sapient human beings, God uses the means of communication. Revelation is the self-communication of the trinitarian persons.

The triune communicative action is a significant aspect of Christian soteriology. A triune God draws people into fellowship through symbols and speech. The openness of God's perichoretic fellowship is the ground for the rise of the divine-human fellowship and the human-human fellowship. The language of inhabitation or indwelling is not limited to the intra-divine relationship alone (à la Miroslav Volf).

The intimacy of the God and humanity relationship is most effectively expressed and coined through the term koinonia. "God is our dwelling place" (Psalm 90). "Our bodies are a temple of the Holy Spirit" (1 Corinthians 3:16, 6: 19). We participate in the divine mystery through the eucharistic meals and drinks. Through the communion taking place through the sharing of the body and the blood, we are in God and God is in us. According to St. Paul (1 Corinthians 1:19), God has called us "into fellowship" with Christ.

The ground of communion is given in Jesus Christ, who is fully divine and fully human, and actualized through the Holy Spirit. The Christ event indicates a primal example of God's self-transcendence as well as God's self-limitation in relation to humanity. Jesus Christ represents God's self-giving love in reaching out to humanity and restoring communion with them. The self-emptying (kenosis) act of God in Jesus Christ opens the ground for mutual understanding and covenant between God and humanity. In Jesus Christ, the communion between God and humanity is realized. Jesus Christ is the person "in whom everything was created and is now being restored to communion with God."[21]

In this line of thinking, one may argue creation was a divine activity which opened the possibility of communication between God and humanity by granting freedom and otherness to humanity, that is, to grant a space to humanity to be particular and to be other.[22] Likewise, redemption means the restoration of the proper space and relationship among God's creatures, human and nonhuman, and consummation is the fulfillment of personhood in love and communion in a cosmic realm.

God's salvific action is most adequately understood as communicative action. Communicative engagement is the method which God relies on in dealing with humanity. Persuasion, which is performative in nature, is an integral aspect of communication. Communicative action is based on persuasion. Persuasion is a nonviolent way of influencing others, whereas compulsion is supported by threat and/or the use of violence. By sending his Son, the Logos, to the world, God showed that God decided to redeem us by persuasion rather than coercion. The Logos is the Word of God who seeks to persuade the world. Persuasion involves a risk for oneself. It exposes oneself to the possibility of being rejected.[23] When God invites human beings into communicative-covenantal relationship, God allows Godself to be vulnerable to human beings in opening the relationship. God has experienced the pains and hurts of rejection and betrayal through the insincerity and unfaithfulness of human beings. Yet God proves consistently and continually God's sincerity by being faithful to covenant.

Habermas' idea of communicative action affirms this fundamental communicative disposition of human existence. Habermas' insight that understanding is the *telos* of the speech act points toward this primordial (but often lost or distorted) ontological orientation (yearning) of a being to reach out to others in relationship. It affirms the fundamental human desire to have at-one-ment (atonement) with others in a non-oppressive, but liberating and loving relationship.

B. The Trinity, Communication, and Habermas

From a trinitarian perspective, however, one may say that Habermas' theory, despite the pragmatic value of its proceduralism, is limited in understanding the existential and religious meaning and the scope of communication for human existence. As Rudolf Siebert and Helmut Peukert point out, Habermas' ethics is not able to account for the question of death—the limit-condition of any human communication. In order to solve this problem, according to Siebert and Peukert, communication should be conceptualized in the context of the universal community of communication, such as the trinitarian Kingdom, which is more inclusive than the present linguistic community. That is, it should encompass the whole of humanity and history.[24] They contend that the logic of the universal redemption of validity claims, if it is to be genuinely universal, must encompass every human being of the past, present, and future. The logical conclusion of Habermas' communicative rationality and the possibility of validity-redemption will be futile and illusory unless a promise of the final reconciliation of things and the consummation of justice and vindication for victims are secured. Only under the presumption of the consummation of history in the full advent of the trinitarian Kingdom does the redemption of validity make sense. Covenantal-communicative ethics, in the matrix of the social doctrine of the Trinity, suggests communion as the deeper structure and disposition of human communication which points to communion with a triune God, others, and the self. Communication is deeply tied with human yearning for union beyond the present historical and social realm. One asks, "Why should we communicate at all?" Communion, in the trinitarian Kingdom of God, is an inclusive category of human existence because it encompasses the whole aspect of human interactive life, including spoken and unspoken speech. Human communication, in its best moral form, is analogous to the trinitarian perichoretic communication. Accordingly, human communication obtains a deeper structure and comprehensive orientation when it is located in the context of the human desire for communion which goes beyond death. Communication may be understood as a concrete, penultimate human practice, yet necessary and indispensable in history to approximate communion.

From a Christian perspective, the theory of communicative action makes more sense when it acknowledges the triune God as its foundation and goal. For, as Bradley N. Seeman points out, without postulating some independently existing moral reality, such as God, Habermas' theory faces a danger of endless, prolonged regression of divergent moral constructs.[25] In this respect, one finds C. S. Pierce's idea of an "unlimited community of investigators," to which Habermas partly owes his methodological insights, very suggestive. Like Habermas, Pierce argues that the unlimited community of investigators comprises all people who will participate in the investigation of reality. Every investigation aims at the obtainment of truth. Truth is the final arbiter and adjudicator of differences. Pierce, however, unlike Habermas, introduces the proposition that human moral understanding is not a pure sociological or cultural epistemological construct. There exists an external reality behind every investigation. This reality is pivotal for his project of the unlimited communicative of investigation because it is not merely a temporal human consensus which determines the truth, but the reality has a certain structure and power to refute and repudiate human constructs and opinions. In short, reality ultimately speaks for itself.

The investigation of moral realities is analogous to that of scientific studies. In scientific investigation, the success and predictability of a scientific theory depend on the existence of the outer physical or social realities which refuse to succumb to any erroneous or mistaken human scientific constructs. Without postulating this existence, any explanation of scientific success and continuity will be impossible. Similarly, in human moral exploration, one may contend that moral beliefs are not merely human constructs. The existence of a moral reality is at least partly testified in the convergence of several fundamental moral rules across various cultures (prohibition of torture, killing of an innocent, impurity in marriage, simony, lying, etc.) and by the existence of fundamental human moral sentiments, such as conscience.

For Christians, one could say, the triune God constitutes this external moral reality. For Christians, the Logos given in the order of creation, and God's ongoing action in the power of the Spirit provide a certain moral constancy for an investigative community. In many places, scripture witnesses to God's faithfulness and sincerity as the bedrock of moral constancy. That is, moral reality exists in the created world in the form of creational order and God's ongoing self-communication and witness in the power of the Holy Spirit. As the unlimited community of communication searches for common moral principles applicable for humanity, its investigations may converge because of the constancy of the triune God's creational and ordering economy. Otherwise, its moral constructs may continuously clash with the self-communication of God in history (which constitutes the external moral reality) until they are corrected.[26] The moral reality of God, through the self-witness of the Logos and the Spirit, resists any systemic distortion or false human moral constructs. God in God's own self-communicative work participates in the unlimited community of communication as the final judge and vindicator.

God is a moral power who watches over and judges all human moral enterprises. As the Old Testament testifies, God intervenes in history constantly, correcting the course of history by challenging human misunderstandings and distortions of truth and justice. This idea of the independently existing God constitutes, in Pierce's term, the "secondness" of human moral investigations. From a Christian perspective, God constitutes the eschatological point of convergence for various moral investigations. For Christians, communicative action is not entirely futile by virtue of the continuous self-communication and self-witness of God. Regarding this essentially public nature of human moral existence, Jesus warned, "Nothing is covered up that will not be uncovered, and nothing secret that will not become known. Therefore whatever you have said in the dark will be heard in the light, and what you have whispered behind closed doors will be proclaimed from the housetops." (Luke 12:2-3)

Every human communication points toward the unity in the universal communicative community of the trinitarian Kingdom. This trinitarian vision is transcommunal and eschatological in its nature and scope. The trinitarian Kingdom indicates a fully reconciled community which advances through the work of the Logos and the Holy Spirit. God is "a unifying unity" who brings reconciliation to God's creation. We are invited to participate in this process as God's covenantal partner.[27]

However, one cannot overlook the praxiological value which Habermas' communicative ethics contributes to the trinitarian theology. His ethics is instrumental in implementing the theological vision of the triune Kingdom in a social-political context. First, one may easily find that there is a strong affinity between the doctrine of social Trinity and communicative ethics in terms of their underlying moral ethos. The trinitarian Kingdom of God presents the ideal of an open, inclusive, and liberated form of life which is consonant with Habermas' idea of the "ideal speech situation." The trinitarian fellowship of perichoresis is the background and context of Christian covenantal-communicative action.

Specifically, the idea of perichoresis provides a dynamic and creative category of personhood and sociality for Christian ethics, based on mutuality, inclusiveness, equality, freedom, and interdependence. Mutual dependence, reciprocity, freedom, and equality indicate the symbiotic, covenantal nature of human existence, which reflects the perichoretic life of the trinitarian Kingdom. In other words, the trinitarian Kingdom constitutes the concrete, empirical content of the universal community of communication for Christians by means of which God and humans engage in the praxis of emancipation and reconciliation, anticipating the full realization of the Kingdom in the end of history.

Habermas contended that communicative action takes place against the counterfactual presupposition of a universal community of communication. From a Christian perspective, the trinitarian Kingdom of God rather than the transcendental epistemological illusion functions as the basis and goal of Christian communicative praxis for emancipation and reconciliation in a way analogous to Habermas' idea of the ideal speech community. The Kingdom was concretely revealed in God's salvific action in Jesus Christ, through his incarnation, crucifixion, and resurrection, and affirmed by the work of the Holy Spirit. The trinitarian Kingdom constitutes a universal community of communication for Christians in which God and humans participate as covenantal-communicative partners.

Christian communicative action is embedded in the context of God's trinitarian Kingdom and its communicative action toward humanity. The history of the trinitarian Kingdom embraces not only the history of Christian community but also the history of all humanity and creation itself. From a Christian perspective, the whole of humanity constitutes a single covenantal community, a universal community of communication. Scripture holds that humanity is God's covenantal partner. That is, God speaks to all humankind in various ways, either through historical or natural events. In addition, God's covenants with Noah and Adam show God's care for the whole of creation, including non-human creatures.

Christian communicative action refers to cooperative ecumenical Christian praxis in response to the action of the triune God in history. Christian communicative action is enacted through ongoing reciprocal,

critical, argumentative discernment, on the basis of the ultimate covenant
of God in Jesus Christ. In Jesus Christ, God not only has affirmed our
humanity, but also has accepted every human being as God's covenantal
partner. The trinitarian Kingdom of God constitutes the primordial covenantal community, and the ultimate horizon and *telos* for Christian ministry and dialogical engagement with others. In this trinitarian framework,
the covenant obtains its cosmic horizon and concrete discursive context
with the whole of humanity as participants. The eschatological Kingdom
of the Trinity provides the cosmic covenantal context for social ordering,
justice, and symbiotics. As such, the trinitarian Kingdom of God serves as
a theological basis for the critique and reconstruction for social relationships. All human forms of covenants must be analyzed, assessed, and
criticized in light of this prototype covenant. Margaret Farley states,

> If the ultimate normative model for relationship between persons
> is the very life of the Trinitarian God, then a strong eschatological
> ethic suggests itself as a context for Christian justice. That is to
> say, interpersonal communion characterized by equality, mutual-
> ity, and reciprocity may serve not only as a norm against which
> every pattern of relationship may be measured but as a goal to
> which every pattern of relationship is ordered.[28]

Every form of covenant is tentative, provisional, and thus subjected
to the critique and empowerment of the primordial covenant of God in
Jesus Christ. Social covenants embody and approximate the divine covenant. Every social covenant needs to be examined in light of God's Kingdom. The relationship of human covenants and the divine covenant is
analogous to that of customary social conventions and the ideal speech
situation in Habermas. Other covenants are relative and secondary to the
divine covenant. Historical social covenants are dependent upon and derived from God's covenant; therefore, they must be judged and illuminated
by it. The new covenant is already achieved in Jesus Christ, but its historical fulfillment awaits the *eschaton*. The dialectical relationship of the
"already" and the "not yet" is also analogous to the relationship of actual
dialogue and the ideal speech situation. Actual dialogue presupposes and,
at the same time, partially realizes the ideal speech situation.

Covenantal theology, reconstituted in a trinitarian conceptual
scheme, provides a more consistent doctrine of God's sovereignty and a
better understanding of covenant. The trinitarian understanding of God
and Kingdom more explicitly manifests the communicative basis of human

sociality. Upon this horizon and basis of Kingdom, Christians engage in various forms of communicative praxis in order to bring liberation and reconciliation among various conflicting groups. We are not taking the divine covenant as an idealistic form or a utopia. Rather, the divine covenant has a historical anchoring point in the church as the body of Christ. Christians become co-workers of the divine communicative action by inviting other people to the universal covenant of God in Jesus Christ.

Communication is an instrument and means to approximate and restore communion. Jesus Christ, the Logos, is God's communication toward humanity. Preaching is a communicative (illocutionary) act used for mutual understanding between God and humanity. It raises validity claims on the objective (the nature and destiny of the universe as God's creation), the intersubjective (ethos, morality), and the subjective (faithfulness, sincerity) worlds. It proposes questions of truth for reality, rightness of relationships, and sincerity of the heart. God's communication in Jesus Christ constitutes the criteria for human communication. Human understandings of truth, rightness, and sincerity are critically examined in the context of God's covenant in Jesus Christ who is the Wisdom, Power, and Logos of God.

The Holy Spirit refers to the power and presence of God in the world in order to bring reconciliation and emancipation in God's creation. In the Christian tradition, the Holy Spirit has been understood as the principle (or agent) of union, justice, and life.[29] The Holy Spirit is the bond of love and the power of mutual submission. The Spirit unites the Father and the Son in love. The Spirit is the incorporating power of God who welcomes us into the inner life of God.[30] The Spirit opens our lives to God in Jesus Christ. Through the Holy Spirit, we participate in divine life as disclosed in Jesus Christ. The Holy Spirit is also the power of justice and emancipation. The Spirit frees the captives, empowers the outcasts, and liberates the oppressed. Jesus said, "The Spirit of the Lord is upon me, because he has anointed me to bring good news to the poor. He has sent me to proclaim release to the captives and recovery of sight to the blind, to let the oppressed go free, to proclaim the year of the Lord's favor" (Luke 4:18-19). It is the Spirit who calls us out of our self-centeredness, isolation, and self-obsession into the life of mutual affirmation, love, and fellowship. This activity of the Spirit reflects the perichoretic trinitarian life of participating, sharing, mutual caring, self-giving, and self-surrendering.

The Holy Spirit is universally present. The Spirit is not a persona confined to a particular religious narrative. LaCugna says, "The movement of the Spirit of God cannot be controlled, domesticated, or regulated, but the presence of the Spirit can clearly be observed where there is *koinonia*."[31] God's Spirit is not confined to the Christian community, however. The Holy Spirit opens God's communion to all not yet in God's communion. "The Holy Spirit is God's outreach to the creature."[32] The Spirit works through human "fleshliness" and events.[33] The Holy Spirit works in history to bring life, justice, love, and the knowledge of God to human life. The Spirit is a reality claiming and making power. The Spirit attests and gives certainty to our reconciliation with God. The Spirit is the down payment of God's unfailing promise of the coming Kingdom, and the foretaste of the liberated creation and the eternal communion. As such, the Spirit is the source of our hope. Christians are the first fruit of God's triune Kingdom.

V. The Trinity and Interreligious Dialogue

From a Christian theological perspective, the Holy Spirit is the power who is able to bring a true mutual understanding and reconciliation between God and humanity, and between human beings. The universal presence and work of the Holy Spirit means that God unceasingly involves Godself in ordering, sustaining, and renewing God's creation. This universal activity of God was called "common grace" by the Calvinists. If contemporary Christians still believe, as Free Church Calvinists did, that God is the God of the universe, that God's grace and rule pervade every aspect of human life, then we cannot deny the possibility of covenanting with other religious or non-religious peoples.

From a Christian perspective, an interreligious discourse is not nonsensical because of the communicative action of God in history. The whole creation, including all people, is the object of God's communicative work in the Logos and the Spirit. God is at work in other religions as well as secular movements to bring witness to Godself. God's performative action is not limited to the Bible and the church. God is also the God of the Gentiles. The creative, governing, and ordering power of God permeates every human community as well as the universe. Jesus Christ creates his witnesses wherever he chooses to do so. Non-believers often challenge and correct the distortional understanding and propagation of the gospel by the church.

This means that God's revelation in Jesus Christ is the final one, but not the only one.[34] According to Braaten, other religions are *praeparatio evangelica*, preparation for the gospel, in a way analogous to the function of the law. Christians must listen to these extramural witnesses to the Logos, the search for the agreement on the basic moral principles and

laws of the commandment of God, and allow these voices to challenge
Christian complicity with social injustice, the status quo, and insincerity.
Moreover, Christians should provide the space for these perspectives to
illuminate, accentuate, and explain the truth of the Gospel. Karl Barth's
comment is quite valid in this respect when he says,

> We recognize that the fact that Jesus Christ is the one Word of
> God does not mean that in the Bible, the Church and the world
> there are not other words which are quite notable in their way,
> other lights which are quite clear and other revelations which are
> quite real . . . Nor does it follow from our statement that every
> word spoken outside the circle of the Bible and the Church is a
> word of false prophecy and therefore valueless, empty and corrupt,
> that all the lights which rise and shine in this outer sphere are
> misleading and all the revelations are necessarily untrue.[35]

Karl Barth states "our present contention is that what was and is possible
for Him in the narrow sphere is well within His powers in the wider."[36]

The Free Church Calvinists—by positing the common grace as the
universal basis of covenant, politics, and social order—affirmed God's
general revelation alongside Scripture. "The New Testament nowhere
makes the claim that Christ is the one and only revelation of God in history and to humanity."[37] Romans 1:18-32 clearly affirms the general revelation of God apart from the Christ event and Scripture. Christians cannot
deny that God has witnesses for Godself in other cultures and religions.
This does not mean that we deny either place or significance of the gospel
in interreligious dialogue. The Christ event and Scripture provide the criteria of discernment for Christians. We do not understand what God is
doing in other religions and cultures where there is no knowledge of Christ
as given in Scripture. The idea of common grace is meaningful only in
relation to special grace, which guides and directs our interpretive and
communicative process.

It is impossible for Christians to say that non-Christians are completely devoid of the truth. The presence and work of Jesus Christ are not
limited to the church. God's action does not stop at the boundaries of a
Christian community. Every creature is related to Jesus Christ as Logos
and Light. According to the Gospel of John, it is through Jesus Christ, the
Logos, that the world came into being. He is the source of all that exists,
and he is the light that gives light to every one. Despite their different religious affiliations, Christians and non-Christians share one common world

which is the creation of God. Christians and non-Christians share common characteristics as they have been created by the same God.[38] The world created by the Word bears His marks and vestiges. This reality of one common world is increasingly evident in a global society. This provides the basis for Christians to participate in discursive ecumenical engagements with people of other religions. Christians need to listen to what God has shown to other religious communities, what they have received and learned from God through their pursuits of truth.

There is always a risk and vulnerability in open dialogue. Dialogue can bring a profound change to the partners in discussion. Newbegin says, "Dialogue means exposure to the shattering and upbuilding power of God the Spirit."[39] One cannot deny the possibility that a radical reconceptualization of the church's long-held doctrines, perspectives, ecclesiastical self-understanding, and practices may take place as a consequence of the dialogue. Christians may discover and appreciate God's gifts and enlightenment to other religious groups. Christians and non-Christians, in their open encounters, may come to a new common agreement on significant public policy issues and moral principles.

A revelatory experience is not confined to Christians. It is universally found. Tillich says, "God has not left himself unwitnessed."[40] Revelatory experience may occur not only individually but also intersubjectively through mutual encounter and discursive reflection. Nor is the possibility of revelation confined to religious communities. It may take place in secular realms. In the Creator God, the sacred and the secular are not completely separate. In fact, the sacred and the secular may offer a critical judgment to each other, providing occasions of edifying criticism for each other.

The significance of a critical conversation is confirmed by the historical fact that Christianity has grown into its current form by receiving judgments from other religions. That is, Christianity has evolved and enriched itself by critically adopting and receiving various religious and philosophical elements from the surrounding culture. If religion is a ubiquitous human phenomenon, world religions could become significant sources of Christian theological reflection in studying the nature and meaning of God as the Creator and the Sustainer, and the one revealed in Jesus Christ.

In fact, other religions provide rich resources for the human quest for the meaning and purpose of life. The relationship of Christianity and other religions is not inimical but could be dialogical, mutually edifying to each other. Each religious tradition, to different degrees and extents, carries the experience of divine reality and economy. Religions are related to each other in their search for the ultimate meaning, and in the manifestation of the ultimate reality. Christian encounter with world religions may enlarge and refine Christian theological understanding of humanity and God. The process of communication will illuminate a rich and complex aspect of divine reality. The Holy Spirit may use the opportunities of dialogues as the momentum to convict and enlighten the sins and misunderstandings of the church.

Communicative examination is necessary because this world is not morally perfect. Human rebellion and sin constantly distort human understanding of morality. Ambiguity, confusion, and the possibility of distortion characterize each human historical existence. Since every revelation is received under the condition of finitude, anxiety, and estrangement, it is always subject to the possibility of misunderstanding, distortion, and corruption. That is, Christians and non-Christians share not only the goodness of the creation but also the dark aspect of human sinfulness. To ensure the good aspects and to prevent the domination of evil aspects, human communities require constant mutual examination, scrutiny, and honesty before the truth. The divine demands are not self-evident in every case. Also, human perception of God's demands is always limited. It is bound by history and in many cases distorted by human self-interests and egoisms. The situation requires clarifications and illuminations, which are differently appropriated and articulated by different cultures and traditions.

Thus we see that God's revelation is not limited to Christians. Nor does it mean that Christians engage in dialogue with predetermined answers and solutions, only to dictate them to others. By engaging with other faith traditions, Christians are also equally challenged by others regarding our own moral misunderstandings, insincerity, and hypocrisy. We rediscover the meaning of the Christ event and the gospel in a new perspective, from a new angle, and we are challenged to reformulate our understanding on a different terrain. The communicative process provides an opportunity for Christians and others to gain a better mutual understanding and acceptance as well as a mutual critique on systematically distorted aspects of our religious traditions. We do not compromise or give up the essential truth claims of the Gospel, even as they are redefined, reconstructed, and rearticulated by the challenges raised by others.

VI. Summary

Habermas' communicative ethics envisions the implicit idea of the

universal covenantal community which is commensurable with the trinitarian Kingdom of God of a social trinitarian theology. In the matrix of
the trinitarian theology, covenantal-trinitarian theology provides a much
richer and deeper theological ground for communicative ethics. Couched
in the framework of the social trinitarian understanding of God, the idea of
covenant embraces the basic methodological insights of communicative
ethics without sacrificing Christian theological particularity and identity.
Also, by instituting a trinitarian Kingdom of God as the ground and context of covenant, covenant renders a more enduring and transformative
basis for Christian ethics.

Notes

1. Paul Tillich, *Systematic Theology*, vol.1. (Chicago: University of Chicago
Press, 1951), 211ff.

2. Ibid., 251.

3. The recent discussion of a social doctrine of Trinity has been kindled by
various intellectual and practical sources: a renewed interest in the Cappado-
cian theology, the liberationist-feminist theological search for a liberated human relationship and community, and a new awareness in the socio-cultural
studies on a relational nature of human life, knowledge, and identity.

4. Catherine Mowry LaCugna, *God for Us: The Trinity and Christian Life*
(New York: HarperSanFrancisco, 1992), 243.

5. Colin E. Gunton, *The One, The Three, and the Many: God, Creation and the Culture of Modernity* (New York: Cambridge University
Press, 1993),163.

6. Jürgen Moltmann, *The Trinity and the Kingdom: The Doctrine of God* (New
York: HarperSanFrancisco, 1991), 157.

7. Ibid., 96.

8. Ibid., 156.

9. LaCugna, *God for Us*, 274.

10. Moltmann, *The Trinity and the Kingdom*, 158.

11. Ibid., 250.

12. Ibid., 251.

13. Gavin D'Costa, *The Meeting of Religions and the Trinity* (Maryknoll: Orbis Books, 2000), 122.

14. Yet, according to Scripture, the witness to the Logos is not limited to the Spirit. The Spirit does it together with the disciples: "But when the Counselor [the Spirit] comes, . . . he will bear witness to me; and you also are witnesses, because you have been with me from the beginning (John 15:26-27).

15. Moltmann, *The Trinity and the Kingdom*, 56.

16. LaCugna, *God for Us*, 299.

17. Ibid.

18. Ibid.

19. Ibid., 250.

20. Ibid., 290.

21. Ibid.

22. Colin Gunton, "Trinity, Ontology, and Anthropology," in *Persons, Divine and Human: King's College Essays in Theological Anthropology*, ed. Christopher Schwoebell & Colin Gunton (Edinburgh: T. & T. Clark, 1991), 56.

23. David S. Cunningham, *These Three Are One* (Malden: Blackwell Publishers, 1998), 308.

24. Cf. Helmut Peukert, *Science, Action, and Fundamental Theology: Toward a Theology of Communicative Action* (Cambridge: M.I.T. Press, 1984); Rudolf J. Siebert, *The Critical Theory of Religion: The Frankfurt School: From Universal Pragmatics to Political Theology* (Berlin, New York, Amsterdam: Mouton Publishers, 1985).

25. Bradley N. Seeman, "Pierce, Habermas and Moral Absolutes," *Journal of Interdisciplinary Studies*, 12/1, 2. (2000), 45-68.

26. Ibid., 47.

27. In bringing reconciliation and peace, the Spirit sometimes works through the non-cognitive media of human communication. Religious stories, songs, hymns, arts, and folk tales are instruments through which the Spirit liberates a person's self-centeredness and self-enclosure, and elevates human souls to a higher ground. Through these media, the Spirit appeals to and awakens human conscience to love and justice.

28. Margaret Farley, "New Patterns of Relationship: Beginnings of a Moral Revolution," *Theological Studies* 36, (1975): 645-646.

29. Karl Barth says that the Holy Spirit is the togetherness of the Father and the Son. Through the Holy Spirit, the act of the mutual impartation and self-giving between Father and Son takes place. The Holy Spirit is also the bond of union between God and human beings. The Holy Spirit realizes the objective revelation of God in Jesus Christ subjectively in human hearts (*Church Dogmatics.* vol. I/1, ed. G.W. Bromiley and T. F. Torrance (Edinburgh: T. & T. Clark, 1949), 470).

30. LaCugna, *God for Us*, 298.

31. Ibid., 299.

32. Ibid., 297.

33. Cf. Michael Welker, *God the Spirit*, trans. John F. Hoffmeyer (Minneapolis: Fortress Press, 1994), 163ff.

34. Carl E. Braaten, *No Other Gospel: Christianity among the World's Religions* (Minneapolis: Fortress Press, 1992), 65.

35. Karl Barth, *Church Dogmatics*, vol. IV/3, ed. G.W. Bromiley and T. F. Torrance (Edinburgh: T. & T. Clark, 1949), 97.

36. Ibid., 118.

37. Braaten, *No Other Gospel*, 65.

38. Leslie Newbigin, *The Open Secret* (Grand Rapids: W. B. Eerdmans Publishing Co., 1978), 207.

39. Ibid., 211.

40. Paul Tillich, "The Significance of the History of Religions for the Systematic Theologian," in *The Future of Religions*, ed. Jerald C. Bauer (New York: Harper & Row, 1966), 81.

CHAPTER 4

COVENANTAL-COMMUNICATIVE ETHICS

I. Methodology

A. Covenantal-Communicative Ethics and Four Sources of Christian Ethics

Ethical methodology is concerned with the way a moral agent reaches a decision, evaluating and examining available options and courses of actions. The process of decision-making inevitably engages with authoritative sources which an agent embraces. In Christianity, Scripture, tradition, reason, and experience are usually understood as the four major authoritative moral sources. That is, Christian decisions acquire a theological legitimacy through its reference to these normative sources. Through a varied accenting and weighing of the four sources of ethics which are the quadrilateral of Scripture, tradition, reason, and experience, a particular moral decision is reached. Ethical methodology in this process presents a rational way of discerning moral issues and guiding individual and collective human actions. Different methodologies of Christian ethics imply the different emphases and focuses on the four sources. This means that different Christian ethical methodologies inevitably carry in them different accents and focuses on the understanding of God, the world, a moral agent, and the relationship of faith and reason.

Covenantal-communicative ethics, with its emphasis on the communicative process, has significant merits compared to other methodologies of Christian ethics. In the public sphere, covenantal-communicative ethics takes experience and social science as its starting points for ethical engagement with other, non-Christian groups. As a method of forging common morality in a postmodern society, it seeks the overlapping consensus (covenant) among different participants regarding mutually regulative moral principles. Although experience and social science are relatively prioritized, however, covenantal-communicative ethics refuses to give any uncritical privilege to them over the others. When covenantal-communicative ethics is employed in various levels of ecclesiastical polity, such as session, classis, synod, assembly, and council, its theological dimension, such as Scripture and tradition, will be more explicitly highlighted.

However, whether an occasion of public or ecclesiastical engagement, covenantal-communicative ethics puts the four sources in a creative tension and mutual critique. It recognizes that each source of Christian ethics is exposed to the danger of "systemic distortion of communication," thus unavoidably requiring intersubjective critique and communal discernment in forging a new mutual understanding. For example, for Protestants, Scripture is probably the most authoritative source. Yet the plurality of narratives opens multiple possibilities of interpretation. In addition, biblical writings include the already distorted communication of each particular culture and history in which they were composed. The process of interpretation is exposed to the possibility of further communicative distortions. Tradition is important. Yet tradition may be biased against a particular race, gender, or ethnicity in its process of formation and use. Moreover, Christian tradition is not monolithic. It includes diverse sets and strands of beliefs, values, practices, and principles. Our understanding of tradition, as it is the case with Scripture, is conditioned by history and mediated by our particular epistemic values and interests.

Similarly, experience could be discrete, often reflecting cultural limitations and parochial interests and perspectives. The findings and theories of social sciences do not always guarantee scientific objectivity and consensus: indeed, they are limited with regard to the ultimate questions of human life. They often serve a particular social interest instead of the common interest. The reality of plurality and distortion, prejudice, and parochial perspective makes intersubjective criticism and adjudication an indispensable process of practical reasoning. Communicative ethics relies on diverse criteria, such as comprehensiveness, coherence, sincerity, relevance, appropriateness, and adequacy among others, in the process of intersubjective adjudication.

B. Method

Covenantal-communicative ethics presents a discursive methodology of moral adjudication for Christians in their various ecclesiastical and public engagements. Covenantal-communicative method is built upon communicative requisites engrained in the communicative process. As the process of communicative action and covenanting showed, communicative requisites indicate the minimal procedural normative requirements which are indispensable to make the process of mutual engagement fair and just. When these requisites are ignored or suppressed, the morality and sanctity of the process itself is questioned, not to mention the products of the process. As various forms of liberation theology have effectively demonstrated, human construction and application of universal morality could be colored and biased by dominant political, economic, and cultural interests. In order to correct unequal power relationships in moral adjudication, universal participation and fair, equal opportunity of speech must be protected as an integral process of moral reasoning. Communicative requisites refer to this procedural requirement. The idea of covenant shares this procedural interest, although its history has not always explicitly formalized this demand.

Covenantal-communicative ethics, by benchmarking these requisites, increases the opportunity for the process of covenanting to be fair and just. These communicative requisites refer to *the necessary elements of modernity.* Habermas shows how these elements can be reconstituted on a formal-pragmatic basis rather than a foundational one. These elements include the more explicit and positive acknowledgements of individual creativity, freedom, equality, and universal participation. They are also necessary in protecting the minimal common ground of human existence: basic freedom and the rights of individuals which are now accepted as moral values of global consensus. These elements are concretely embodied in the ideas of *an equal and fair process of adjudication, the universal participation of all concerned,* and *intersubjective dialogue as a constitutive process in constructing a common morality.* Attention to these aspects is necessary to construct a common order of symbiosis (life together) in a pluralistic society on the basis of dialogue rather than violence or domination.

Covenantal-communicative ethics proceeds through intersubjective, discursive examination and exchange of validity claims. Covenantal-communicative ethics takes justification as an indispensable process of practical reasoning. Justification means to provide reasons (warrants, evidences, and explanations) for accepting claims. It means a redemption of the most valid—coherent, relevant, adequate—claim among available options. Justification is the constitutive process of rationality. A justificatory process usually includes intersubjective argumentation, critique, and explanation. Justification indicates a very rational structure of human life.

Communal life requires justification, because it is the process of resolving discords, misunderstandings, and differences, in order to reach an intelligible understanding and acceptance. It is a rational process of reaching understanding under the given limitations of time, energy, and resources. Thus, any decision with public implications requires the process of justification. There is, however, no conclusive justification of any claim. The validity or cogency of a claim is relative to other claims. Justification and mutual examination are necessary aspects of human social existence in history, especially under the condition of human sin. Public life is enacted through justification, the redemption of reasonable claims which leads to the achievement of agreement and consensus.

Covenantal-communicative ethics seeks to discover commonly sharable moral principles through discursive discernment. It brings the normative claims of various communities under mutual examination. It brings a critical reflection upon the background understandings, particular needs and wants, and practices and experiences of people and communities. Rational discursive cooperation assists religions to discover and critically reconstruct the universal moral ethos implied in their own traditions. Covenantal-communicative ethics brings diverse sets of religious beliefs, experiences, and practices into mutual dialogue for the discovery of the universalizable moral principles. A covenantal-communicative process discovers the points of contact or overlap among the different religions. An intersubjective search and cooperation may create tentative principles of agreement that can be accommodated in various traditions. Mutual critique and examination proceed in the light of the presently shared idea of the right and the good. Certain religious practices, such as the circumcision of women, can be subjected to mutual criticism. Once a universalizable principle is selected, it is brought back to the concrete test for particular traditions and situations. As will be discussed later, a contemporary international ratification of universal human rights attests to this important possibility of mutual agreement on global regulation and coordination.

C. Common Grace and Common Moral Experiences

As mentioned in the previous chapter, covenantal-communicative engagement takes place under the theological premise that the universe is created and sustained by the triune God. God as the Spirit and the Logos is present in the universe. Christians are able to dialogue with other religious peoples on the basis of this universal presence of the triune God. Traditionally, this universal presence of God in the Spirit and the Logos is referred to as common grace. Common grace implies the activity of the triune God in sustaining, ruling, and renewing God's creation. From a Christian perspective, every human being is living by virtue of God's redeeming, governing, renewing activity, namely by common grace. God's grace is not delimited to any single or several elected religious communities. God gives rain and sunshine even to the wicked. The common grace indicates God's sovereignty despite human depravity and ignorance. It implies the faithfulness of God toward all of God's creation. God, in God's freedom, does not desert God's creation, leaving it in total chaos. God maintains at least a minimal order because total chaos means the denial of God's sovereignty.

Covenantal-communicative action is possible because of God's universal presence and activity in history. Specifically, this implies that communicative engagement is possible on the basis of human moral experience. That is, moral experience provides a common basis of discourse for both Christian and non-Christian communicative action. Free Calvinists believed that common grace was registered in the human conscience in the form of moral experiences. Hauerwas and communitarians argue that the idea of common grace and common moral experience is illusory and even dangerous for a particular Christian conviction. They contend that moral experience makes sense only in the context of a particular historical community and narrative. Christians cannot deny the fact, however, that if they believe in God's universal presence and ongoing activity in history, moral experience is not limited to Christians. There could be certain aspects of human moral experience which could be redeemed to be "common" through dialogical examination and public discernment. This does not mean that there is a universal moral experience which is immediately available to human reason.[1] From a covenantal-communicative perspective, common grace is no longer defined in terms of the intuitive knowledge of morality through an innate human faculty that exists independent of culture. Human moral experiences, as registered in human conscience, are partially shared and transmitted in the form of tradition, social wisdom, and moral principles, although always susceptible to misappropriation, manipulation, misapplication, and distortion. That is, the human experience of divine reality as it is mediated by human language, culture, and symbols.

The possibility of convergence on mutual moral awareness increases as our world becomes more and more interdependent through globalization. In a global society, the possibility of a shared moral awareness and experience across the different cultures exists just as much as the possibility of conflicts, as our interaction and exchanges increase and intensify. The situation of global interdependence forces us to reflect collectively upon common moral concerns and social issues in search of a possible social cooperation. Social cooperation is urgent and ineluctable in our society where nuclear technology, ecological deterioration, population explosion, and religious-ethnic conflicts pose real threats for every member of humanity. In short, the world as a whole throws question on its fate and destiny. Globalization offers a new possibility of ecumenical moral conceptualization. This concern is addressed by several globally-oriented religious and secular moral movements, such as global ethics, ecological ethics, and human rights. They seek to secure a minimal moral order as the basis of human interactions. A shared human moral experience provides a basis for discovery or construction of common moral principle. It is true that a shared experience is still interpreted through the lenses of various different religious and cultural frameworks. Yet, there is also a high possibility that different traditions come to agreement on the minimal moral standards that regulate and cooperate actions. For example, the international ratification of universal human rights after World War II, the creation of the World Trade Organization, the expanding role of the United Nations in international affairs all attest to the trend and development of global consciousness in contemporary society.

D. Covenantal-Communicative Ethics and Rules, and Goals

Covenantal-communicative ethics seeks the construction of universal principles in relation to the common interests of humanity. In doing so, it conceives the relationship of rules and goals in a dialectic and synthetic framework. In covenantal-communicative thinking, goals and moral principles are not mutually exclusive, but rather complementary and interdependent of each other. As we have seen, covenant is achieved as covenantal parties pursue goals that are higher than merely immediate and personal ones. Covenantal communication seeks the shared larger goals of the participants. Covenantal-communicative ethics acknowledges that our moral life requires more than letters of laws and moral principles. We need goals to flourish and thrive. If moral principles delineate the boundaries of human actions, goals usually express the expectations and aspirations of our individual or collective life. When goals are believed to be worth living for, they provide exhortations and motivate the actions of those who are striving toward them.[2] Let us not forget that goals are deeply involved in the formation of human aspirations, desires, and dispositions.

Covenantal-communicative ethics helps us to understand moral principles in the context of goals. Moral principles set the minimal expectations of covenantal partners. Moral principles express the commitment of covenantal parties to the shared goals. Guiding and circumscribing their moral choices and actions, moral principles inform the moral structure and form of covenant. In short, moral principles specify the terms of interaction. They set the boundaries of how goals should be pursued by the covenantal partners. They spell out what each party expects from the other in forming a covenantal relationship. As such they function as the standard in deciding whether commitments are kept and respected by the partners. By observing the agreed upon principles, the intended goals are realized. However, these moral principles are not fixed once and for all. Covenantal parties may agree to renew and revise the rules in light of goals in response to significant changes in their circumstances and environments.

E. Law and Gospel

This discussion of rules and goals provides profound insights for reconceptualizing the relationship of law and gospel. This relationship has long been the major subject of Christian theological ethical investigation. The covenantal-communicative approach offers a new insight on the relationship of law and gospel. Disclosing the divine will for humanity, one may argue, both law and gospel are different media of God's self-communication in history. Law obtains a positive function in the context of God's loving relationship with humanity, which is love. Adam, humankind, was already in communion with God before the law was given. The fact that God created Adam in God's image ("in our image" in Genesis 1:26) implies that from the beginning it was God's intention to have a communicative relationship between Godself and humankind. God had communicated with Adam in a loving relationship (Cf. Genesis 1:28, 2:15) before he gave him a commandment not to eat the fruit of the tree of knowledge. This indicates that the law is given in the context of communion. Law presupposes and predicates on love.

Conversely, this implies that even in the relationship of love or communion, there is mutual moral responsibility and obligation. Law represents boundary, guideline, and a mark for mutual respect, in realizing the love.[3] The existence of law indicates that any relationship, including the God-human relationship, requires a proper and just form and structure. Love is partially realized through law, just as law is an aspect of love. Love does not abolish the law but fulfills it. Even living under God's

grace, human beings are required to walk and live in the way God designates, which is law. Hence, law and gospel are not in conflict with each
other. Law and gospel are complementary in God's economy. If law designates the minimal standard of order and justice, gospel describes its
source and *telos*.

If law and gospel are interrelated in fulfilling the divine will, covenant is a crucial relational theological-political category that mediates law
and gospel. Covenant indicates a structure and form of mutual transaction
that respects both the integrity and the common interest of the parties. It is
not an imposed structure against the free will of the parties. Rather it establishes the structure on the basis of the parties' free decisions. In this
way, by protecting the freedom of each party, covenant is open and in
continuity with communion.

F. Covenantal-Communicative Ethics and the Covenant of Grace

In a covenantal-communicative framework, the covenant of grace
obtains a new theological meaning. Early Calvinists understood this covenant in a purely unilateral and unconditional way, thus disregarding the
participation of human agency and reciprocity. However, a covenantal-
communicative ethics refutes this idea. The covenant of grace is an aspect
of the overall triune economy. Both the covenant of works and the covenant of grace are different aspects of one trinitarian economy. If the covenant of works (laws and justice) is an aspect of the trinitarian economy
that preserves the order, the covenant of grace, more positively, refers to a
free grace of a triune God who intends the restoration of communion. The
ultimate aim of this covenant is not forgiveness, but communion through
reconciliation. That is, we are forgiven and regenerated *for the sake of
communion with God*. The covenant of grace is predicated on and points
toward divine-human mutuality.

Therefore, in the covenant of grace, there is an expectation of a human response. The achievement of the communion requires regeneration
of humanity from the slumber, sloth, and power of sin into a new, sanctified relationship. In the unity of the regeneration and sanctification process, the covenant of grace precipitates the communion. As the regenerated
are drawn to the sanctification process, the sanctification process requires
human participation and voluntaristic moral endeavor. Whereas regeneration is unconditional, sanctification is conditional. In the integrated whole,
the two processes are inseparable for Christian life. Regenerating grace is
also sanctifying grace. If regeneration is the beginning of the salvation,
sanctification is its fulfillment. The sacraments of baptism and the Eucha-

rist are the symbolic seals of our covenant with God. And regular participation in the Eucharist functions as the renewal of the covenant.

The covenant of grace does not nullify or erase human freedom. The covenant of grace is necessary for the fulfillment of God's ultimate goal, which is communion. By forgiving sinners, the covenant of grace creates a condition for genuine human freedom and responsibility which is the indispensable basis for the covenantal mutuality. That is, the covenant of grace clears and removes the enslaving power of sins and their effects which are the barriers of covenant. This removal is achieved through the imputation of Christ's righteousness, and this, in turn is the consequence of the covenant between the Father and the Son, *pactum salutis*. In this covenant, the Father proposes the Son as the Mediator, and the Son agrees to sacrifice himself to make satisfaction for human sins, and to create new righteousness. In His covenant with the Father, Christ, the second Adam, functions as the representative of humanity. On this unconditional basis of grace, all human beings are invited as covenantal partners of God for new creation. Holiness and righteousness cannot be achieved by coercion, or imposition of the divine will. Human beings need to be empowered and motivated to live righteously. New desires, new affections, and newly transformed hearts arise in grateful response to God's salvific grace. The covenant of grace alone is not sufficient for God's salvific economy, for if salvation is the communion of God with human beings, it requires the free, voluntary, self-determining participation and submission of humanity to God.

The reciprocal nature of the covenant of grace is congruous with the relational nature of the triune God. The covenant of grace is the result of the pact which takes place within the Godhead itself, namely between the Father and the Son, and subsequently between the Son and believers. A relational, perichoretic God is a personal and covenantal God. God's action is not unilateral. The triune, relational God always anticipates a response from humanity when He interacts with human beings. Covenant refers to this form of relationality. In covenant, humanity interacts with God. Relationship becomes covenantal when human beings respond to God's initiating love and grace with a willing heart.

The covenant of grace is understood as God's desire to restore God's original communion with humanity which was broken by human sin. In Jesus Christ, God restores the original communion with humanity. The Christian doctrine of atonement addresses this fundamental alienation and distortion of the human situation. The Letter to the Ephesians says, "He [God] might gather together in one all things in Christ both which are in heaven and which are on earth—in Him" (Ephesians 1:10). In Jesus Christ there are no longer Jews and Gentiles, women and men, slaves and masters. Atonement (literally at-one-ment) intends the restoration of relationship between God and humanity. Jesus Christ is the Word who came to reconcile (re-council) the alienated world to God. God initiated a new covenant in Jesus Christ. In Jesus Christ, God graciously condescended Himself to reconcile humanity. Jesus Christ represents God's new covenant with humanity which fulfills the covenant of creation. Through faith in Jesus Christ, we enter into a new relationship with God. God makes communication and reconciliation between Himself and humanity possible through the power of the Holy Spirit. Yet, God's new covenant does not abrogate God's faithfulness toward God's creation. Rather, a new covenant points toward the ultimate communion and reconciliation in the *eschaton*.

This implies that the relationship of common grace and special grace is not conflicting but complementary. Special grace illuminates and confirms common grace. Theoretically at least there should be fundamental unity and continuity between the two by virtue of the unity of the triune God and God's action in history. God's covenantal grace is the grace which creates a new relationship—ordering, sustaining, redeeming, renewing, and sanctifying human beings and communities.

II. Conscience

Conscience is a dimension of the human self which is central to our moral experience.[4] It defines human beings as moral beings in the deepest sense. According to Timothy O'Connell, conscience pertains to the three distinctive aspects of the self: moral capacity, process, and judgment.[5] First, conscience indicates the capacity of critical moral awareness of the agent. Second, conscience often refers to the process of moral reasoning through which a person discerns right and wrong, good and bad. Finally, conscience is understood as the locus of one's moral judgment on one's action.

In human history there have been diverse explanations on the origin and nature of conscience. Calvinists and liberals view conscience as a faculty, an independent, autonomous, infallible entity of moral judgment. For Calvin, conscience meant the subjective dimension of the divine revelation given to individuals through the order of creation. Conscience is "a universal endowment, part of man as man, an element of the *imago dei*."[6] Conscience performs the function of a universal moral judgment to distinguish between good and evil. For Calvin, conscience is the sense of divine judgments, "the knowledge of the will of God" (*cognoissance*) inscribed in the heart of a person. This view has not changed much for the Calvinists. They continue to understand conscience as the faculty of the universal public knowledge of good and evil in human hearts.

However, this foundationalistic understanding is being challenged by postmodern ideas. Postmodernists, feminists, and poststructuralists, inspired by the critical tradition of Nietzsche, Freud, and Marx, present a sociological, historicist view of conscience. For them, conscience is a social construct. They argue that human conscience is inevitably bound by the contingency of time and space. Conscience is neither a self-enclosed, introspective entity nor an independent faculty of moral revelation or intuition. It reflects and manifests the reigning authority and moral sentiments of society, such as patriarchy, bourgeois social values, and the will to power.

In this section, I shall show how the idea of communication contributes to understanding the moral phenomenon of conscience. I argue that conscience, in its function, takes a communicative form. The communicative idea of conscience will show a dynamic and relational nature of a human moral agency with a more balanced perspective on freedom and relationality. Moving away from the foundationalistic and individualistic understanding of conscience, a dialogical, communicative understanding of conscience more adequately explains the formation and growth of the moral self in the matrix of his or her environment. It will show that conscience pertains to a self-reflective, self-dialogical process of moral reasoning of the agent that is intimately related to moral maturity and virtue formation. The form of morality that a mature conscience develops is postconvenient in nature.

Conscience discloses a structure of moral reasoning that is congruent with Habermas' communicative action. Conscience shows a social, intersubjective aspect of the self. In engaging an imaginative, but real dialogue between I and Me, conscience discloses a communicative structure of a person as a free, equal, and reciprocal being. Conscience refers to the innermost moral dialogue of the self with him- or herself. The word "conscience" is derived from the Latin word, *con-scientia*, meaning "knowing with," or "common knowledge." Its etymology shows that conscience is not monological but relational, dialogical knowledge. Conscience refers to a critical self-awareness, self-examination that arises in interaction with God and others.

According to Paul Lehmann, conscience means "a knowing in relation," "a bond betwixt two;" conscience names "the pivotal personal center of man's [sic] total response to the dynamics, direction, and personal thrust of the divine claim upon him."[7] As a self-reflective moral process, conscience is not the isolated, pre-given faculty of the individual. In conscience, the self is still open to the relationship with others. It is formed in the matrix of particular social relationships. The operation of conscience takes a communicative form. It is an ongoing process of self-moral understanding in relation to others. Eric Mount notes, "Since conscience is a way of 'knowing with,' it is not only 'knowing with' others in shared community; it is knowing through discourses that carry mixed signals about ourselves and others."[8]

Conscience, in its function, is essentially performative or illocutionary. In conscience, one excuses, defends, argues, charges, and rebuts. In conscience, the self is exposed to honest encounter/confrontation with himself or herself in scrutinizing his or her thoughts, motivations, and intentions of activities. In conscience, the self is related to the self more extensively and thoroughly. The self examines its action in consistency with his or her past history. In conscience, the self is vulnerable to the claims and charges presented by self-knowing truth. The dialogue within the self takes place usually in relationship with social authorities and norms internalized in the self. It takes the form of the conversation between I (subjective-impulsive) and "me" (socialized, normed self). There is a moral measurement and criticism of one's action in light of moral ideals and standards because conscience contains "the presence of something general in the particular."[9] The self examines itself in light of social rules and goals. An immature conscience judges itself uncritically according to the rules and goals. Yet, a mature (post-conventional) conscience may take a critical attitude toward the rules and goals.

In conscience, one enters an imaginative inner communicative action with concerned others (family, neighbor, colleagues, societal norms, etc). According to Berry Harvey, in intertestamental Jewish literatures, conscience was understood as the *elenchus*—"an inner forum provided by God that accuses and instructs the individual in the struggle against sin and for a virtuous life before God."[10] Conscience in operation shows an analogous structure to communicative action. In an inner dialogue, the self takes a critical distance from itself. This distance does not imply an absolute isolation. Rather it is a distance coming from the reflection of the self before social norms and the truthfulness of its action. It includes the self-dialogue with surrounding moral authorities and tradition for the redemption of guiding principles of one's action. Truthfulness to oneself, sincerity (or the transparency of motivations and intentions to the agent) is the significant aspect of this process. Conscience operates under the premise of self-truthfulness or self-transparency. The agent, through scrutiny, detects one's true motivations. In conscience, one bears responsibility toward one's motivations/intentions. Motivations and intentions are significant for the integrity and value of moral actions, and consequently for the formation of character and virtue. Without the moral approval of the self on motivations and intentions, conscience cannot become fully free and rest.

Another similarity of conscience to communicative action is found in the relational nature of conscience. Conscience is formed in the matrix of relationship. Relationality is the context of conscience formation and operation. Conscience arises in response to problems, issues, and transactions facing a person. Conscience is not the site of the independent, final moral certainty divorced from the matrix of relationship. Conscience is formed in the self's engagement with various social, cultural forces, conveyed through significant others, such as parent and peer.

Since conscience is a product of a creaturely human existence interwoven with the events and occurrences of history and practical concerns, there is no guarantee that one's conscience is always right. Individual conscience is fallible. There could be a poorly or an erroneously formed or operating conscience. For example, a damaged radar screen provides erroneous data, which is inevitable, in the same way, a poor or an erroneously formed conscience is unreliable in reaching a rightful moral decision or judgment. For this reason, appeal to conscience alone cannot be a moral guarantor. That is why one needs to submit the decisions of one's conscience to a communicative community for mutual scrutiny and validation.

The idea of a poor or an erroneous conscience implies that conscience is not a fixed faculty. It is developmental. Conscience is a process, not a completion or perfection of decision. It is a personal morality in the process of one's constant becoming (or growing). It is on the pilgrimage, the journey toward maturity and perfection in *eschaton*. It makes a provisional decision. Our conscience sees but a poor reflection as in a mirror, not face to face yet (1 Cor. 13:12). Individuals, as they grow up, reflexively participate in the formation of moral convictions.

The kind of conscience arising from this maturating process is post-conventional in nature (Cf. Kohlberg; Habermas). Post-conventional conscience is the kind of conscience developed out of communicative process. If conventional morality means uncritical acceptance of the present and past authority and tradition, post-conventional conscience reconstructs traditions and authorities in light of new challenges posed by changes in technology, social structure, and institutional transformation. Post-conventional conscience is characterized by a cognitive, reflexive stance of the agent toward rules, principles, traditions, and ethos. It exercises a healthy hermeneutical suspicion as well as affirmation toward rules, principles, practices of one's own tradition and community (*a la* Stanley Hauerwas). By doing so, it critically appropriates rules, principles, and traditions in a new historical context. Through the exercise of post-conventional conscience, core values and the spirit of these rules, principles and traditions are redeemed without being trapped into literalism or legalism.

A mature, post-conventional conscience shows actual critical balance and unity of reason and will, societal norms and freedom in the self. Conscience is the locus of the self's identity where the polarizing forces of freedom and accountability are contested and reconciled. Conscience indicates a constant attempt of the agent to harmonize or integrate one's actions with the demands of societal norms. Conscience has to do with the maturity of moral agency. Conscience involves the whole being of the moral agent. In conscience, thinking and acting, knowing and doing, judgment and involvement become one integrated reality. This process usually includes the deconstructive and reconstructive process of presuppositions and foundations of conventional rules and principles. Self-critical and reflexive dimension is a crucial element here. That is, some form of free reflection and critical distance from convention must be involved in this process. When the development of communicative attitude is inhibited or disrupted, an authentic internalization of rules and the development of virtues are not possible. Communicative process is critical for the development of mature moral agency. Conscience becomes mature through the growth in the ability for self-reflection, judgment, and prudence. Mature conscience and the formation of agency (character and virtues) are intimately related. Conscience is an aspect of the virtue formation. Virtues are formed through the mature exercise of conscience. Virtues include a critical, communicative process in their formation. Virtues are not the blind acceptance or imprint of the external authorities.

How is conscience related to the trinitarian theology? From a Christian theological perspective, conscience is not simply a social artifact or construct. For Christians, conscience implies the fundamental experience of the divine and human encounter. Conscience, in a Christian context, is neither autonomous nor heteronomous, but theonomous. Conscience is not the colonizing agency of society occupying one's heart, nor is it an unerring, infallible, intuitive moral faculty given for every person. Conscience has its ground in and accountability before God. A theonomous dimension of conscience shows that although it is formed through the socialization process, yet it is not completely socialized. John Newman's observation is relevant here. He says,

> [Conscience] vaguely reaches forward to something beyond self, and dimly discerns a sanction higher than self for its decisions, as is evidenced in that keen sense of obligation and responsibility which informs them. Hence, it is that we are accustomed to speak of conscience as . . . voice, or the echo of a voice, imperative and constraining, like no other dictate in the whole of our experience.[11]

One may say that conscience is the vestige and reflection of the relational image of the triune God. Conscience functions in the tripartite context of human relationality of the self, God, and other human beings. Conscience means the fulcrum of human moral responsibility. It functions as a tribunal or a seat of judgment. It attests this fundamental aspect of human communicative ability and accountability, namely a person's covenantal relationship with God and others. It constitutes the deepest inner sanctuary and the living bond between God and a person. The torment or pang of conscience speaks about this experience. It happens when human beings violate the boundaries divinely arranged for their good.[12] St. Paul says,

> When the Gentiles, who do not possess the law, do instinctively what the law requires, these, though not having the law, are a law to themselves. They show that what the law requires is written on their hearts, to which their own conscience also bears witness; and their conflicting thoughts will accuse or perhaps excuse them on the day when, according to my gospel, God, through Jesus Christ, will judge the secret thoughts of all (Romans 2:14 -16).

Conscience becomes a post-conventional when it discovers God as a covenantal and dialogical partner. In encounter with God, the boundary of the self's identified community can be expanded into the universal community of communication. There are occasions when social norms and authorities are challenged as a consequence of the self's dialogue with God. Because of his or her relationship to God, the self is not completely socialized, not an automaton of social engineering.

For Christians, the reference point of conscience is God. Our relationship to God is the most fundamental and foundational one in the development of moral agency of the self. God as the most comprehensive and inclusive reality, reality above reality, Being of Beings, guides our search for integrity in the self's social interaction with others. God is the judge of our motivations and intentions.

The kind of conscience which the triune God creates is postconventional. It is a mature form of morality which is able to harmonize the situational variances with the demand of rules and principles. Just as the Spirit constantly reorders and rearranges social relationships in accordance with the Logos, the same Spirit works in the lives of individuals in order to form a post-conventional form of morality. The Spirit reinterprets the authoritative rules and principles in a new context. [13] In postcoventional morality, rules and laws are neither intuitively known through rationality nor heteronomously imposed. St. Paul's distinction of letters of laws and spirit of laws is informative in this respect. His idea indicates the movement from a conventional form of morality to a post-conventional form of morality. Rules and laws are not followed uncritically. Yet the agents are invited to exercise their prudence and wisdom to understand and practice them in accordance with the spirit of the laws. St. Paul recognizes that this exercise is safe and possible with the assistance of the Holy Spirit who was the author of the laws and rules.

A historical function of conscience is congruent with the creative ordering work of the triune God in the Logos and the Spirit. Conscience is related to both the Spirit and the Logos, which come to one in many cultural guises and forms. In conscience, the self receives many summons from cultural *logoi* (norms and rules of society) in various life situations. But the self does not uncritically succumb to these norms and rules. In response to summons, one's spirit attests and affirms or rejects and refutes these norms and rules.

The above discussion sheds a new critical insight on Hauerwas' idea of virtues and character. He tends to view the latter as a self-enclosed entity without allowing the function of reflection and reasoning as integral of its developmental process. The formation of virtues requires moral exemplars to imitate. These exemplars are important for the beginning stage. As the agent matures (as it moves from an uncritical acceptance of authorities to a more mature, critical understanding of them), it exercises more moral prudence (and critical freedom) toward tradition, narrative, and community. It examines societal rules and principles and is able to appropriate and interpret them without compromising their original spirit. Cognitive components are integral to the exercise of prudence. This particular cognitive component is operative in the form of inner communication of a moral agent.

III. The Church

A Christian communicative action takes place primarily in and through the church. The church is the sacrament of the trinitarian Kingdom, the mystery of communion of human beings with the triune God and other human beings. The mutual participation and fellowship between God and humanity takes place in the church. The church presents a new historical form of human solidarity created by the economy of a triune God. It is a perichoretic community where identity and difference, individuality and communality are respected at the same time.

The foundation of the church is the trinitarian perichoretic economy. Karl Barth said that the church is the historical-earthly existence of Jesus Christ. More accurately, one may say that the church is the historical existence of the divine perichoretic fellowship, *koinonia*. That is to say, the reciprocal and loving fellowship of the triune God is the basis of the *koinonia* as a historical community of love, hope and faith. The fellowship or *koinonia* of the church corresponds to the perichoresis of trinitarian persons. The church was created in and through the cooperative work of the trinitarian persons. God's unity, therefore, becomes the basis for the unity and reconciliation of humanity. The church is a historical product of the cooperative praxis of the trinitarian persons. It reflects and manifests the communion of the trinitarian persons. The church is built upon the triune God's perichoretic fellowship (*koinonia*) and economy.

The church implies a new form of intersubjective community. The sociality of the church is actualized in the reciprocal intersubjectivity. The church as the community of communication of free, equal, and reciprocal persons echoes the triune *koinonia*. The communicative intersubjectivity is the determinant of the church. Emulating the trinitarian perichoresis, intersubjective reciprocity determines the relationality of persons in the church. The sociality of the church is distinguished from other—authoritarian or contractual—forms of sociality by its reciprocal, communicative character. A hierarchical model of the church is rejected in this understanding. The unity of the church lies not in its uniformity coming from hierarchical control, but a communicative, cooperative unity arising through the freedom of the members in Jesus Christ.

This communicative insight is visible in St. Paul's epistles. For example, in his letter to the church at Corinth, he uses the term *parrhesia*, meaning openness, confidence, and freedom of speech. This word characterizes the sociality of the church.[14] The Spirit of God enables and empowers *parrhesia*. Where the Spirit is, there is freedom. The mode of authority exercised in the church should be communicative. It should be also shared among various parts, for the church's authority is not an imposed authority but a persuasive one, winning the hearts of its members. The exercise of Christian authority, in tune with the triune God, is made through persuasion, a loving appeal to hearts.

Communicative ethics proposes an organic and democratic understanding of the Church. The church composes various parts with various functions and roles endowed with spiritual gifts (charismata). There is no hierarchy among the different gifts or the parts of the body of the believers. Even apostleship is no exception. It is one of many gifts and tasks given to the church. Each part is adjoined in the body with Jesus Christ as its head. There is functional differentiation among various parts of the body, but among them all, there is freedom and equality. Even so, no part is independent of the others. They exist in functional interdependence and reciprocity. The spiritual gifts must be used and exercised for the sake of the common good of the church.

In building the church, the Logos and the Spirit cooperate perichoretically. The church is determined both christologically and pneumatologically. As Jesus Christ was led by the Spirit in his earthly ministry, so the Spirit builds the church in conformity to Christ, the Word. Whereas the Logos institutes the church, the Spirit enlivens and energizes it. As the triune God is one and three at the same time, similarly unity and diversity are harmonized in the being and mission of the church by the perichoretic work of the triune God. The freedom of the Spirit and the structure of the Logos are in seamless cooperation to build the church in a dynamic and ordered form. The Spirit transcends history, yet it is the Spirit of truth, so it follows the tracks of the Logos. The Spirit respects the personal and particular aspect of individual members and their talents and gifts. The Logos provides the rational structure for mutual engagement and coordination. That is, by virtue of the co-inherent work of the Spirit and the Logos, the church obtains rational as well as organic, affectionate aspects at the same time. The notion of the church as the body of Christ is sensible only in light of the communicative balance and unity of the Spirit and the Logos. To refer to the church as the body of Christ means this organic, dynamic and differentiated nature of relationship.

The church signifies a new solidarity of humanity in Jesus Christ. Zizioulas said that the church is a person, and every human person is an ecclesial being.[15] German theologian Dietrich Bonhoeffer defined the

church as a "collective person" of Jesus Christ who exists as a congrega-
tion.[16] LaCugna is correct in saying, "The ecclesial hypostasis—
graced person—experiences the body as a means of true communion,
transcending individualism and exclusivism, and pointing to the future
realization of universal communion."[17] The church is a community of free,
equal, and reciprocal individuals motivated toward mutual understanding
and love.

Even so, the church is still imperfect. Unlike the triune intersubjective perichoresis, the intersubjectivity in the church is neither infallible nor
sinless. It is the intersubjectivity among fallible sinners. Despite its ground
in the economy of the triune God, the church's historical existence is exposed to a moral precariousness and ambiguity. It is constantly threatened
by sinful desires, egoism and ambitions. The church is always exposed to
the dangers that selfish, narrow loyalties may cloud its understanding and
mission. History shows that it is implicated with various forms of sins and
mistakes, such as imperialism, colonialism, and witch hunts. Because of
its fallibility and sinfulness, the church requires constant critique, scrutiny
and repentance. This is why the church needs to be a communicative
community. The communicative theory takes seriously the sinful dimension of the empirical church, its exposure to systematic distortion of
communication. It critically reflects upon the current cultural practices,
social formations, and institutional structures in light of God's action in
Jesus Christ. The scope of the church is both cosmic and particular. The
church's communicative action is placed between the "already" and "not
yet" of the trinitarian Kingdom. The communicative church is the church
as pilgrim, in a journey toward perfection and fullness promised in the
triune life, despite its present imperfection. The church, in her communicative engagement and discernment, should emulate the trinitarian Kingdom and its perichoretic communion.

The covenantal-communicative method directly resonates with the
spirit of the Reformation, *ecclesia reformata semper reformanda*—"the
church reformed and always reforming." It provides a concrete method of
the church's self-renewal through discursive praxis and engagement. In
other words, the church is formed and reformed through the ongoing
communication with God and with other human beings within and without
the church. Communicative action is a historical step toward solidarity
and communion. Communication is the penultimate dimension of the ultimate communion of God with humanity in Jesus Christ. Communicative
ethics is understood, in this cosmic context of God's history of action, as a
pragmatic, practical methodology. It has its legitimate place in history as

a provisional and penultimate human endeavor to cooperatively discern the will of God and approximate the ultimate unity promised and given in God's kingdom. Communicative praxis challenges and renews the tradition of the church and envisions a new form of a liberated life for humanity. It is self-critical. Covenant indicates a partial historical realization of trinitarian communion and an eschatological sign of the destiny of the whole humanity for communion with God and other beings.[18]

Communication takes place in the context of Christian liturgy and sacrament. Christian liturgy and sacraments point to a deeper structure and the ultimate ground of human communication: the life of God. Baptism and the Eucharist show an analogical structural similarity to communicative action with the dialectical tension of separation (the detachment from the old, conventional relationship) and reintegration (incorporation into a new relationship). Holy Communion is the sacrament of communion taking place in the church by the power of the Holy Spirit. It is a sign of God's kingdom in inclusiveness, reciprocity, freedom, love, and equality. It states a new form of sociality—freedom in relation, and relation of free persons. Holy Communion precipitates the transfiguration of all humanity from solitariness and isolation to loving community, and from tyranny and oppression to freedom, at the same time. Baptism also becomes a concrete event and basis for a true communion among persons. Baptism also transforms isolation and separation into communion. The metaphor of the church as the body of Christ indicates the corporate-communal dimension of Christian life. In Jesus Christ, human beings earn a perspective to be self-transcending toward others. In baptism, a human being obtains a new capacity for communion, self-transcendence, and love.

This communicative dimension is implied and captured by a traditional Christian understanding of the church. As its root, *ecclesia*, indicates, the church shows a strong ethical consonance with communicative action. The church is a public sphere and institution, called out of the world to discuss and reflect upon the worldly concerns and issues in light of God's reign. In *ecclesia*, human beings are equally companions in the search for divine truth and its realization. The uniqueness of individuals is not subjugated to or dispensed to the collective ideal and doctrine. Individuals are equally invited into conversation. The Spirit moves through the interaction of its members, thereby *koinonia* is activated. In the process of reaching understanding, in the search for the concrete, the will of God, the talents and resources of members are mobilized and actualized into *diakonia* (service). In communicative discourse and praxis, through *koinonia* and *diakonia*, the collective personhood of Jesus Christ is being increasingly realized in history with concrete form and shape.

The covenant-communicative praxis indicates a prophetic, liberating, and reconciling activity of the church, enacted in light of the divine covenant in Jesus Christ. Communicative action imparts a concrete social political dimension to the life of the church. The church is the community within communities, the primordial communicative community that inspires, empowers, and guides to reconstruct existing social relationships in the image of the Kingdom of God. The church, as a distinctive community, is called out of the world and keeps a critical distance from the world, but provides a critical energy and perspective on the world. It is not a strategically oriented community.

The church is called to perform a prophetic and a reconciling ministry in society. It interprets the purpose and meaning of life under God. Like prophets who stood against unjust or unfaithful kings and emperors, the church is to rail against regimes or institutions which do not respect the basic requirements of laws and agreements. The purpose for its prophetic role is not to abolish or replace the regime, or to build an alternative polity as detached from the state, but to engage in public discourse by reminding and pointing to the ultimate source and ground of morality, polity, and community.

As we have seen, one finds the impulse of this communicative praxis in the Free Church movement. During the Reformation and the eras that followed it, the church positioned itself as the community within communities. The church engages in communicative praxis by holding political authority, social mores, conventions, and cultural ethos and practices accountable to the divine rule. The church plays a similar role and function in a postmodern society, when the church returns to its original calling and mission to overcome various social, economic, and cultural divisions.

We may call the Free Church movement a theologically motivated and covenantally enacted communicative praxis. Its liberating and ordering impulse has spread, challenging all kinds of systematically distorted communication within and without the church. The Free Church was one of the first communities of communication in a modern sense.

Human rights in a communicative context are stipulated against the background of a universal community of communication. When the church's right to be a fully communicative community—free, equal, and reciprocal in search of the realization of the divine will—is ensured, other rights are communicatively legislated on this basis. The church is the community that provides the most universal, cosmological, and inclusive horizon for one's moral decision and action, and the concrete loci of coop-eration. The church as the universal community of communication and mutual acceptance, freedom, and equality, is the prototype and model for a reconciled and liberated human community. Each member of the church is free and equal before God, and to each other. Their freedom is given and bound only by God. The church provides the anchoring point for indi-viduals in forming and reforming social institutions and structures.

This trinitarian-covenantal model of ecclesiology overcomes the limits of the still hierarchical model of the Roman Catholic Church and the implicitly authoritarian ecclesiology of communitarians such as Stanley Hauerwas. The trinitarian-communicative conception of the church upholds a dynamic, organic, and relational aspect of the church's being and mission. It respects the public mission as well as a particularis-tic theological basis of the church. On the trinitarian basis, the church is able to engage in the public realm without compromising its unique theo-logical identity.

IV. Communication, Covenant, and Communion

By engaging the social doctrine of the Trinity with Habermas, cove-nantal-communicative ethics clarifies the significant interrelationship of communication, covenant, and communion. It shows that if covenant is the structure of communication, communication is the process of reaching covenant, and communion the goal of covenant and communication. A trinitarian communion is the foundation, process and goal of covenantal-communicative ethics. As we have established, covenant and communica-tion and communion have analogical reference and root in a trinitarian life of perichoresis.

From a Christian perspective, the interrelation of the three notions is critical to a proper understanding of the nature of human moral existence and social life. Communication is an integral process of self-realization in relationship whose ultimate goal is communion. Communication is indis-pensable because it is the expression of one's being-ness. In a sense, all living beings express themselves. All beings aim at self-realizations through communication.[19] A being is known to others in communication. Without communication, it has difficulty being known; consequently it experiences difficulty in establishing an appropriate relationship. Commu-nication is the ultimate medium of a relationship, and thus self-realization. Through communication, a person enters a relationship with others. Rela-tionship is an indispensable aspect of human existence, which becomes a meaningful and living reality through communication. Communication presumes the existence of the other. A speech in communication is not the property of a speaker alone. As soon as a speech is made, it becomes a common possession of the speaker and the listener. That is, a possibility of bond exists in communication.

Communication takes either a verbal or a nonverbal form. It could also be cognitive or symbolic. Symbol or metaphor is an indispensable aspect of communication. It is a significant means of self-expression and realization. A shared symbol embodies and signifies a bonding reality between different parties. Symbol or utterance is the extension of a being. A being reaches out through symbol and utterance. Symbol, as communication, renders what is present (invested) there. Symbol presents and contains what is signified. Symbol or utterance has a referential value. Hence, sincerity is probably the most significant moral value or criterion for communicative action. With a false presentation, a being ultimately frustrates and blocks the way to self-realization, for itself and the others with whom it is communicating.

Communion refers to the state of being in unity spiritually and intellectually (and physically in the case of marriage). Communication is the expression of the desire to be in communion with others. We enter fellowship with others through communication. Communion presupposes communication because communion requires the cooperation of two or more persons, divine or human, and this cooperation takes place through the agreement of informed wills. The process of cooperation includes the surrender and conformation of our own wills to God's will. Yet this surrender and conformation arise not through coercion but through persuasion, hearkening our hearts. Communion is neither a fixed nor an enclosed state. It refers to an ecstatic, living union of different persons. It is renewed and deepened through communication. Communion presupposes freedom and differentiation. Communion does not mean the collapse or absorption of one's being into another being; rather, it indicates the dynamic unity in a highly differentiated plurality of beings. Communion presupposes a mutual understanding and agreement of different parties through communication. A being is fully realized in communion because in communion the forces of identity and difference are finally in harmony.

Communicative process is crucial to overcome the distortive power of sin and to adjust to changes which are intrinsic aspects of contingent human existence. Sin causes the disruption of relationship and communication between God and humanity. Communicative action is necessary to restore a broken or distorted relationship. The Pentecost event shows that God's redemptive work began first with the restoration of communication.

It affirmed each dialect and vernacular rather than subsuming all difference into one.

Covenant is the structure of mutual obligation which is established through successful process of communicative action. Communication is the integral aspect of covenant. Communication indicates the capacity to enter into covenant with others. As Eric Mount aptly puts it, "Covenant provides the context in which argument and dissent are allowed."[20] That is, covenant inevitably includes the process of communication. Covenant is essentially relational and dialogical. Covenant presupposes otherness or differences as it is the process of overcoming disagreement. When its communicative dimension is properly spelled out, one can see clearly that covenant is intimately associated with a dialogical reflective moral process.

If communion is achieved through communication, communication in turn requires the freedom, equality, and reciprocity of the participants. Communication aims at reconciliation. Conversely, the conditions of reconciliation need to be clarified by communication. If communion is the consummation of relationality among particular and different persons, it is achieved through communication.

Communion does not exhaust our individuality and freedom. Communion presupposes differences and individual identity (freedom). Communion does not exhaust a personhood and its freedom. Just as the triune communion is the communion of the differentiated trinitarian persons, the communion of God with humanity is also the communion which respects differences. A genuine communion respects freedom, equality, and reciprocity. In this respect, communication and communion are intimately related. Communion is achieved through communication. If communion refers to the unity between different persons, it is achieved through their communication. Communication clarifies the conditions of communion. The intrinsic *telos* of communication is mutual understanding, a step toward communion. In relationship to communication, communion is not an uncritical merging or collapse of individualities, but cognitive conscious and voluntary self-giving that arises through mutual understanding.

Covenant provides a provisional, mediating structure between communication and communion. Covenant gives semi-permanency and structure to relationship and communication. Communion needs to rely on a certain established ground and basis, although the former always surpasses the latter, but never detours it. Communication clarifies the routes to covenant. Through a communicative process leading to covenant, various mutual interests, needs, and desires are presented, examined, and tested. Through this process, the possibility of constructing the common interest and the common good arises.

V. Society

A. Covenantal-Communicative Ethics and Structuration of Society

Covenantal-communicative ethics adequately captures the dynamic nature of human agency and societal formation, both in terms of its transformative possibility and of its stability/constancy. It dynamically illuminates an essential social process of human world-building and world-maintaining activity. According to Anthony Giddens, social practices take on a recurrent, accumulated character. All social practices, including religious ones, are situated in three significant dimensions: temporality, space, and constraint of a tradition.[21] In combination, these three dimensions pose the possibility of continuity and discontinuity, stability and change. The notion of structuration adequately catches the process of human world-building activities and its given constraints. Structuration encompasses both active and passive aspects, personal and collective sides of human agency.[22] Structuration does not regard social system/structure as an impervious and fixed reality. Rather, it considers social reality as a reformable or a trans-formable one. Human freedom and action suggest that possibility. However, human freedom and action are not unbounded. They are not open to every kind of possibility. Human freedom and action are constrained and guided by established structure of tradition, the limitations of time and space. Social structure gives a certain continuity and pattern to human actions. Tradition is a proper form of social structure with several normative sets of social practices.

Covenantal-communicative action (covenant made through communication) indicates a primordial social mechanism of structuration. It attends to both constant (enduring) and contingent dimensions of social existence. In covenantal-communicative action, social structure is open to change and reformation, and the agent finds an anchor point in social action. Covenant recognizes that human society requires some enduring structure/system for its stability and predictability, yet it acknowledges that the possibility of change always exists in social practices. In covenantal-communicative thinking, neither structure nor agency is absolute. They are mutually implicated. Just as social structure is a human construct through a long collective endeavor, human agency is shaped through a socialization process. One way to overcome the theoretical dilemma posed by the bi-polarity of totalitarian repressive structure and chaotic/libertine freedom is to understand social process as structuration. Covenantal-communicative action indicates a structuration process of society for growth and adjustment. Covenant indicates a formal agreement through which the structuration process obtains a certain public recognition and normativity. It is situated in time and space. Yet covenant suggests a certain patterned and structured paradigm of human inter-transaction which renders indexical meaning to time and space. Covenant respects the open and provisional nature of social structure and human agency. Agent and structure presuppose each other; they are interdependent. Yet, from a Christian theological perspective, this structuring, world-building activity of human beings does not happen in an absolute moral vacuum or total arbitrariness. It is constrained by the triune economy of creation, redemption, and sanctification.

B. Covenantal-Communicative Ethics and Social Spheres

The idea of covenantal spheres provides a more complex view of the public and consequently public engagements for Christians. A Christian moral life does not end at the doorstep of the sanctuary. It continues beyond. Christian ethics studies how we can best live out the demands of the gospel in various realms of our life, such as family, school, local community, hospital, political party, corporations, and governmental agencies, as a father and mother, employee, Sunday school teacher, choir member, social worker, firefighter, or business manager. A different social context demands a different response of Christian faith in fulfilling the will of God. The idea of social sphere refers to this distinctively differentiated and enduring domain of human social action.

The idea of social spheres moves beyond David Tracy's idea of the three public spheres for Christian theology: church, academia, and society.[23] Church and academia are merely two of the many social spheres. Society has a variety of other publics. The idea of covenant helps to understand this complex and interconnected nature of social spheres. This also helps to overcome the monolithic, reductionistic danger of liberation ethics, reducing all forms of social evils to a monocause of either race, gender, or class. Covenantal-communicative ethics helps us to see the operation and function of oppression in various social spheres by identifying the moral requirements of the various spheres.

The methodology of covenantal-communicative ethics is useful in adjudicating the conflicts among various covenantal institutions. It provides a theological and methodological framework that respects the historical-pluralistic nature of social institutions and their principles of distributive justice. Covenantal-communicative ethics establishes justice through mutual critique and agreement. In a covenantal-communicative framework, the authority of each institution (or sphere sovereignty) is understood in covenantal terms. A particular content of authorities and responsibilities of each institution—its purpose, scope, and limitations—is determined through public discourse in reference to the ultimate reality.

A political sphere is usually the place where the adjudication of conflicts of authorities takes place. The political sphere plays a coordinate function in drawing and guarding the boundaries between special covenants and their distributive principles by defining, clarifying, and reinterpreting the shared meanings of goods. The political community constitutes a world of common meanings, or in the lifeworld to use Habermas' term.[24] It "establishes an unavoidable setting for the consideration of distributive justice."[25] Without this political community, there is no definite collective agency of decision-making on the distribution of social goods and the recognition of particular covenantal rights.

As for various spheres of society, covenantal-communicative ethics indicates a methodology of public adjudication of distributive principles within various social spheres and of boundaries among spheres. It effectively responds to a historicist concern of Walzer and a theological interest of Kuyper. In adjudicating the conflicting claims of sphere sovereignties and rights, it explores the possibility of transcultural agreement on distributive principles of justice under the stricture of the historical contingency of every human understanding of justice. A covenantal-communicative methodology investigates the theological meanings of social goods and their boundaries for the construction of a plausible theory of sphere and sphere sovereignty in attending to diverse human cultural experiences. It stipulates the participation of all concerned people in the process of investigation and mutual deliberation of the meanings of the social goods and boundaries. As Walzer points out, the discernment of certain internal principles (intrinsic notions) of social goods "cannot be determined by philosophical arguments among ourselves—nor even by philosophical argument among some ideal version of ourselves."[26] This stipulation is based on the belief that without the inclusion of all concerned parties, and without acknowledging their freedom and equality in the decision-making process, the very process of public adjudication itself is morally flawed, thus making a just society impossible.

By creatively and constructively engaging the four sources of Christian ethics, the covenantal-communicative method helps to find valid and rightful terms of interaction as well as autonomy among different spheres in different contexts. That is, it defines not only the negative terms of mutual noninterference (independence) but also positive terms of mutual interaction. It helps to cross-examine the practices of spheres in light of mutual tradition, experience, and canons.

A covenantal-communicative ethics of sphere carefully discerns how God's trinitarian economy has been displayed in various spheres of society. In discerning and searching for distinctive logic, patterns, or grammar of various spheres sharable by common humanity, it examines the meaning of contemporary social life in conversation with experiences of other religious traditions and cultures. In the framework of the trinitarian doctrine, it brings diverse cultural conceptions of goods (with basis in the doctrine of creation) into a reflective conversation with biblical understandings of goods (with basis in the redemptive event of Christ). On the basis of the given perichoretic unity among the three persons of God, covenantal-communicative ethics seeks the coherence between human experience of common grace in history (God's revelation in creation) with Christian knowledge of special grace in Jesus Christ, because the God of redemption is none other than the God of creation. If common grace provides a universal theological basis for communicative engagement among diverse human communities, special grace, given in Scripture and Christian tradition, informs, clarifies, and guides this engagement. One may say, then, that this public theology of sphere is built upon communicative endeavor to discern the living Logos within various human logoi through the mediating, illuminating power of the Holy Spirit.

In a covenantal-communicative framework, Kuyper's idea of sphere sovereignty is understood as covenantal sovereignty which obtains its legitimacy by its referential value to the Ultimate Reality (for Christians, the sovereignty of a triune God), and by its normative acceptance by people. The specific stipulation of the authority and responsibility of each sphere—its distributive principle and boundary—indicates the terms of covenant agreed upon by the members of society. If common grace, as Kuyper argued, means divine grace operating in every aspect of human life, it provides a universal theological basis for communicative engagement of diverse human communities in search of common moral grounds and distributive principles of justice. That is, covenant is possible on the basis of the trinitarian belief that a considerable degree of goodness and moral possibility exists today, despite human depravity and cultural differences, because of the ongoing self-revelation (self-communication or self-witness) of a triune God in every human society. Common grace indicates this ongoing self-witness of a triune God for justice, peace, and order.

Covenantal-communicative ethics is helpful in understanding the nature of modern social institutions and their inter-spheral relationships. Many modern institutions take covenantal forms. They are formed by and run through the covenant of members: government by elected officials and qualified public servants, church by consistories and presbyteries, university by association of trustees and faculties, and business by trustees. As such, each institution has covenantally-defined tasks, goals, and responsibilities. Institutions become the sources and spaces of positive freedom for members, where they can participate and realize their potentials. Yet each institution is not an isolated, competing structure. It exists in a symbiotic, covenantal relationship with others. The boundary between spheres is negotiated and redefined through the communicative covenant of members. The body social is constituted by covenants of different institutions and spheres. As such, society as a whole takes a confederate form, namely a covenanted symbiosis of various institutions serving and working for the common good of society.

These observations lead us to conclude that the idea of sphere justice has a communicative-covenantal structure, and becomes more explicitly operative and functional under the presumption of covenant. The idea of covenant provides a theological and methodological framework which not only embraces Walzer's historicist thrust and pluralistic understanding of distributive justice, but also responds to the challenge of public adjudication of conflicting principles of distribution resulting from the situation of religious-cultural pluralism. In covenantal-communicative ethics, Walzer's theory of sphere justice becomes more consistently historical, and Kuyper's theory attains practical political and moral relevance without losing its theological potency.

Covenantal-communicative ethics presents a public theology of spheres. The communicatively derived concept of spheres is to be conceived as social covenant. Society through public discourse comes provisionally to a certain shared, agreed upon understanding of the boundaries, limits, and authorities of each social sphere. Boundaries are redrawn and new goals are placed under new realms of sovereignty. These decisions are not permanent, however. They are only provisional, and thus subjected to future revision.

A covenantal-communicative understanding of spheres responds to the challenges of a postmodern, global society where the adjudication of social conceptions of goods and spheres is indispensable as various goods are shared, divided, and exchanged across traditional national boundaries.[27] A covenantal-communicative ethics of spheres is not an insidious imposition of religious control over society. It intends to be a reasoned, intelligible theological response to the religiously constitutive nature of human existence, which is in constant search for the meaning, goal, and purpose in various domains of human existence. Covenantal-communicative ethics provides a coherent public vision and guidance to people who, otherwise, might suffer from fragmentation and anomie. It helps to transform spheric activities into meaningful social embodiments of vocation. The primary task of this covenantal-communicative ethics is to clarify and illuminate the nature and meaning of social goods and spheres, and their interrelationship by bringing various sources of ethics (the quadrilateral of Christian ethics) into constant mutual critique of and conversation with each other. It explores the possibility of a common understanding of sphere justice, critically examining various cultural conceptions of social goods in terms of their distortive dangers as well as transformative possibilities in the future. Covenantal-communicative ethics specifies the meaning of social goods, prophetically criticizing new forms of sphere idolatries (injustices) and seeking to reintegrate various segments of life into a meaningful public vision for common life. As such, it provides adequate guidelines and directions for the use and exchange of social goods in a global society.

Notes

1. This is the major difference from the Calvinists' view of morality. Calvinists understood common grace primarily in terms of the divine laws implanted in human conscience. This perspective is no longer viable in a postmodern situation because of its foundationalistic tendency.

2. Robin Lovin, *Christian Ethics: Essential Guide* (Nashville: Abingdon Press, 2000), 54ff.

3. Cf. Paul L. Lehmann, *The Decalogue and a Human Future: The Meaning of the Commandments for Making and Keeping Human Life Human* (Grand Rapids: W. B. Eerdmans Publishing Co., 1994).

4. Anne E. Patrick, *Liberating Conscience: Feminist Explorations in Catholic Moral Theology* (New York: Continuum, 1996), 35.

5. Timothy E. O'Connell, *Principles for a Catholic Morality* (New York: Seabury Press, 1978), 89ff.

6. Edward A. Dowey, Jr., *The Knowledge of God in Calvin's Theology* (Grand Rapids: W. B. Eerdmans Publishing Co.,1994), 56.

7. Paul L. Lehmann, *Ethics in a Christian Context* (New York, Hagerstown, San Francisco, London: Harper & Row Publishers, 1963), 354.

8. Eric Mount, "Conscience in Process," an unpublished paper, 4-5.

9. Ibid., 14.

10. Barry Harvey, *Politics of the Theological: Beyond the Piety and Power of a World Come of Age* (New York: Peter Lang, 1995), 61.

11. John Newman, *An Essay in Aid of a Grammar of Assent*, ed. Charles Frederick Harold (New York: Longman, Green and Co., 1947), 82.

12. Lehmann, *Ethics in a Christian Context*, 356.

13. As will be discussed later, in a Christian theological understanding, the formation of conscience is related to the particularizing Spirit. As the localizing, particularizing power, the Spirit is deeply involved in the process of virtue formation and conscience. The Spirit personally attends to our moral development. Human moral development is a part of the sanctification process which is led by the Spirit. The Spirit, the perfecting power, communicatively engages with our spirit in the process of moral reasoning, practices, and reflection. The Spirit is involved in the maturation of our conscience. Yet the Spirit does so always in the context of community.

14. David F. Ford, "Faith in the Cities,"in *On Being the Church: Essays on the Christian Community*, ed. Colin Gunton and Daniel W. Hardy (Edinburgh: T. & T. Clark, 1989), 245.

15. John Zizioulas, *Being as Communion: Studies in Personhood and the Church* (Crestwood, N.Y.: St. Vladimir's Seminary Press, 1993).

16. Dietrich Bonhoeffer, *The Communion of Saints: A Dogmatic Inquiry into the Sociology of the Church* (New York: Harper & Row, 1963), 52.

17. LaCugna, *God for Us*, 264.

18. Ibid.

19. Karl Rahner, *Theological Investigations: More Recent Writings*, vol.4. (Baltimore: Helicon Press, 1966), 229.

20. Mount, *Covenant, Community, and the Common Good*, 137.

21. Anthony Giddens, *The Constitution of Society: Outline of the Theory of Structuration* (Berkeley: University of California Press, 1984), Chapter 1.

22. Peter L. Berger calls these active and passive sides "externalization" and "internalization," respectively (*The Sacred Canopy: Elements of a Sociological Theory of Religion* (New York: Anchor Books, 1990), Chapters 1-2).

23. David Tracy, *The Analogical Imagination: Christian Theology and the Culture of Pluralism* (New York: Crossroad, 1991), 5.

24. Walzer, *Spheres of Justice*, 28.

25. Ibid., 29.

26. Ibid., 314.

27. The approaches of Walzer and Kuyper are limited in dealing with these problems. They are more concerned with the distinction and protection of a sphere than its inevitable interdependence and interaction with other spheres.

CHAPTER 5

COVENANTAL-COMMUNICATIVE ETHICS IN CONVERSATION

This chapter engages covenantal-communicative ethics with prominent contemporary Christian ethics: particularly narrative ethics, Catholic human rights theory, and liberation ethics. It will show that covenantal-communicative ethics, in the matrix of the doctrine of the Trinity, presents constructive understandings of the theological notions of virtue, character, and human rights. It also creatively responds to some difficulties that liberation ethics and Catholic ethics face in a pluralistic situation. It suggests a communicative process as the political method of not only social critique (the critique of systematic distortion of communication) but also collective will formation (solidarity) to achieve the goal of integral liberation.

I. Narrative Ethics
Among various responses to postmodernity, Stanley Hauerwas' voice is prominent. Challenging the history and tradition of American mainline churches' public engagements, he is proposing a new style of ethics that is solely grounded in a particular Christian history, narrative, and tradition. It is worthy and fruitful to engage covenantal-communicative ethics with his ethics in order to clarify their respective differences in terms of method, content and structure.

A. Stanley Hauerwas' Critique of Liberalism
Hauerwas does not see any possibility of synthesis for even compatibility of liberalism with Christian ethics. He believes that any Christian attempt at integration or synthesis with liberalism inevitably dilutes the uniqueness of Christian convictions and identity. This conviction makes his critique of liberalism and its institutions radical and uncompromising. Hauerwas is critical of almost every aspect of liberalism—its

theory, practice, and institutions such as democracy, justice, human rights, and so on. He thinks that any accommodation of liberalism is harmful for Christian communities. By separating the agent from its narrative context, he believes, liberalism is directly culpable for the erosion of a community, for the impoverishment of individual identity and character, and for the fragmentation and anomie of social life. Hence, Hauerwas' primary concern, therefore, is not to change nor to improve a liberal society, but to safeguard the church from the fragmenting and disintegrating forces and impacts of liberal society.

According to Hauerwas, liberalism espouses a foundational model of ethics. Liberalism is motivated by the "impulse deriving from the Enlightenment project to free all people from the chains of their historical particularity in the name of freedom."[1] In its epistemology, liberal ethics is based on the premise that a right and correct moral decision can be reached by the impartial reason alone, that is, independent of any particular tradition, culture, and historical background of the agent. Liberalism takes a philosophical stance that the question of truth and falsity can be solved by appeal to a neutral first principle or proposition which is self-evident, indubitable, and incorrigible. Liberal ethics was originally invented to solve the problem of the social order brought about by pluralism. Hauerwas notes that liberal foundationalism eventuates out of a "hunger for absolutes."[2]

Hauerwas concludes that liberal foundationalism cannot solve the problem of order and truth. Rather, it aggravates the problem as it is conducive to violence and fragmentation. Needless to say, the foundational presumption of liberal ethics is detrimental to Christian faith and life. Liberal ethics is inherently intolerant, oppressive, and inimical to historical contingencies and particular traditions. It relegates religious convictions to the margin of society by reducing them to a subjective or private motivation underlying human behaviors.[3]

B. Narrative and Character

Hauerwas' ethics is more than often called *narrative ethics*. According to Hauerwas, the content of a particular ethic is correlative to a particular narrative of a community and its religious convictions.[4] A particular moral conviction of a community is shaped and transmitted through its narrative. Narrative envisions a particular good the community pursues. It shows how a particular community understands the self, the world, and God in their relationships. By describing and illuminating the way things are, a narrative constitutes the matrix of our understanding of truth and falsity, right and wrong. A narrative is the most significant frame of reference for a community. The members of a community interpret their experiences through the lens of a narrative. Narrative as a fundamental framework and the basis of moral decision even defines the scope and content of moral inquiry itself.[5]

Hauerwas contends that narrative is neither incidental nor accidental to Christian belief; it is a constitutive aspect of Christian faith.[6] Christian ethics is correlative to its narrative. Narrative is especially adequate to convey and express the in-depth meaning of religious convictions of a Christian community. In short, Christian convictions take a narrative structure. Narrative displays the grammar of Christian convictions. Non-narrative forms of ethics are not able to account for the particularity of Christian moral life. The nature of Christian ethical life cannot be construed unless this narrative nature of Christian life is properly acknowledged and explicated. Narrative provides a horizon for Christian moral thinking and action which cannot be provided by any universal moral notions or principles. There is no more fundamental and effective way to speak of God and God's relationship to humanity than in a narrative form. In narrative, the knowledge of God, the world, and the self are understood coherently. "Neither God, the world, nor the self are properly known as separate entities but are in relation requiring concrete display. That display takes the form of a narrative in which we discover that the only way to 'know' God, the world, or the self is through their history."[7]

Closely related to Hauerwas' idea of narrative is his understanding of character. Hauerwas says that natural morality is best understood as a form of character, not as a form of universal moral law. From Hauerwas' perspective, agency indicates the descriptive ability of the self as a member of a particular narrative community; it is a power to make sense of its life in the perspective of narrative.[8] Moral agency is neither identical with nor reducible to individual autonomy. Rather, it implies one's ability to inhabit character.[9] This ability primarily refers to a social skill which one learns by participating in the communal practices of a particular community.[10] Morality is the predicate of character which is informed and shaped by the narrative of a community. For Hauerwas, the question of *who* we are precedes *what* we should do; what we do is determined and derived from who we are. Actions and decisions are dependent on who an agent is, namely character.

According to Hauerwas, ethics is not primarily concerned with a disconnected series of choices or decisions but with the development of character. Character indicates a particular trait of a person which has a

durable and coherent quality. Character denotes the "qualification or de-
termination of our self-agency, formed by our having certain intentions
(and beliefs) rather than others."[11] Having character means having a coherent sense of self. It is distinguished from other changing qualities of the
self such as emotions and moods. The development of character requires
long term discipline and training in a community constituted by a particular vision.

Character, as the enduring power of agency, gives the agent a coherent disposition and direction, corresponding to the narrative. Our capacity to claim our lives and be responsible for our actions is the result
and the function of our character. Such capacity develops as the agent
lives through the challenges of life in a manner consistent with narrative
convictions.

> Our character is the result of our sustained attention to the world
> which gives coherence to our intentionality. Such attention is
> formed and given content by the stories through which we have
> learned to form the story of our lives. To be a moral person is to
> allow stories to be told through us so that our manifold activities
> gain a coherence that allows us to claim them as our own.[12]

Character is "the form our agency takes through our beliefs and
intentions."[13] Character is concerned not with actions or consequences but
with the being of the actor, his or her intention, dispositions, and tastes.
Moral actions follow and flow from character. This implies that the question of identity is not only involved in the problem of ethics from the out-
set but is the primal determinant in the process of making decisions. The
actions of a person have a particular content and shape as they correspond
to the particular identity and character of the person. One is able to understand the true nature of such actions only when one looks carefully into
who the agent is and what his or her motive and intention are. This indicates that moral situations are not something that confronts the agent from
without. Rather, they are defined by particular moral agents nurtured
within community.

For Hauerwas, character is the source of a moral decision. One's
moral decision inevitably reflects one's moral character. In the face of
life's complexity, character ultimately determines what will count as a
moral problem, what course of action to take, and, accordingly, the very
nature of one's moral understanding and judgment. As conviction and
ethical reasoning cannot be separated, moral problems cannot be defined

in a uniform way for everyone. Even when some actions appear to be identical, they are not necessarily so when they are performed by different persons. Some questions are never considered to be moral questions for some people if their particular moral convictions do not categorize them as such.

Hauerwas argues that individual character is a display of narrative. Narrative shapes the agency. That is, for him, narrative is the resource from which one derives the power to have character at all.[14] For by virtue of embeddedness in a narrative community, individuals have "the power to be one thing rather than another, in short, to be persons of character."[15] Narrative constitutes an interpretive framework for the agent to describe, discern, and judge a moral situation and take adequate moral actions. The kind of narrative one is taught is therefore crucial for the formation of one's character. The extent and power of any agency relies on the adequacy of narrative.[16] Constituted by narrative, the agent is enabled to integrate his or her life in a particular time and space. Narrative gives coherence and unity to the agent by enabling the individual to relate and interpret the present in light of past experience and in anticipation of the future. In other words, the agent attains a transcendent and holistic perspective over one's action through the horizon provided by narrative.

C. Critique of Stanley Hauerwas

Hauerwas dismisses any Christian discourse of universal order as a Constantinian preoccupation. He comments that the question of order is not a primary concern for Christian ethics. Hauerwas ties the question of order with foundationalism. Yet, he argues, the end of foundationalism does not necessarily lead to despair, confusion, moral nihilism, or cynicism. Hauerwas proposes the virtue of peace as a political alternative to the question of order. The resolution of conflicts and violence does not rely on coercive order. Rather, it is only through the truthful and uncompromising commitment to peace, exemplified by the church, that the source of the problem can be attacked.

But Hauerwas' position still begs the questions: "Does the end of foundationalism mean the end of the question of order?" "Can postmodern society survive without any shared basis of order?" "How is a peaceful life possible?" One must acknowledge that Hauerwas' ethics is very limited when dealing with these problems. The question of order remains with us whether or not foundationalism is dead. Postmodern society suffers from various forms of conflict and strife as encounters among different religions, cultures, and classes increase. This situation threatens not only a minimal degree of peace and order but the very survival of humankind. Tension and disagreements have become an indelible characteristic of contemporary human life, even among people of the same religion, tradition, and community. The conventional ideas and practices, and traditional beliefs are increasingly subjected to public scrutiny as a community and its members interact with communities and people of other traditions. This situation makes extra-textual dialogue and criticism an inevitable aspect of postmodern social life. The ideas of democracy, justice, and human rights obtain a certain institutional significance and practical necessity in a pluralistic situation because they secure a minimal degree of morality and order in society. This also provides the conditions necessary for public conversation and decision-making. Further, if one accepts Hauerwas' suggestion that we confine ourselves to our own community and history, this raises questions of whether peace and justice in global community life are possible, given its pluralistic and interdependent nature.

Hauerwas offers no positive evaluation of the common historical experiences involved in the rise of liberalism in western society.[17] For example, the idea of religious freedom was embraced, after the Thirty Years' War, as a pragmatic solution to the destructiveness and cruelty of religious fanaticism and intolerance. Jeffrey Stout is correct in saying, "It is precisely because we fall so far short of rational agreement or objective certainty in religious matters that the right to religious freedom obtains in our society. Religious liberty is justified by conditions of discord and uncertainty that might not always obtain."[18]

Hauerwas' attempt to purify Christianity from liberalism goes too far. Max L. Stackhouse contends that some aspects of liberal thought are not alien to Christian faith but intrinsic to it. He says,

> Christianity has a liberal element at its core. Following Jesus, Christians have been willing to challenge tradition when it becomes legalistic, ethnic, or impervious to prophetic insight. . . Christianity, in other words, does not imply trusting religion as a given. It demands critically interpreted and socially engaged theology in which philosophy and ethics and social analysis play decisive roles.[19]

Similarly, Michael Quirk points out that the difference between Christianity and liberal society may not be as deep and distant as Hauerwas emphasizes, given the historical relationship between the two. Especially, as Hauerwas contends, if liberalism implies a particular form of the good with its own history and tradition, then the dialogue between Christian tradition and liberalism cannot be rejected because there is no reason Hauerwas should exclude the liberal form of life as a possible conversational partner.[20] If this is true, the liberal Christian ethical approach to the question of relationship between the church and the world retains its legitimacy.

Likewise, publicity and peaceableness are not necessarily as contradictory as Hauerwas implies. In its history, publicity has been one of the distinctive aspects of Judeo-Christian narrative as attested by Christian confession of God as the Creator and the prophetic witness toward justice. Persuasion, which is the mark of public theology, presumes a nonviolent relationship between speaker and listener. For example, Martin Luther King, Jr.'s public engagement aimed at the persuasion of white America, yet it relied on nonviolent resistance. Similarly, narrative ethics and public theology are not antithetical. As will be discussed later, even gospel stories could be understood as public performative action intending mutual understanding and persuasion of the audiences.

For these reasons, public theology cannot be relinquished as a mere product of Christian surrender and compromise to the liberal moral ethos. It has a pragmatic, practical need and consideration. Democratic values such as tolerance, fairness, freedom, and equality may never be sufficient to guide Christian lives, but they are nevertheless indispensable to public life for humanity. They are the products of human historical experiences that, without a common moral ground, would render the adjudication of conflicts impossible, and endanger the very existence of society. Thus, if the liberal institutions are destroyed, then we are faced with the age-old problem of how to coordinate the warring religious communities and ethnic groups. Even if the philosophical foundation of the liberal project is undermined, this does not mean the pragmatic usefulness of its institutions has ended. Thus the question is not whether liberal institutions are outdated, but how to reformulate them on a more historicist basis when society is in desperate need of social order, peace, and justice.

D. Communication and Narrative

Covenantal-communicative ethics acknowledges that a narrative provides the vision, the motivation and the matrix where human ethical decisions and activities are shaped. Yet, the narrative is not immune to the possibility of distortion and mistakes. Its use and interpretation should be subjected to a critical analysis and communal scrutiny. The narrative cannot be taken as an *a priori* of Christian moral decision. The Trinity and communication should be prolegomenon to Christian ethics. They provide a broader and more inclusive understanding of divine action and biblical texts than narrative. Not every text in Scripture takes a narrative form. There are epistles, psalms, and proverbial teachings. Yet it must be noted that all biblical narratives, such as Torah, wisdom literature, psalms, gospel stories, and epistles, are written with a communicative intention and purpose, namely persuading audiences into the salvific reality of God. For example, epistles encourage or exhort the readers to remain faithful to Jesus. Their intentions were to persuade or strengthen the addressed communities in their religious convictions and identities. In order to achieve this, they employ various rhetorical strategies such as missionary, ethical, pastoral, and anti-heretical polemics. In this respect, I argue, even parables and gospel stories are more adequately understood under the rubric of communicative action of God. Gospel stories have a performative (illocutionary) structure. They report a particular intersubjective discursive engagement between an evangelist and his or her community. They are produced with particular audiences in mind. Gospel stories are situational and local in their character. They were written for particular audiences in particular situations experiencing particular sets of theological and ethical problems. The author wants to come to an understanding with those audiences regarding his or her own conviction regarding Jesus Christ, so that they may also come to share it.

Communicative engagement was integral to the process of narrative construction. Scripture is the outcome of a longstanding process of communicative reflection (engagement) of the believing community of the Jewish and Christian communities, in appropriating and interweaving various elements from surrounding cultures into a coherent whole. Communication included the diachronic and synchronic reflection on the human experience and analysis of divine action. It included the multiple voices of various individuals and groups of people of different class, gender, and cultural and philosophical backgrounds. Canonization indicated a reaching (converging) toward a certain consensus on the nature and meaning of divine action. The gospel writers reconstructed various strands of oral traditions.[21] The object of reflection was the divine action. The purpose of gospel stories is to win others through persuasion to the reality of God's reign revealed in Jesus Christ. They are not intended simply to provide information or to impose prescriptive rules, but to bring the audience to a new level of understanding and insight so that they may agree to them.[22]

E. Narrative and Moral Principles: A Covenantal-Communicative Perspective

Covenantal-communicative ethics offers a more adequate understanding of the relationship of moral principle and narratives than that of Hauerwas. Covenantal-communicative ethics acknowledges the interdependent, dialectical nature of their relationship. There is an ongoing dialogical interchange between moral principles and narratives.

Narratives usually constitute the interpretive context of moral principles. Narratives are useful in identifying and illuminating the broad scope and rich interpretive possibility of moral principles. They are helpful in viewing moral principles in their mutual connections and in light of the complexity of human existence. However, this does not imply that a Christian moral life is possible without moral principles. Narratives do not exhaust moral principles. Moral principles are necessary to prevent misuse, distortion of narratives for an immoral purpose. They could be instrumental in criticizing a distorted or misguided ethos (such as racism or sexism) of a community in interpreting a narrative. Moral principles are conceived as the middle axioms that provide guidelines for action and decision by mediating the scriptural world and various ethical situations. They indicate the minimal moral standards and boundaries that any narrative should not override. Narratives are constrained by moral principles. The question of morality cannot be reduced to narrative.

Although, as Hauerwas contends, every moral principle may require an interpretive narrative framework, this interpretive framework is not fixed permanently. The meaning of narrative is not exhausted by one interpretation. Narrative always possesses "meaning potentials." Covenantal-communicative ethics acknowledges the multiplicity and diversity of biblical stories and narratives. It refuses to reduce the complexity and richness of Scripture to any single, universal, moral narrative, or principle. It recognizes that Scripture does not offer all the prefabricated answers to moral problems, although it may disclose a pattern of God's action in history—judgment on human immorality, injustice, and oppression.

Hence, in a covenantal-communicative ethics, narratives and moral principles serve as mutual constraints and illumination. They could be appropriately understood only through a continuous discursive examination and critique of a community open to others. In a covenantal- communicative ethics, the stipulative meaning of some moral principles is open to an interpretive revision. As situations change, the meaning and applicative scope of these principles may change. Through a communicative process, moral principles are constantly refined in response to the complexity of a moral situation and in coherence to narratives.

The doctrine of the Trinity provides the most distinctive, particular-istic, as well as universal, public framework for Christian actions. It re-spects the organic and the prophetic, the particular and the public dimen-sions of the church's ministry. It enables the church to obtain a holistic and balanced perspective on these two distinctive dimensions. In the trini-tarian framework, the prophetic-moral dimension is always in a critical tension, mutual check and balance, with the sacramental and the mystical dimensions. Through the trinitarian economy, the prophetic, the mystical, and the sacramental dimensions are indispensable for the faithful and ef-fective ministry of the church. In an analogous way to the perichoresis of the trinitarian persons, in the one triune economy, the three dimensions are intimately related for the holistic experience of God's salvation.

In the trinitarian framework, both the public witness and the liturgi-cal life are equally necessary. If the liturgical life provides richness and depth for the public ministry, then the public ministry embodies the liber-ating and empowering spirit of liturgy in concrete social actions. The or-ganic understanding of the relationship of worship and justice in the Trin-ity helps us to prevent unjust (discriminating, oppressive, misogynic) practices of liturgy and the uncritical assimilation of Christian life into a secular culture and ideology.

Under the rubric of the trinitarian economy, Christian worship and social justice are inextricably related. Both worship and just action are different forms of response and service to God. Worship is the event and process through which our experience of salvation is continuously re-newed, maturated, and energized. Just social actions are the occasions where our salvation is actualized in social realms. If worship is a mystical, intimate, ecstatic event of communion with God, then just actions are for-mal and rational aspects of that communion. Worship and justice share the same goal: holiness. If the aim of worship is the holiness of a worship-per and a worshipping community, then just actions intend the holiness of society. Through holiness, the world is reconciled with God.

The triune God is the common formal referent of worship and jus-tice. The triune God is the goal of our worship and justice. Worship and justice are reciprocating and cross-fertilizing. Worship and justice are in-dispensable components of our growth toward communion with God. The demise of a worshipful life leads to the impoverishment of the Christian ethical imagination and inspiration. Vigen Guroian declares,

The deterioration of Christian worship and disciplines of prayer deprives the church of tools of discernment and creativity to build ethics from within the ecclesial body itself, and so there has been wholesale borrowing from these secular ethics [of Kantian, Lockean, Millsian, Hegelian, or Marxist]. In a variety of ecclesial locations, the fundamental antinomy of being 'in the world but not of the world' loses its edge while simultaneously the eschatological horizon of Christian belief is overlaid with a transparency of one or another secular ideology.[23]

Christian worship life should be examined by the criteria of justice. Worship has a moral function. As a communal practice, worship produces a particular cultural ethos and pattern of life. This ethos generated by worship must be subjected to communal critique and public judgment. People can worship God even practicing or condoning the worst form of social evil and injustice, such as slavery and segregation within the community. A worship life that does not engender just actions ends up as a narcissistic self-indulgence.[24]

This dialectic relationship of worship and justice shows that a trinitarian approach adequately addresses the critique raised by Stanley Hauerwas against public theology. Hauerwas contends that when cut from its liturgical roots and sacramental practices, public theology is exposed to the danger of assimilation to the surrounding secular ethos of liberal democracy. He declares that a particular Christian tradition and narrative should be the sole foundation of Christian ethics. In light of our discussion of the Trinity, though, Hauerwas' approach faces a problem. In preoccupation with the distinctive identity of Christian tradition and narrative, his ethics does injustice to the universal, creational dimension of a trinitarian economy. Covenantal-communicative ethics shows that the church does not have to choose between publicity (universal rules and principles) and particularity (narratives and sacraments). They are equally aspects of divine self-communication. Grounded in the Trinity, the church may accept both publicity and particularity as the equally indispensable aspects of the church's ministry. Hence, it belongs to the covenantal-communicative task of the church (the art of *phronesis*) to determine how to artfully balance and coordinate these elements in response to various problems and concerns within and without the church.

F. Covenantal-Communicative Approach to Character/Virtue

1. The Spirit and Moral Formation

For Hauerwas, schooling and life in the narrative community are critical for the formation of character. Narrative imparts a specific pattern or structure on the life of the agent. A moral agent obtains the continuity and structure of his or her morality through narrative. Without the narrative, ethical life will be experienced as a mere unconnected series of decisions. In this section, I contend that as our discussion indicates, the Trinity, informed by covenant and communication, provides a more plausible ground for character formation and virtue. Specifically, I argue that Hauerwas' low doctrine of the Holy Spirit (pneumatology) impairs a more viable Christian understanding of character and virtue.

From its early history, the Christian community believed that the Spirit plays a significant role in the formation of Christian character and virtues. That is, the particularizing work of the Spirit is inextricably related to the process of Christian character formation and virtues. In short, one may say that Christian virtues are the result of the Spirit's work. In Galatians, St. Paul identifies the nine primal virtues as the fruits of the Spirit. The Spirit is involved in a constant human quest for wholeness, integration in the face of various forces of dehumanization and alienation.[25] The Spirit helps us in our striving toward the fullest realization of a person or a community in every relationship. This effort to grow or reach is called by various terms, such as "divinization" or "sanctification." In other words, the Spirit, "the perfecting cause of the creation" to use the phrase of Colin Gunton, is involved in every stage of our spiritual growth (maturity) as a particularizing power of God. The Spirit cares for us not only in our various situations and conditions, but also in various levels and phases of our moral and spiritual developments.[26] St. Paul assures us on this caring work of God in the Spirit: "No testing has overtaken you that is not common to everyone. God is faithful, and he will not let you be tested beyond your strength, but with the testing he will also provide the way out so that you may be able to endure it"(1 Corinthians 10:13). The Spirit respects our limits and capacities in leading us to further growth in righteousness and love in the steps of Jesus Christ.

Unlike Hauerwas' assertion, our character is not the product of narrative schooling alone. Although Christian character, as Hauerwas argues, is shaped in a Christian community by a particular Christian narrative, it is not determined by it. For Christians, the primary agent of character formation is neither community nor narratives, but the triune God. The triune God may use the community and a narrative for this purpose. The triune God, through the collaborating works of the trinitarian persons, molds and forms our character and virtues in a balanced and mature way. Specifically, the Spirit patterns our moral character after Jesus Christ. The Spirit edifies us into a sanctified life in imitation of Jesus Christ. As God is holy, Christians are called to be holy. In its perichoretic relationship with the Logos, the Spirit forms Christian virtues and affections in accordance with a normative pattern of the Word. The Spirit guides and helps Christians to make their actions consistent with their normative demands of the Logos. The Spirit informs and guides our deepest motives and intentions in accordance with the divine will revealed in the Logos.

If we analyze this process from a human side, character grows out through the praxis of the faith. It arises through the continuous spiritual and moral endeavor of an individual Christian toward excellence against various challenges. Christian character is the result of a reflective as well as a practical action of an individual Christian. Christian character is not a result of uncritical and ritualistic religious activities; rather it is informed and guided by a critical reflection and knowledge in the living God. Through the ongoing process of reflection-action, Christian character increasingly emerges as a fuller, more authentic form and content, namely a theonomous, post-conventional being.

This implies that character is revisable. It is not formed once and for all. It develops and reconfigures through the passage of one's life journey. Individual agency plays a significant role. The relationship of character and decision-making is not entirely antithetical. A decision reflects and displays one's character. Yet the reiteration of decision-making in a certain direction makes a profound impact on one's character formation, for decision-making inevitably affects the self's moral dispositions. Just as there is no decision-making from which the self's moral disposition is absolutely absent or exempt, there is no decision-making which does not affect one's future character formation and virtue development.

Rules are not inimical to virtue formation as Hauerwas implies; rather, they are integral to it. Character without the constraints of rules would be incoherent and arbitrary. Rules play a significant role in virtue formation because they present explicit normative constraints and directions for the behavior and conduct of the agent. Like narrative, rules also intervene in the formation of our aspirations, desires, and habits. Rules are important because they provide the criteria of human action.

As relationality is a distinctive nature of a personhood, Christian character is shaped in the context of a self's relationship with God and others. Hence, Christian character requires a certain rightful structure or form in its historical embodiment and realization. Without a rightful structure, a quest for a personal integration will be futile. The question of character cannot ignore the concern of justice because the latter presents a structure of relationship between moral beings. This indicates there exists an intrinsic link between Christian character and justice.

These two aspects, character and justice, are related to the macro and micro dimensions of the work of the Spirit. On a macro level, the Holy Spirit works to bring justice and liberation in history and society. On a micro level, the Holy Spirit works for the sanctification of individuals, through the formation of the proper moral volitions and characters. These two dimensions are inseparable. That is, the Spirit works in the way not to enclose individuals to themselves but to lure them to participate in the liberating work of God in history. The Logos provides significant moral guidelines for this link between micro and macro works of the Spirit by identifying the fundamental patterns/order of social interaction and relationships.

Through its sanctifying and liberating work, the Spirit brings God and humanity into communion. In LaCugna's words, the Spirit humanizes God, just as the Spirit divinizes human beings, making human beings theonomous and catholic.[27] The Spirit joins us to God and to other human beings in baptism. And this union is remembered and renewed continuously in our worship life.[28]

Through character formation, the Spirit shapes a theonomous human being in the image of Jesus Christ. Jesus Christ is the new image of humanity. LaCugna notes, "Jesus is what our own humanity was created to be: theonomous, catholic, and in communion, in right relationships, with every creature and with God. He is who and what God is; he is who and what we are to become."[29] The idea of a theonomous being overcomes the shortcoming of both the liberal idea of the autonomous individual (poorly socialized person) and the communitarian vision of the self (overly socialized person). A theonomous being is a post-conventional being. A theonomous being understands a particular tradition and narrative, but is not controlled and absorbed by them. In relation to a triune God, a theonomous being could take a critical attitude toward his or her tradition and narrative, and community. This is possible because the Spirit, in its transcendence, enables us to take a post-conventional attitude toward tradition and narrative. Secondly, a theonomous being, formed by the Spirit, arises through a communicative faith praxis (action-reflection process) of a moral agent in relationship to God and others.

2. Covenantal Virtues

a) Fidelity

Covenantal-communicative ethics does not downplay the signifi-cance of character and virtue for ethical life, although its priority may differ from that of Hauerwas. The primal virtue of covenantal-communicative ethics is faithfulness or fidelity. Faithfulness is the basis upon which covenant is established and maintained. Covenantal-communicative ethics understands fidelity as the glue that binds people together, thus the cornerstone of a community. The virtue of trust or fidel-ity denotes a quality of trustworthiness or sincerity in keeping one's prom-ise, and cohering one's words and actions. Faithfulness is an endeavor and will to continue a relationship despite various odds and problems against a covenantal relationship. Fidelity is the foundational virtue because without it the formation and sustenance of the community is impossible. As such, it has a special meaning in the trinitarian economy. God works with hu-man beings through the trust created in a covenantal relationship. The sin-cerity of God's performative action, namely God's promise, is proved through God's faithfulness. On this point, Moltmann says, "God's truth is his truthfulness. Consequently we can rely on his promises and on himself. A God who contradicted himself would be an unreliable God. He would have to be called a demon, not God. The true God is the God of truth, whose nature is eternal faithfulness and reliability."[30]

In a pluralistic society, the question of how to develop the virtue of trust and fidelity is a challenge for every community in searching for a lasting and enduring peace. Without some reservoir of fidelity, namely social capital, a global society cannot function properly. Without it, the very relationship itself threatens to break down. The virtue of trust and loyalty is fostered through a covenantal commitment, for covenant pro-vides a certain dispositional structure in molding virtue or character into fidelity. That is, observance of covenantal requirements can be a practical way of developing the virtue of faithfulness.

b) Honesty

Closely related to the virtue of fidelity is the virtue of honesty. Hon-esty is presumed in fidelity. Yet, it is distinguished from the latter in refer-ring to the sincerity in expressing one's intention and ideas in a covenant-ing process. The virtue of honesty is resonant with Habermas' emphasis on "sincerity" or "truthfulness" in a communicative relationship. Fidelity in a covenantal relationship begins with and grows through honesty in a conversation. Everyone is concerned with knowing whether what he or she is hearing from others is truthful or not. Honesty is a foundation of any meaningful covenantal relationship. While dishonesty increases the level of misunderstanding, suspicion, and fear between the parties of a covenant, honesty increases intimacy and trust between them.

The virtue of honesty encourages the telling of truth regardless of its consequences. To be honest includes the risk of vulnerability one takes in engaging with others in search of truth and the common good. The adage that "Honesty is the best policy" is based on the belief that in the long run truth-telling is more contributive to a covenantal relationship than any immediate expediency achieved by dishonesty. Without honesty, it would be difficult to sustain any other related covenantal virtues. By being honest, one respects the value of integrity and fidelity in relationships. By being honest, one develops the courage to examine one's intentions truthfully and address one's responsibility sincerely. Honesty also inculcates the sense of humility to acknowledge one's indebtedness toward others in various achievements.

c) Solidaristic Catholicity

Catholicity is another distinctive virtue of covenant-communicative ethics. This virtue is derived from the practice of obligation in the universal covenantal community in God. Catholicity is more than a liberal virtue of tolerance. It cares for the well-being of the partner beyond immediate self-interest.

Covenant is different from contract in terms of its scope of unlimited commitment and obligation.[31] Something universal is represented in covenant. In covenantal thinking, responsibility is not confined to the covenantal partners alone. In its dependence on God, responsibility expands to every creature in the universal community of God. Covenant presupposes the moral community of persons which is universal and inclusive in God. Hence, the sense of responsibility in covenant goes beyond all limited causes, loyalties, and ethical boundaries. In the final analysis, the scope of covenantal virtue is co-extensive with the universal community of creation.

Catholicity derives from the covenantal partners' reliance on God. God is the overseer of a covenant. Covenant obliges us to God as the highest source and ground of our existence. Because of this reliance on and accountability before God, covenantal obligation is larger than the letters of laws, although covenantal obligation is usually specified in laws. Covenantal obligation points us beyond the immediate goals and interests of covenantal parties. That is, these obligations include the responsibilities toward people outside the immediate partners of a particular transaction. Covenant connects us to the vulnerable others who may not be the immediate partners of our transaction, but who along the way will be affected by our decisions. This presence of others, "which we cannot fully fathom or control, calls to us, requires our recognition, and obliges our response, even before we place ourselves under obligation or decide to assume responsibility for this other."[32] The poor, the oppressed have a new moral status in this covenantal context. They are the invisible partners of covenant. God listens, and defends their causes.

Covenant brings us to the inextricable, interdependent matrix of solidarity which has claims upon all of God's creation. Every transaction must be examined in light of the solidarity of creation in God. One may say that covenantal obligation is the obligation toward the common good which specifies God's concern for the well-being of every member of creation. Christian ideas of the common good are based on the fundamental interconnectedness and interdependence of every living creature in God. As covenantal obligation extends universally to every living creature, the common good fleshes out the aim and context of covenantal obligation. Covenantal obligation could be properly figured out in light of and in the context of the common good. Every human transaction, to be covenant, must be consistent with and contributive to the common good. The common good helps to spell out the scope and nature of covenantal obligation. It points out our often forgotten obligations to the invisible, vulnerable others. In this respect, the solidaristic catholicity is associated with respect for basic human dignity.

d) Gratitude

Intimately related to the virtue of catholicity is the virtue of gratitude. The covenantal-communicative ethics' emphasis on solidarity has to do with the indebted nature of a human existence in relationship to God. It presumes that one's life is neither self-sufficient nor isolated, but inevitably interdependent. Interdependence implies some form of indebtedness. Covenant, as a structure of interdependence, recognizes the indebted nature of human existence in its core. "Covenant involves an acknowledgment of what we did not create that has made us what we are."[33] Every human covenant must be reminded of its gift character: one's life is possible through the contribution of many known and unknown elements which include the gifts from a previous generation, one's contemporaries, and other species and nature. Every person owes something to others. Indebtedness leads to the emphasis on the responsibility toward others who are not the immediate parties of a covenant. It must take into account the contingent needs of others which the incumbent covenant does not specify. Doxology is a distinctive religious liturgical genre expressing thankfulness toward God, often chanted at the culminating moment of a covenantal ritual, thus acknowledging God as the source and nurturer of the universe. By acknowledging God as the source and nurturer, doxology has a transforming power upon a person. It constantly relativizes his or her social achievements, and therefore is a reminder of one's creaturely status before God.

3. Covenant, Character, and Vocation

A covenantal-communicative approach helps us to understand character and virtue as complex, pluralistic terms in the contexts of various institutions. Especially when one applies this pneumatological insight to a societal level (macro), intermediary associations become the places of virtue formations as well as learning places of the intrinsic rules of respective associations. Each association fosters, embodies, and encourages a certain kind of virtue (as well as a possibility of vice).[34]

Economic institutions foster and inculcate virtues and habits congruent to productive and efficient economic life, such as prudence, frugality, efficiency, etc. For instance, being a corporate manager morally requires both a proper formation of virtue under the stricture of rules and principles of economic activities. In short, virtue takes a multiple, complex form in its formation and manifestation. Unlike Hauerwas' views, virtue and rules are not antithetical, but complementary. Virtue is fostered under the constraints of historically proven rules and principles. Otherwise, there is no distinction of virtue from vice. Rules and principles lose their binding and obligatory power without the undergirding virtues that sustain these rules and principles. In the intrinsic functional connection to rules and principles, virtues become civic, public virtues.

Character takes a practical contour and configuration in a Christian covenantal framework. Covenant provides a crucial linkage between duties and identity, rules and virtues. Covenant, through its emphasis on agency and the provisional nature of social formation, adds a critical-reflexive dimension to virtue in their formations and social functions. In a covenantal theology, virtue is neither an uncritical passive product nor a permanently fixed entity produced by a particular community. The covenantal idea of a dialogical self highlights this dialectical and dynamic relationship of identity and duty, of virtue and rules. The formation of virtue in individuals is not unreflexive. Virtue is formed through a constant self-examination and moral conversation. Conscience, as self-communication, is a significant moral reasoning process that adjudicates and reconciles the strictures of rules and principles with passions and social rules within the agent.

A covenantal-communicative approach more effectively broadens our theological and ethical imagination to understand the significance of social institutions for virtue (character) formation. The notion of vocation is appropriate in describing this association between virtue formation and institutional life. Various intermediary associations and social institutions become the places of vocational virtue formation. Each association fosters, embodies, and encourages a certain kind of virtue (as well as a possibility of vice) as they transmit and share particular institutional practices.[35] In short, virtue takes a multiple, complex form in accordance with the nature of vocational institutional contexts.

4. Vocation

The notion of vocation is useful in describing a covenantal nature of Christian character or virtue. Christian character and virtues take various vocational forms as Christians live out their faith within the diverse institutional structures of a society. Vocation is a personal response and dedication to the calling of God in a particular occupational context. Of course, the vocational dedication requires the development of virtues and habits necessary for a specific occupational task. Vocational virtues and habits are shaped in the context of a covenantal relationship with God (calling) and with its constituency, stakeholders (service or lay ministry). To enter a covenantal relationship means to develop a particular disposition and habit to abide by and fulfill the obligations of covenant. The formation of vocational virtue requires social practices that are stipulated by the moral principles and rules intrinsic to a particular vocation. For instance, being a medical doctor requires both a proper formation of necessary virtues under the stricture of rules and principles intrinsic to medical practices (e.g., nonmalfeasance, beneficence).

This specification of covenantal-vocational nature of character and virtue is more coherent with the relational, historical nature of human selfhood. Hauerwas' idea of character/virtue fails to specify this relational and historical nature of character and virtue formation. Hauerwas tends to discuss character/virtue as the sole function of a particular tradition and a narrative. He fails to identify a relational-covenantal aspect of virtue and character. Although narrative and tradition are pivotal in the formation of character and virtue, they are expressed through a particular covenantal social relationship: teacher-pupil, wife-husband, employer-employee, physician-patient, pastor-congregates, etc. There is a dimension of character or virtue that is required by the very nature of vocation or work in covenantal relationship.[36]

The necessary virtues could be identified in different vocational contexts, such as business, politics, scientific community, education, and family. In other words, there are virtues that are required specifically for physicians, politicians, fathers, and mothers. These virtues take concrete form through the covenantal relationship where the agents are involved. Covenantal ethics presents a more sophisticated, differentiated, complex theory of virtue. Virtues are differentiated along with (in accordance with) the covenantal relationships and contexts. Vocation gives rise to a particular contour and shape of virtues. Michael Walzer's idea of the complex self shares this thrust and insight. Hauerwas fails to discuss the significance of vocational virtues. His idea of virtues seems to be more that of a pre-modern, authoritarian, undifferentiated society. These vocational virtues are critical for the public nature and meaning of Christian discipleship. Christian virtues need to be incarnate concretely in various social spheres as these spheres are conceived as the theatre of the triune economy for justice and the common good.

The idea of virtue is associated with the idea of calling or vocation. Vocation is a covenantal idea. Vocation is the covenantal calling of God for each individual to a special task in promoting the common good. This implies that virtue is informative. It obtains a particular articulation and form in relation to one's vocation. Virtue takes a particular constellation in one's vocational context.[37] For example, Christians must be honest, yet honesty takes shape as various constellations in accordance with various vocational contexts. The virtue of honesty required for physicians is different from that of politicians. As virtue is formed in a particular relational context, the constellation of a particular content of virtue belongs to a realm of covenantal relationship.

The fulfillment of this calling requires more than written laws. It requires a sustaining tradition, habit, and character which enable the agent to withstand all the adversarial forces. As Christians enter a covenantal relationship with others in a particular institutional context, they need to be conscious of and develop a particular set of virtues which is necessary to fulfill their calling in this institution. In the process of forming and nurturing a vocational virtue, one has to notice that there could be a tension and conflict between Christian vocational virtue and the institutional ethos. Various institutions transmit the particular traditions of virtues through institutional practices. That is, in each institution there is a symbiotic moral pattern, a certain operative expectation of life together, an ethos. Through institutional life, one inevitably adopts and obtains habits and values embedded in the practices of that institution. Covenantal-communicative ethics does not accept institutional ethos and habits uncritically. Rather, it takes a critical and post-conventional stance toward the institutional ethos. By doing that, vocational covenant engages in the process of a reconstructive endeavor, affirming and rejecting certain aspects of transmitted habits, ethos, and values of the institution.

II. Catholic Ethics of Human Rights

A. David Hollenbach's Catholic Theory of Human Rights

Among contemporary Roman Catholic moral theologians, David Hollenbach offers one of the most articulate and persuasive theories of human rights. He is considered one of the leading interpreters and defenders of post-Vatican II Catholic social teaching in America.[38] Hollenbach attempts to reconstruct a liberal political project of human rights in the framework of the Catholic common good tradition. According to Hollenbach, the Catholic tradition of the common good does not oppose the historical achievements of modernity, such as pluralism, human rights, and democracy, but rather it helps to sustain and expand these achievements in a more relevant and adequate way in the contemporary social context.[39] Hollenbach contends that Catholic ethics, rather than bifurcating freedom and solidarity, individual rights and communal responsibility, presents a harmonic, integral view of these categories. He says that this harmony of "the idea of human rights with concern for the common good is a crucial condition for any viable moral-philosophical theory in our time."[40]

For Hollenbach, respect for the dignity and worth of every person constitutes the foundation of human rights.[41] Human rights are the claims stemming from the fundamental norm of human dignity. Grounded in the social and relational nature of a person, Catholic theory is that human rights are no longer understood as the claims derived from isolated individuals' inner moral essence or consciousness. Human rights adhere in persons who are created in the image of God. Being a human person is to make an undeniable universal claim upon others and society. Human rights stipulate the minimum moral conditions of human life.

According to Hollenbach, Catholic human rights theory proposes an integral theory of rights in which every aspect of human life—personal, physical, and social—must be affirmed. In his view, any human rights theory which is established solely on a single aspect of human life (such as freedom, needs, or relationship) falls short of reality because it is based on a narrow and limited view of human nature and dignity. Since the meaning of human dignity is conditioned and limited by history and culture, the content and scope of human rights must be determined only in the context of particular historical relationships through a careful study and analysis of the patterns and institutions of society.

By virtue of its communitarian theological anthropology, Hollenbach contends, the Catholic theory of human rights is different from those of liberal and socialist theories. Catholic understanding of human rights is distinctive by virtue of its recognition that the ontological foundation of human rights lies in the reality of Jesus Christ,[42] and that the demands of human dignity are historically situated in the matrix of various social relationships. Hollenbach argues that this theologically informed communitarian recognition of human dignity is the most important Catholic contribution to the human rights discussion today.[43] Hollenbach claims that the Catholic theory provides a more comprehensive and integral understanding of human rights than the liberal and socialist theories of human rights theories. It finds no difficulty in integrating civil-political rights and social-economic rights. Respect for civil-political rights and for social-economic rights is not mutually exclusive; these rights are interrelated around the foundational norm of human dignity. Having their bases in the ideal of human dignity, civil-political rights and social-economic rights protect different aspects of the same moral reality.[44]

Hollenbach contends that there is no necessary logical connection between human rights and liberalism or socialism. Human rights are not exhausted either by liberal or socialist philosophy. Both liberal and socialist rights theories are mistaken in identifying "a limited domain of human existence with the radical foundation of human rights."[45] These theories are based on a very truncated view of human nature, such as an individualistic idea of freedom, or a collectivistic notion of social participation or economic needs. Hollenbach holds that the meaning of human dignity cannot be limited to a single social category. Rather, it requires an integral and comprehensive ground, such as the Christian idea of human dignity.

Hollenbach does not see any conflict between human rights and the common good. Rather, he argues that human rights, from a Catholic moral perspective, cannot be understood apart from the common good. The common good and human rights are mutually necessary. Just as personality and community are mutually implicated, so are human rights and the common good. The rights of individuals cannot be realized in isolation from the good of society. The promotion of human rights is correlative to the promotion of the common good, and vice versa. Rights are understood as claims to share and participate in the construction of the common good. Rights are essential for the realization of the common good as the minimal moral standard of society, because the common good is partly achieved through the protection of human rights. Due to this interdependent nature, Catholic moral theory does not share the liberal idea that the right is prior to the good. Rather, "the right is part of the good, and the achievement of justice is part of the quest for the common good."[46]

Situated in the matrix of the common good, diverse claims of human rights are socially differentiated and coordinated. The common good adjudicates and harmonizes various claims of human rights. A violation of human rights is equivalent to the violation of fundamental human solidarity. Conversely, the claim of human rights must be made not in an individualistic way, but in relation to the common good. That is, if the common good is the context where the claims of rights arise and are tested, human rights designate the minimal necessary conditions for human communal existence in society. Without social protection and respect for this condition, the realization of the common good is greatly threatened and thus impossible. In other words, human rights delineate the necessary social conditions for human individual fulfillment and social union.[47] This condition encompasses every realm of human life—the social, political, economic, and cultural. Hence, human rights become an integral aspect of the common good.

In Hollenbach's view, the common good constitutes the ultimate horizon in which the diverse claims of rights arise, and where they are discerned, interpreted, and adjudicated. The common good specifies and guarantees conditions in which individual rights are adequately realized. The common good takes priority over individual goods, but only in the sense that the former performs a subsidiary function for the realization of the latter. In fulfilling their goods, individuals need the help of society. Society provides those conditions—resources, opportunities, and protection—without which the fulfillment of individual good is inconceivable. Subsidiarity is a necessary guideline for the proper function of a government in relating to its various parts and individual persons.

Hollenbach asserts that the common good sets the demand of human dignity on a par with the need for order and justice at an institutional level, and vice versa. The proper shape of social institutional structures and arrangements is indispensable for the construction and fulfillment of the common good and for the realization of human dignity. Society must judicially and institutionally guarantee the freedom and responsibility of individuals to participate in the creation of the common good and in the redistribution of the benefits of the common good. This insight provides a significant ground for the Catholic synthetic theory of human rights.

Related to the idea of the common good is the Catholic correlative understanding of rights and duties. Set in the teleological framework of the common good, rights are correlated with the corresponding duties and obligations. In Catholic communitarian ethics, rights and duties are two interdependent aspects of the same moral reality. Having rights implies having duties toward others in a reciprocal way. Rights and duties are necessary for the achievement of the common good. The bearers of rights must exercise their rights and duties in relation to others in the context of the common good of society.

Hollenbach says that this synthetic, communitarian view of rights is in the best tradition of Catholic ethics which attends to both political liberty and basic human needs. This synthetic approach has new relevance in the context of an interdependent and pluralistic world. It presents an inclusive and encompassing approach of ethics to a world divided by different ideologies and social systems. In Hollenbach's view, this inclusive synthetic vision is congruent with the historical self-consciousness of the Catholic Church as a transnational and trans-cultural institution.[48]

B. Critique of David Hollenbach

1) Although the Catholic communitarian theory of human rights may have several merits in correcting the dangers of liberal rights theory, it tends to lose the critical-transformative thrust involved in the liberal idea of human rights and democracy. Rooted in the Thomistic organic, teleological tradition, it does not fully appreciate the radical sense of individual freedom and respect for differences.

The propensity toward integration and harmonization under the rubric of the common good and the single norm of human dignity tends to ignore the inherent complexity and conflictual nature of a human social life. The ambitious desire to reconcile various perspectives of human rights often misses the reality of social conflicts and neglects the difficult process of making choices in contingent situations.

One must say that Hollenbach's conception of the relationship between individual rights and the common good is more idealistic than practical. For example, the ideational synthesis of two different ethical traditions of human rights, liberalism and socialism, does not guarantee the reconciliation of two different political perspectives. In the reality of Catholic moral practice, the tension and balance between the individual freedom and the common good is more than often tilted to the side of the latter as indicated by the hierarchical, authoritarian structure of the Catholic Church. Individuals are constrained by the authority of the Church.

Specifically, the internal political structure of the Roman Catholic Church does not genuinely embrace democratic impulses and a pluralistic ethos. Hollenbach's emphasis on dialogue, conversation, and participation seldom finds its meaningful practices within the institutional life of the Catholic Church itself. The Catholic ecclesiastical structure still maintains a pyramid-like, top-down, hierarchical authority which controls every aspect of its institutional life. Decisions are made by the oligarchy of the cardinals and bishops. Power resides at the apex of the pyramid, namely the person of the Pope in the collegiality of bishops. There is an undeniable discrepancy between Hollenbach's claim of participation as a primary condition of justice, and the Catholic Church's exclusion of laity from the ecclesiastical decision-making processes. The Catholic Church shuns the democratic process—discussion, criticism, and argumentation. In short, Hollenbach is silent about the systematic distortion of communication in the church such as the denial of women's rights and the participation of laity in the decision-making process of the ecclesiastical life by the Vatican.[49] The recent disclosure of the sexual scandal of priests proves this point. The continuation of the immoral practices was partially due to the lack of lay participation in the process of decision-making and the supervision of ecclesiastical affairs.

Margaret Farley is correct in pointing out that the Vatican statement that persons are equal before God does not necessarily indicate that they are equal before one another. That is to say, though a woman is equally the creature of God, she may be still treated as though she were inferior to a man. In other words, the norm of human dignity can be asserted by maintaining the inferiority of women and nonwhites. She contends that only the explicit acceptance of the principle of mutuality and coequality would correct this danger lurking behind the notion of human dignity.[50] Thus, this situation begs questions: To what extent is the Catholic Church able to embrace the radical demand of freedom and equality for the revision of its own tradition and hierarchy? How much is the idea of "justice as participation" efficaciously implemented in the Catholic Church and institutions? Can the Vatican magisterium allow itself to become an equal conversation partner with the laity, especially with laywomen, and to expose itself to challenges and criticism? To what extent can it apply standards of human rights equally to its internal practices as it requires of society?

2) Because of its emphasis on human dignity, the Catholic rights theory tends to be anthropocentric. It does not possess conceptual room to include the rights of nonhuman creatures. Moltmann's observation is correct in this respect. He comments, "[H]uman dignity cannot be fulfilled through human rights at the cost of nature and other living things, but only in harmony with them and for their benefit."[51] For example, Moltmann states that the present formulations of human rights, such as *The Universal Declaration of Human Rights of 1948*, and *International Covenants on Human Rights in 1966*, are not sufficient to encompass the problems of contemporary society. Moltmann continues, "[H]uman rights have to be harmonized with the protective rights of the earth and other living things and have to become a part of these."[52] In this respect, a covenantal understanding of human rights is more comprehensive and adequate. God's covenantal relationship with humanity includes the stewardship of the earth and other creatures. The land exists in solidarity with the fate of human beings in covenantal relationship with God.

C. Covenantal-Communicative Ethics and Human Rights

1. Human Rights as the Common Morality: Communicative Basis

Covenantal-communicative ethics presents a more plausible explanation for the emergence and the evolution of international human rights in modern history. Human rights function as part of the common morality of a global society. From a covenantal-communicative perspective, universal human rights, such as *The Universal Declaration of the Human Rights of 1948* and the two subsequent international stipulations, i.e., *The International Bill of Rights* and *the Covenant on Civil and Political Rights*, indicate a minimal moral consensus among various religious and ethnic groups. If we examine the historical development of the idea of human rights in modernity, we see that it was motivated by the collective human experience of evils and atrocities during the two world wars. The modern theory of human rights was established on the basis of collective reflection on the common human experiences of religious persecutions, colonialism, racial oppression, and genocide.

The international community felt an urgent need to develop a common moral standard and language to check and condemn such atrocities. Later, the category of human rights, through communicative discourses of international society, was expanded further to include new generations of human rights such as socio-economic rights, cultural-communal rights, and potentially ecological rights in the future. This process of expansion shows that the binding authority of universal rights comes significantly from the communicative consensus of international society.

Today, the intensification of global interdependence adds a further impetus to the need for a global moral standard. As interdependence is increased and intensified, more specific regulative ideals and principles will be needed. The impacts of globalization and interdependence are morally ambiguous. Interdependence often heightens the possibility of conflicts and clashes of interests. In this context, human rights represent the agreement of members of the global community on the basic moral issues commonly confronting the world. The covenantal-communicative approach draws the normativity of human rights not from the analysis of individual consciousness, but from a communicatively achieved consensus. Human rights are the public expression of overlapping moral expectations and ethical visions of participants. The moral status of human rights as international moral norms is not predetermined nor imposed. It functions as the "null hypothesis"; it is achieving its status as an international moral language through a wide reference and use among members of the international community.

International human rights need to be constantly improved through discursive engagement in their scope and content. Discursive engagement includes the process of critically examining the operative assumptions both of international human rights and of each religious and cultural tradition regarding the notions of human dignity, personhood, the good, and community. Through critical conversation, the participants may come to a better knowledge of the possibility of congruence and the reality of discrepancy between the assumptions of a particular religious tradition and those of human rights. They may also inquire about how congruence and discrepancy are embodied in religious, social, cultural practices and institutional configuration. This process may lead them to probe what practical recommendations and suggestions can be made to encourage and bolster those aspects of the religious norms and practices which are consistent or compatible with the idea of human rights.

This strategy of communicative ethical approach to human rights utilizes what Abdullahi An-Naim called the retrospective enlightened interpretation of traditional cultural norms: that is, each religious and cultural tradition retrospectively reexamines and recasts its traditional norms and practices in light of the ratification of universal human rights.[53] This process leads to the retrieval and reconstruction of norms in conformity with the underlying anthropological and political assumptions implied by universal human rights. Hence, in this methodological framework, the meaning and applicability of human rights are neither fixed nor closed. They are open to further revision, elaboration, and expansion through the addition of new types (generations) of human rights as human social interaction and conflict take a new form and content.

Covenantal-communicative analysis of the rise of international human rights is supported by Sumner B. Twiss' theory of the two-level approach. Like Habermas, Twiss understands contemporary human rights as the outcome of the gradual moral consensus achieved by the international community. He emphasizes "the importance of mutual commitment to open-mindedness," "a willingness to be changed by reasoned argument," and "a commitment to giving equal respect to all dialogical partners" as significant moral elements in the process of stipulating international human rights. [54]

On the basis of his analytic study of the history of international ratification of human rights since World War II, Twiss argues that the idea of human rights is not necessarily antithetical to particular religious identity and cultural tradition. Human rights can be justified internally by particular religious and cultural traditions. In solving the common social, moral, and ecological problems identified by the subject matter of human rights, religious groups may gather and critically examine the assumptions and perspectives of their respective religious traditions in conversation with internationally ratified human rights. According to Twiss, religious communities may recognize within their traditions viable moral elements and social values that are consistent with the idea of universal human rights. [55] Through the search for the analogues of human rights within their religious cultural traditions, diverse religious communities may come up with agreement on the shareable moral principles of human rights for international interaction and regulation. Twiss argues that once the existing norms of human rights are accepted as a primary moral frame of reference for mutual transaction, despite disputes and disagreements on the specifics and details, they have regulative and stipulating authority over members.

The communicative values of inclusiveness, fairness and equality have a significant meaning for contemporary discourse on human rights. Human rights need to be rooted in indigenous values, morals, and convictions. That is, universal human rights become truly universal when the members of the global community adopt and affirm them as their own. In other words, universal human rights will qualify as universal morality only if they are consistent with a local understanding of rights. In this respect, religious roots and sources of human rights, for example, human dignity and covenant of creation, need to be more explicitly identified and inculcated and nurtured in each religious tradition through various forms of rituals and practices. Without these roots and practices, the tree of human rights cannot thrive much longer. It may end up as a transient international diplomatic invention. In order to avoid this, international human rights need to be tested and proved on local levels before they are imposed upon others as universal rights. To procure its moral authority and legitimacy as global ethics, the concept of human rights must recognize and protect the local rights of tribal traditions, and indigenous cultures. This insight, in turn, provides a perspective into why the ratification of cultural-communal rights is significant as we discussed above.

2. Human Rights: Covenantal Justification

Through its emphasis on dialogical reciprocity in freedom and equality, the covenantal-communicative approach also helps to reconceptualize the idea of human rights from a Christian theological perspective. It is well known that covenantal theology has exercised a formative influence in the historical emergence of human rights.[56]

For Christians, the moral obligations of human rights are grounded in God's covenant with humanity. Human rights are moral claims and expectations that arise from God's universal covenantal community. The universal covenant of God expresses God's good will and intention in creation. God created the universe in love and declared, "It is good!" From a Christian perspective, every creature is a member of this creational covenant. In other words, all creatures are born into this covenant whether or not they are aware of the fact. In this respect, this covenant has an unconditional inclusive character. The inclusiveness is confirmed again in Jesus Christ as Christians confess Jesus Christ as the Second Adam, a new catholic humanity. Whether they acknowledge it or not, viewed from this vantage point, every human being is mutually involved in a covenantal relationship. As the members of this covenant, they have obligations and responsibilities toward one another. This covenant affirms the value and worth of every living creature.

This universal covenant constitutes the context of Christian communicative engagement. In a way analogous to Habermas' idea of the "ideal speech situation," this universal covenant for Christians refers to the original moral reality of God's creation as well as the eschatological hope of its final and full restoration.[57] Christian communicative praxis takes place in the context of this inclusive covenant and points toward its fulfillment. The universal covenant designates and signifies the common good of the creation.

From a trinitarian perspective, this universal covenant is the product of the trinitarian economy. The universal covenant community is the extension of the eternal trinitarian life in the historical realm. It is the reflection and embodiment of the trinitarian *koinonia* in the creaturely reality. The triune God initiated and established a covenant which respects the differences and dignity of all creatures in the way the three persons do to each other.

Human rights begin with the fundamental recognition and respect of others as the members of the covenant community. They are the entitlements arising from membership in the universal covenant. It is the moral design of God which requires human beings to respect one another. To harm or to kill others is to offend the fundamental solidarity of humanity given by God. The affirmation of the membership is the beginning of the respect for the sanctity of each member. Each human being has worth as a member of God's covenant community. And as Michael Walzer notes, membership is the primary social good which a society distributes. To affirm the membership of each person means to value him or her individually, irreplaceably, and equally with the same kind of worth that God has granted.[58] Human rights are justified as the affirmation of the basic sanctity and dignity of human beings as the members of God's covenant household, creation. Stackhouse claims, "Individual rights were given a firm foundation—indeed, a divine foundation—in the membership of God's *humanum*."[59] As we have discussed earlier, from a trinitarian perspective, the *imago dei* means that we are, as created in the image of a *triune* God, God's covenantal partner. To recognize the membership of other persons in God's covenantal community is to treat their worth equally to one's own. The recognition of membership is the foundation of human rights, because on the basis of the membership one can claim one's freedom and equality, access to the resources of the earth, and different cultural styles. When membership is not recognized, the denial of all these claims automatically follows.

It is important to note that the close moral association of the idea of membership in the universal covenant and human rights is resonant with Habermas' idea of communicative ethics. Habermas observes that the struggles of human rights are closely related to the struggle for recognition of the full members of society. Habermas says that historically, communicative ethics is expressed in the variety of forms of "struggle for recognition." According to him, the struggle for recognition is the fight for acceptance as full members of society by being able to participate in a decision-making process, or as full human beings with universal human rights and freedom. The struggle usually proceeds with the critique and contest of the dominant social norms.[60]

Hence, human rights delineate minimal moral expectations and obligations which human beings share as they belong to the same moral community of God. The Scripture never uses the term "rights," nevertheless, it is implied in the covenantal claims and obligations of human beings toward other beings. Since human rights arise from membership in the universal covenantal community, and since covenant indicates the bond of all human life, human rights are not individualistic but relational. Solidarity and interdependence are given in the membership of the covenant community of God, just as they are affirmed by the relational nature of every human being in the *imago trinitas*. There are responsibilities and obligations corresponding to claims of rights.

Covenantal thinking is fruitful in identifying the requirements of human dignity in concrete social contexts. Each human being, created in the image of God, is endowed with a transcendental worth and dignity. Yet, the protection of dignity is neither monolithic nor one-dimensional. Human beings fulfill themselves through various institutions and associations. The dignity should be understood and protected in various social relationships, namely in various covenantal institutions. In other words, from a Christian perspective, many modern institutions take covenantal forms. Institutions such as family, union, university, corporation, government, medicine, and so on are best understood as covenants instituted in society with special purposes and goals. They are created to serve particular needs within society, and thereby they promote the common good. Each institution has covenantally defined tasks, goals, and responsibilities. Institutions become the sources and spaces of positive freedom for members to participate and realize their potentials. Yet each institution is not an isolated, competing structure. It exists in symbiotic, covenantal relationship with others. The boundary between spheres is negotiated and redefined through the communicative covenant of members. The body social is constituted by covenants of different institutions and spheres. As such, society as a whole takes a confederate form, namely a covenanted symbiosis of various institutions that serve and work for the common good of society. As we will discuss later, covenantal-communicative ethics is helpful in understanding the nature and dynamics of modern social institutions and their mutual relationships.

The conceptualization of social institutions as special covenantal institutions is useful to protect human dignity in concrete social contexts. A covenantal approach to human rights is useful in recognizing the variegated aspects of human dignity, human rights, and their protections. God's covenant with a human being is concretely found in the plurality of social institutions. Human beings have various claims and moral obligations to one another in their covenantal social activities. These claims and obligations are embodied in various institutional covenants, namely special covenants, to use Joseph Allen's term. Special covenants refer to the covenants that arise out of special kinds of historical transaction and arrangement between two or more parties.[61]

Special covenants include the relationships ranging from the permanent to the brief duration. They also encompass the primary and intimate relationships as well as the secondary, formal relationships.[62] Among special covenants, institutional covenants refer to the kind of relationships that obtained an enduring and lasting quality in society. In other words, they are the relationships affirmed into social institutions.

Special covenant spells out the basic conditions and requirements for protecting dignity in a particular institutional covenantal context. That is, the nature and structure of human rights and corresponding obligations are informed and determined by the special covenants, more notably by institutional covenants. In other words, our responsibilities attain their particular contents and shapes in accordance with the covenants rooted in particular social institutions and transactions. These responsibilities are communicated not only through the form of professional codes, standards, and ethics but also through the duties of various offices of an institution.

Every special covenant presupposes and is bound by the universal covenant in creation. The former cannot override the latter. It should serve the concretization and the promotion of the latter. The relationship of the special covenant and the inclusive covenant corresponds to that of the particular good and the common good. A special covenant is commissioned to carry out a particular task for the promotion of the common good of the universal covenant community. The common good designates the comprehensive good that comprises the dignity, worth, and well-being of all living creatures.

By virtue of its relational insight, covenant is useful in explicating the correlative rights and duties. In each institution, there is a correlative right and duty pertinent to a particular covenant. For example, in marriage, the right of the wife is reciprocated by the duty of the husband, and vice versa, as they belong to a covenant relationship under God. The covenantal idea of rights is correlative in nature, with the corresponding claims and duties. Claims of rights should be examined in a particular covenantal context. Claims are not abstract. They are grounded in the particular covenantal relationships. The nature of claims depends on the nature of obligations from which the claims are derived. And obligations are inscribed in particular sets of relationships. The covenantal approach is fruitful in understanding rights in a relational term. Rights are differentiated along the covenants that people enter into. In other words, different covenants give rise to different claims, and thereby different scopes of obligations for participants.

Contemporary enumeration of human rights makes more sense when viewed from a covenantal perspective. Civil-political rights and social-economic rights pertain to claims and obligations belonging to various differentiated social covenantal domains and contexts. They define the minimal covenantal obligations of society to protect the freedom and the needs of individual members for their political, associative, marital, economic, and cultural-civic life.

Covenantal understanding affirms the necessity of protecting minimum development of one's capacities and potentialities for the protection of human dignity. Human dignity cannot be protected by one institution alone. Covenantal institutions protect various aspects of human dignity as an individual conducts his or her life in various institutions of society. The protection of human dignity requires cooperation and collaboration among these various social institutions. The right of property, right to work, right to marry, right to be secure from arbitrary arrest, these and others delineate the rights of individuals grounded in variegated covenantal relationships. All these special covenantal rights are circumscribed and bound by the universal covenant of God in creation. That is, the claims arising from a special covenantal relationship, such as the right of the husband or the employer, cannot override the obligations embedded in the universal covenant, most notably the sanctity of a person. This implies that even if the content of rights and duties may differ in correspondence to the nature of a particular covenantal relationship, it could never supercede or abolish the basic human worth. All social-institutional covenants are secondary and subordinate to the universal covenant.

To conceive institutions as special social covenants helps to understand the changing (evolving) nature of the institutions and to clarify the morality required to be involved in their interactions. The premise is that a social institution not only forms a covenantal community itself, but also inevitably stands in covenantal relationships with other institutions of society. The possibility of conflicts always exists among various claims of the institutions. The process of communicative deliberation is to weigh and judge the claims by discursively examining the values and obligations involved in the inter-covenantal relationship. The ethical judgment includes the identification of the intrinsic purpose of each institution in relation to God's universal covenant, and the analysis of the nature of its interaction with other institutions. This reasoning process uses various ethical resources, such as shared experiences, social studies, and commonly accepted moral criteria and principles (e.g., subsidiarity). The goal is to protect the integrity of each institution, and thereby the common good of society, by drawing and setting the boundaries and terms of interaction among social institutions. This process of communicative deliberation has the effect of recovenanting each institution with other social institutions and the body politic.

Another merit of the covenantal concept of social institutions and human rights is that the approach shows how the domination of one institution over other institutions is inevitably tied to the violation of human rights. A claim of one institution may unfairly override or intrude on those of others, thus breaking a covenantal agreement among the institutions. The intrusion creates the condition of violation of human rights by threatening the integrity and sovereignty of each institution.

Michael Walzer's idea of sphere justice explicates this moral problem. The idea of "blocked exchange" in Walzer concretely spells out the kinds of exchange which should be prohibited in society.[63] "Blocked exchange" indicates society's shared understanding (covenantal decision) of inconvertibility, and the unmarketability of goods. Some goods, such as human organs and basic freedom, should never be up for sale. This concept expresses the core moral beliefs of humanity on the limitations of certain transactions of social goods.

Walzer observes that the American Bill of Rights historically embodies social agreement on a series of blocked exchanges. It is noteworthy that some universal understanding of blocked exchange begins to take shape in the international community in the form of universal human rights. Basic political-civil rights such as freedom of the press, freedom of speech, freedom of association, and freedom of body should never be for sale. Similarly, economic rights for basic material needs, such as food, shelter, and healthcare are critical to prevent any economic bargain out of desperation. Together they specify the basic, minimal conditions for human existence in collective life.

a) Civil-Political Rights

In covenantal-communicative ethics, civil political rights are associated with the covenantal obligations of human beings in a civil and political realm. The civil-political rights encompass rights such as the rights to life; liberty and freedom of movement; equality before law; presumption of innocence till proven guilty; privacy; freedom of thought, conscience, and religion; freedom of opinion and expression; freedom of assembly and association; to not be subjected to torture, slavery, and forced labor; to choose freely a partner in marriage; and to have a family. Among these rights, from a covenantal-communicative ethics' perspective, the right to free speech could be directly inferred from a communicative structure of covenant. Human beings are created to be free to choose the course of their actions. This freedom is most adequately expressed in their decision to enter into a certain covenantal relationship. The entrance into the covenant includes the process of communication such as the exchange of opinions, vows, and promises. This communication presupposes the free expression of one's beliefs, intentions, and ideas. That is, the right to free speech is to protect the basic freedom of a person in the process of covenantal communication. From its formal aspect of covenantal-communicative ethics, one could argue that every person has a right to be equally treated in the process of discourse. This right is one of the most fundamental kinds of human rights. It is intrinsic to covenant. Theologically speaking, to be God's covenantal partner means that each person is entitled to the freedom to say "yes" or "no" to the promissory proposals and suggestions. Communicative process presupposes certain stipulations of basic freedom of agency to participate in the decision-making process. Civil-political rights protect the moral agency of the covenantal partner— his or her freedom of speech, freedom of association, freedom of body, and freedom of conscience. These rights are closely associated with the moral protections for individuals involved in the process of covenanting: each partner is to participate in discourse to freely express his or her opinion; the equality of each person should be protected by the law.

The idea of covenant is intimately related to the right to freely form an assembly or association, as we have seen in the explication of Max L. Stackhouse on the formative function of the free churches for the emergence of modern institutions. That is, the right to freely express one's opinions, to freely form one's conscience and thoughts are associated with the right to freely form an association around the idea of covenant, for covenant is a mechanism of free thought, free expression, and free assembly under reciprocity and equality. Theses rights should be protected concretely from potential violations and intrusions by the judicial rights such as the right to legal recourse, the right to presumption of innocence till proven guilty, the right to appeal a conviction, the right not to be tortured, and so on.

One may say that civil-political rights specifically delineate the moral meaning and implication of our membership in God's covenant community. To be members means to be entitled to free and equal participation in the decision-making process of a community, protected by the law. Therefore, as covenantal-communicative ethics postulates on the equal freedom of each individual, one may say that civil and political rights are the claims which arise from a covenantal membership of each person in God's creation community. Human beings are created as God's covenantal partners, namely communicative-dialogic partners. We have discussed that in a covenantal-communicative ethics, the most fundamental moral obligation is to recognize the other as an equal member and partner of a covenant. This fundamental relationality makes a constitutive condition and a regulative context for human social relationship.

b) Social-Economic Rights

The idea of covenant is also useful in explicating the nature of social-economic rights, the second generation of the human rights. Social-economic rights are concerned with the basic obligations in the socio-economic realm. Espoused mostly by the socialist countries of Eastern Europe before the collapse of the Soviet Union, social-economic rights emphasize that human beings are entitled to minimum wages, equal pay for equal work, the provision of basic needs, such as food, shelter, medical service, and work. If civil-political rights focus on the procedural, democratic, and thus communicative aspects of covenant, social-economic rights uphold the fundamental dignity of human beings in their basic economic material living situations. It is expressed through the emphasis on collective societal accountability for the provision of basic material needs of every member of society. To regard each person as a member of the universal covenant community of God means to meet the basic physical and economic needs of each person. As a member of God's universal covenant of creation, every member has a legitimate claim to share the material provisions and blessings of the earth. God stipulates this sharing of the gifts and blessings of the earth. For the earth and its blessings belong to God. Each member has a covenantal obligation toward other members' in meeting their basic needs and necessities. Similarly, each person has a right to work. From the beginning, Christians understood that work was a part of God's providence. As a vehicle for creative activity, it is instrumental for human self-fulfillment.

c) Cultural-Communal Rights

Cultural-communal rights, the third generation of human rights, accent the significance of one's cultural identity and tradition for his or her well-being. As we have discussed above, these rights are necessary for the empowerment of the marginalized cultural traditions and ethnic groups today. Without the positive affirmation of one's culture and tradition, one cannot lead an authentic human life. God affirms and protects human beings in their diverse cultural expressions and ethnic pluriforms. Pluriforms are necessary for the fullness of the creation. Since diverse cultural and ethnic expressions are part of God's creational design, they should be respected. There is no intrinsic hierarchy among different races, ethnicities, and languages. Ethnicity is a gift of God. It is given to enrich one another.

The international ratification of cultural-communal rights can be more adequately explained by covenantal-communicative ethics. The ethos of cultural-communal rights is congruent with that of covenantal-communicative ethics in their shared concern for freedom, equality, and reciprocity of the participants. As we have discussed, covenantal-communicative ethics is an ethical methodology which protects the communicative rights of the weak and the marginal against the monopoly of information and media by the rich and the powerful. One may say that today cultural-communal rights intend to protect and empower the membership and the participation of the weak and the marginal groups, so that they may not be further marginalized or excluded from public discourse and any decision-making process. In other words, the ratification of cultural-communal rights is necessary for the empowerment of the marginal cultural traditions and ethnic groups into the process of public discourse. A major challenge of a global society is how to safeguard the rights of self-determination of small countries, tribes, and indigenous peoples against the exploitative aspects of globalizing forces. In this respect, the ratification of cultural-communal rights proves the significance and adequacy of the covenantal-communicative approach to the question of human rights.

d) Ecological Rights

The covenantal-communicative insight is informative for the understanding of ecological rights. Ecological rights argue that in the onslaught of continued human exploitation and destruction, some form of moral and legal protection also must be applied to nonhuman creatures. That is, their rights must be recognized and affirmed. Other creatures, animals and plants, do not exist merely for human consumption. Human beings are in an interdependent, solidaristic relationship with other creatures. Although other creatures may live without humanity, humanity cannot live without other creatures. Our survival and flourishing depends on them. The survival of other creatures also depends on human beings because human beings, when they misuse power, could destroy all the inhabitants of the earth. As co-dwellers on the earth, humanity and other creatures have common interests to protect the mutual well-being and cultivate the conditions of the earth to make it hospitable for every member of the creation. Just as covenant is possible between the unequal relationship of God and humanity, covenant between human-nonhuman is also possible on the basis of their reciprocity and mutual dependence.

Jürgen Moltmann makes a relevant point on this matter. The earth belongs to God and to every species. Rights of nature should be acknowledged as an integral aspect of global morality. Rights of nature could be adequately explicated in the framework of covenant. Non-human species are members of the divine covenant, as equally with human beings. Their dignity and worth should be protected because of their membership in divine covenant. In making a covenant with Noah, God declared, "As for me, I am establishing my covenant with you and your descendants after you, and with every living creature that is with you, the birds, the domestic animals, and every animal of the earth with you, as many as came out of the ark" (Genesis 9:9-10). Other creatures have their dignity and rightful places as the creation of God. They have rights to the share and protection of the common resources of the earth for their well-being.[64]

Human beings have a moral responsibility toward other creatures and the earth. Human beings are created as their covenantal partners. We are accountable to God for our treatment of nonhuman species and our use of the earth. When we mistreat and abuse them, their cries reach God. God, humanity, and the earth are in the tripartite covenantal relationship. Covenant, through its openness to and awareness of the well-being of non-immediate partners of the incumbent covenant, includes land and nature as integral members of divine covenant. For example, the covenantal membership of the land or the earth (and human solidarity with them) was the tenet of Israel's religious belief. Israel's understanding of who and what they were was inextricably related to the land entrusted to them by God. The land was understood as a moral and theological entity. It functioned as the moral thermometer of the inhabitants. The Old Testament ethics cannot be properly understood outside this solidaristic relationship. Christopher J. H. Wright is correct in saying that in Israel's understanding "the land was personified as the agent of God's blessing or curse, inasmuch as it is described as 'vomiting out' the present inhabitants for their wicked ways, and quite capable of repeating the performance on the Israelites if they imitate them" (Leviticus. 18:24-28; 20:22-24).[65]

Unfortunately, the demise of "God" in modernity inevitably led to the demise of solidarity with the earth. The earth and nature began to be treated as the objects of conquest and exploitation. Covenantal-communicative thinking is helpful in overcoming instrumental, technological rationality and its domination of nature. Aesthetics is the realm of communicative imagination and insight in the conversation with nature. Through the aid of poets, artists, and musicians, human beings may enter imaginative conversation with other creatures, at least vicariously. Such insights and imaginations, through the voices of poets, artists, and mystics, squarely challenge the modern, anthropocentric instrumental rationality which takes nature as mere "unclaimed human property" or human possession.

D. Summary

In this section, the idea of universal human rights, with its three generations, was discussed in relation to the covenantal-communicative method, as a form of global ethics. I showed how effectively covenantal-communicative ethics explicates the rise and evolution of universal human rights. Covenantal-communicative ethics shows that the idea of human rights is more adequately accounted for by covenant and communication. The international ratification of the three generations of universal human rights affirms the validity of the communicative approach to the common morality. The history of human rights shows an increasing inclusion of a different kind of rights through a communicative argument, discernment, and finally ratification.

The idea of covenant shows that the recognition of the sanctity of human dignity and the affirmation of a covenantal membership are inseparable. Communicative covenant mediates human individuality and relationality. Human worth is not individually innate, but relationally configured in various institutional contexts and their relationships. From a covenantal perspective, human beings are sacred because they are created as God's covenantal partners. However, this does not imply that the demands of covenantal relationship are self-evident to human eyes or immediate to human experience. As God's relationship with humanity is historically situated, the requirements of God's covenant do not exist transcendentally from human cultures and languages. The requirements of dignity and sanctity should be discerned and ratified through a communicative examination, yet human rights are not purely constructive. They have referential values and an objective basis in God's covenantal relationship with humanity. Thus, human rights are partially referential and partially constructive.

A covenantal-communicative approach presents a more adequate and consistent theory of human rights than that of Catholic ethics. The category of covenant is more comprehensive and adequate than the single normative category of human dignity in conceptualizing the idea of human rights in a historical, contextual, and integral term. Especially when viewed from a covenantal-communicative perspective, the Catholic idea of human rights is limited to account for the dynamic and interdependent relationships among different generations of human rights. The idea of covenant is useful in understanding the mutual relationships of the three generations of human rights. From a covenantal-communicative perspective, each generation of rights is indispensable for the protection of human dignity in each sphere, such as civil-political, economic, and cultural. Each generation of human rights lays out the basic moral requirement, namely the covenant of each sphere, consequently delineating the spheric boundaries among the spheres.

The three generations of rights are also mutually necessary for the protection and respect of a basic human dignity in its wholeness and totality, that is, in the contexts of its integral existence and expression. Just as the stipulation of each generation of rights constitutes the covenant of a distinctive social sphere, the three generations of human rights are understood covenantally in the interdependent relationships of social institutions. Therefore, the relationship of different generations of rights is that of mutual checks, balances, and edification for the protection of human dignity in totality. The vision of the trinitarian Kingdom of God provides a theological framework for the adjudication of various claims of rights. In light of the trinitarian Kingdom of God, various generations of human rights are brought into mutual critique, correction, improvement and enhancement. Hence, the idea of covenant advances a Christian understanding of human rights a step further than Hollenbach's, while embracing Hollenbach's historical, contextual, and relational idea of human rights.

III. Liberation Ethics

As mentioned in the Introduction, a global society is afflicted with several salient moral problems: the eruptions of racial and ethnic conflicts, the increasing gap between rich and poor, and the intensification of ecological exploitation driven by the boundless greed for profits. These problems tend to victimize the vulnerable and powerless members of society as the society loses its traditional form of mutual institutional constraints and check and balance through globalization. The suffering and pain deepen and become unbearable for many as a society loses the basic social safety net or traditional communal supports and assistances. The complex and interlocking nature of oppression and subjugation taking place in a postmodern, global society requires a much more rigorous social analysis and ethical discernment to understand the nature of challenges and the effective political collaboration among affected groups to overcome the challenges.

A liberation ethics is the methodology of Christian ethics which responds to these social situations of oppression, subjugation, and exploitation from a Christian theological perspective. It is based on the premise that the solutions to these problems require liberating works by religious communities, in collaboration with other social movements, and a certain spiritual guidance and direction from various historical religions and traditions could be instrumental in achieving the liberation of people from inhumane conditions. Liberation ethics is deeply informed by Karl Marx's theory. His idea of ideology critique (that is, human ideas and concepts are not neutral, but inevitably reflect the interests of material and social relationships) is carried on by liberationists. However, recognizing the danger of Marx's economic determinism, liberationists expand the Christian critique of oppression in various other social realms, such as racial, ethnic, gender, and ecological relationships.

In this section, I attempt to show how the methodology of a covenantal-communicative ethics offers insights and suggestions on the overcoming of one major challenge which liberation ethics faces in a postmodern social situation, namely plurality. It is the challenge to understand how different systems of domination delicately intersect with and reinforce each other, to the advantage of the oppressors. The pluralistic and complex reality of a global society shows that any reductionistic, monocausal explanation of oppression is inevitably limited and deficient. For the phenomenon of "oppression" today is too complex to be boxed into the singular category of oppressed and oppressor. It is hard to reduce all forms of oppression to a single root cause. Furthermore, despite its shared goal of liberation, liberation ethics is no longer a homogeneous, monolithic camp. It is a school of Christian ethics with diverse voices, emphases, interests, and concerns.

The challenge for liberation movements in a postmodern society is how to respect the particularity of each unique concern and justice struggle without impairing the necessary cooperation and collaboration among diverse movements. One eminent danger for a liberation movement is its apparent myopic insensitivity to other forms of oppression, concerned only with its own agenda. The process of overcoming this danger is to recognize and accept one's own limited experiential perspective in light of multifarious aspects of human experience and pluriforms of oppression. The danger for liberation ethics is to universalize one's own limited experience as the only legitimate experience, at the expense of other legitimate experiences. This new experiential exclusivism is the ironic repetition of the false universalism of First-World white male theology that liberation ethics has vehemently criticized. In other words, liberation ethics must address the issue of diversity and difference in human experience.

As a matter of fact, domination often pivots around suppression of difference. That is, domination often takes the form of the refusal to accept and acknowledge difference. Acknowledgment of difference is crucial in dissolving the domination which usually relies on the absolutist or foundationalist logic of philosophy and morality. From a covenantal perspective, the affirmation of differences means the recognition of others as authentic members of a universal covenantal community of God. Without this affirmation or recognition of others, liberationism may end up as another form of moral exclusivism.

To avoid this pitfall, liberationists continuously need to expand their hermeneutical perspective by engaging with other experiential dimensions of oppression and liberation. This includes the critical examination of their own theological and cultural assumptions, values, methods, and ethical commitments. The process of dialogical engagement will show how one form of oppression, such as racism, is interlocked with other forms, such as sexism and classism. The process of dialogue will help participants to see the limits as well as the possibilities of one's own experience of oppression for the integral, holistic liberation of humanity.

One inescapable challenge for liberation ethics in a pluralistic society is to ask, How can necessarily different liberation movements and theologies support one another in their individual distinctive processes of social, economic, political, and spiritual transformation? Or more realistically, how can various liberation movements avoid getting trapped into the divisive tactics of a ruling group? Today, the analysis and explanation of various forms of oppression require communal discernment, intersubjective critique, and mutual examinations. Dialogue among liberation movements is not an option, but a necessity today. In other words, liberation movements today cannot be effective without conversation and alliances with other movements. The interlocking nature of various forms of oppression necessitates the cooperation and collaboration of all concerned. As Susan Thistlethwaite and Mary Engel notice, "Recognition of the necessity for such an ongoing dialogue is fundamental."[66] Dialogue will provide the opportunities for mutual understanding, critique, and support. According to them, this process would increase the deepening of the understanding of one's own social locus and experience, and commitment to one's particular justice struggle in connection to other struggles.

This implies that liberation ethics in contemporary society needs a methodology which attends to the concerns of plurality and inequality simultaneously. The task of liberation in a global society requires a careful analysis of various forms of oppression and its ongoing mutations. A more integral and comprehensive method of ethics is required to ground our liberating praxis in a global horizon. The analysis of oppression in a global society requires the study of how old forms of social evils and contradictions of racism, sexism, and classism are now mutating today, and how they are interlocking and mutually reinforcing each other through new structural, institutional configurations. Communicative ethics responds to this complex situation by including various concerned parties in the achievement of a holistic form of liberation. It is exactly in this area that covenantal-communicative ethics could make a contribution. Covenantal-communicative ethics aims at the methodology of discourse for the formation of solidarity and alliance among diverse groups. By identifying these connections, contradictions, and complicities of various forms of oppression, communicative critique helps us to forge a properly integral perspective. Communication is the phase of liberal praxis which enables us to see these connections and contradictions. In addition, the communicative process helps to keep liberation ethics from sliding into an ideological doctrinaire of a mono-cause, mono-oppression, mono- liberation, which shuts down all the differences, all the experiences of oppression and all the forms of oppression.

Intersubjective rationality provides the formal-pragmatic ground to exercise a critique of neo-liberal ideology and instrumental rationality reigning in a global society in the form of a technological control, scientism, and commercialism. The communicative requisites of free, fair and reciprocal dialogue indicate the minimal procedural requirements that are indispensable to making the process of mutual engagement fair and just.

When these requisites are ignored or suppressed, the moral sanctity of the process itself is questioned, not to mention the products of the process. As various forms of liberation theology have effectively demonstrated, human construction and application of universal morality are often colored and biased by dominant political, economic, and cultural interests. In order to correct unequal power relationships in moral adjudication, universal participation and fair, equal opportunity of speech must be protected as an integral process of moral reasoning. Communicative ethics explicitly identifies and highlights these procedural requirements that empower freedom, equality, and universal participation. Attention to these aspects is necessary to construct a common order of symbiosis in a pluralistic society on the basis of fairness and dialogue rather than domination and violence.

Covenantal-communicative ethics centers on critical mutual examination. For the cooperation and alliance among oppressed peoples and groups, some form of self-criticism and self-transformation is indispensable. Thistlethwaite and Engel conclude, "The future of liberation theologies will depend on whether or not they take up this challenge to be open to criticism (both internal and external) of their own assumptions about experience."[67] This self-criticism and self-transformation would be more effective through dialogical engagement and mutual critique, which is communicative. In addition, the process of mutual examination will deepen one's particularity and increase solidarity through mutual understanding. Communicative ethics fosters the ethos of respecting identities and openness to dialogue.

Communicative praxis serves the visions of liberation and social cooperation. In covenantal-communicative ethics, the ideal of liberation is harmonized with reconciliation without sacrificing the necessity of social order and cooperation. By institutionalizing the participation of all concerned parties and using mutual critique as the normative requisites of the political process, communicative praxis serves the purpose of effective political transformation through the formation of the common will and solidarity.

Communicative methodology could be instrumental in forming cooperation and alliance among the oppressed groups. The agreement among various oppressed groups may take a form of covenant (alliances or confederacy) around the shared vision and goal of liberation. The covenant, a structured form of solidarity, could be instrumental in offering the structure of ongoing collaboration among the groups in achieving the goal of liberation. In addition, the achieved solidarity among the oppressed through covenant is indispensable in checking and counterbalancing oppressive forces. As history has taught us, oppressors never freely give up their power and privileges. Only when challenged by countering forces of the oppressed in solidarity do they enter the process of communicative-covenantal engagement with the oppressed for a fairer and more just form of social arrangement. As such, covenantal-communicative ethics becomes a coherent political methodology of Christian praxis in response to the moral demands of justice and solidarity in a global society.

Covenantal-communicative ethics and liberation ethics share some similarities in terms of their political and ethical ethos. Covenantal-communicative ethics attends to various political and moral concerns of liberation ethics, such as critique of domination, suspicion of tradition, community, power, and emancipation. Covenantal-communicative ethics strongly affirms the subjectivity and self-determination of a moral agent. Covenantal-communicative ethics and liberation ethics also share the legacy of prophetic social criticism. They institute the hermeneutic of suspicion as the core process of their ethical methodologies in achieving an emancipated society. They are aware that human moral discourse is not a pure system of linguistic exchange. The discursive practice, like other socio-cultural practices, cannot be separated from a power relationship. The discursive practice takes place in a concrete social relationship of power and domination.

However, there are some noticeable differences as well. Unlike liberation ethics, covenantal-communicative ethics prioritizes dialogue over violent means of achieving liberation. It introduces a new moral element— a collaborative, discursive engagement as the integral process of political praxis. If covenantal-communicative ethics provides a methodology of collaboration and alliances for the task of an integral liberation, liberation ethics, on the other hand, adds realistic edges to the communicative process by emphasizing the hermeneutical significance of the oppressed. One area of contribution that liberation ethics could make to the communicative approach is that the former makes the inclusion and solidarity with the oppressed as a requisite of any social analysis and ethical deliberation. This implies that the authenticity and the sincerity of any claim of justice and common morality will be suspect unless the participation of previously marginalized or excluded people in the process of a decision-making is guaranteed. Although Habermas emphasizes the participation of all concerned, he does not grant any preferential treatment or hermeneutical privilege to the oppressed. Without an emphasis on the participation of the oppressed, especially given the inequality of power, communication may be slanted and skewed toward those who control the means of communication and resources of information and propagation. This reminds us that only the firm procedural assurance (guarantee) of the full participation and representation of the oppressed in the process of formulating the order and the common morality will serve the purpose of liberation and solidarity simultaneously.

IV. Covenantal-Communicative Ethics and Liberation/Reconciliation

Stressing intersubjective critique as a constitutive process of ethical reasoning, covenantal-communicative ethics helps to synthesize the two prominent theological visions of liberation and reconciliation into a coherent political praxis of dialogue and change. In envisioning the universal distortion-free community of communication where humanity is fully liberated as well as reconciled, communicative praxis suggests a concrete political method approximating this vision. It presents a progressive, reformist, and democratic form of politics that moves beyond a Marxist-Leninist paradigm of self-righteous, revolutionary class struggle, or a liberal, *laissez-faire* individualism.

Liberation and reconciliation are not antithetical but complementary demands in Christian faith. They are placed in a dialectical tension. Covenantal-communicative ethics concretely relates the two visions of liberation and reconciliation through affirmation of diversity in public discourse. Public discourse is instrumental to the task of liberation. At the same time, in order for public discourse to be "public," it should welcome the participation and contribution of all concerned. Only through the participation of all concerned, can justice be served and the common good enhanced adequately. Covenantal-communicative ethics' stress on the participation of all concerned partially attends to the postmodern sensibility toward diversity and difference. It espouses that the achievement of liberation and reconciliation is not possible without the acknowledgment and acceptance of differences and pluralities of positions. Yet, at the same time, covenantal-communicative ethics points out that the difference should not be equated with an "anything goes" relativism that paralyzes public discourse and engagement. Plurality should be a liberating plurality, just as unity should be a genuine reconciliation based on the consent of all members of society. Universal participation and communicative critiques are indispensable aspects of politics in regulating and harmonizing the demands of the ethical values of liberation, diversity, and reconciliation.

By emphasizing dialogue and critique, covenantal-communicative ethics rejects both the exclusivistic danger of liberation and a deceptive form of reconciliation. Covenantal-communicative ethics rejects any facile form of solidarity or the pretension of love achieved at the expense of justice. It points out that reconciliation is costly, requiring the confession of sins and repentance. Forgiveness and acceptance into fellowship are only subsequent to atonement. Certainly, mutual critique could assist the awareness of sins and repentance. The ultimate aim of liberation is love and reconciliation, the communion of all humanity in a triune God. Yet love and reconciliation cannot be fulfilled at the exclusion or marginalization of the others. Liberation is an indispensable aspect of the reconciling process which, in turn, presupposes and anticipates a liberated form of life. That is to say, an authentic liberation is fulfilled only when all of humanity is reconciled, and a genuine reconciliation is possible only when each and every individual is free to be a full member of the community, and free to realize his or her God-given talents. If any theology prioritizes reconciliation at the expense of liberation, it risks becoming the ideology of the *status quo*, masking various forms of oppression. Conversely, any theology that upholds liberation at the expense of reconciliation is exposed to the danger of self-righteous exclusivism.

Covenantal-communicative ethics responds to the moral challenges of liberation and reconciliation in a more methodologically consistent way than other approaches. Although the full realization of liberation and reconciliation is eschatological, both are approximated through the communicative praxis of the members. Covenant is a crucial social mechanism that mediates this process.

Notes

1. Stanley Hauerwas, *Against the Nations: War and Survival in a Liberal Society* (Minneapolis, Chicago, and New York: Winston Press, 1985), 18.

2. Stanley Hauerwas, *The Peaceful Kingdom: A Primer in Christian Ethics* (Notre Dame: University of Notre Dame Press, 1983), 10ff.

3. Ibid., 12.

4. Hauerwas rejects any idea of a metanarrative. He observes, "There is no 'story of stories' from which the many stories of our existence can be analyzed and evaluated." (*A Community of Character: Toward a Constructive Christian Social Ethic*, Notre Dame: University of Notre Dame Press, 1981, 96.)

5. Stanley Hauerwas, *Truthfulness and Tragedy* (Notre Dame: University of Notre Dame Press, 1977), 20.

6. Stanley Hauerwas, *The Peaceable Kingdom*, 25.

7. Ibid., 26.

8. Ibid., 16.

9. Ibid., 40.

10. Ibid., 42.

11. Stanley Hauerwas, *Character and the Christian Life: A Study in Theological Ethics* (San Antonio, Texas: Trinity University Press, 1975), 115.

12. Stanley Hauerwas, *Vision and Virtue: Essays in Christian Ethical Reflection* (Notre Dame: University of Notre Dame Press, 1974), 74.

13. Hauerwas, *The Peaceable Kingdom*, 39.

14. Hauerwas, *Character and the Christian Life*, 43.

15. Ibid., 41.

16. Ibid., 43.

17. These include the historical struggle against hierarchy and authoritarianism, the common endeavor to avoid religious war, and the various material, social, and political conditions involved in the Enlightenment, such as the growth of social mobility, differentiation of social structure, growth of the city, technological advances, etc.

18. Jeffrey Stout, *Ethics after Babel* (Boston: Beacon Press, 1988), 226.

19. Max L. Stackhouse, "Liberalism Dispatched vs. Liberalism Engaged," *Christian Century* 112, no.29 (1995): 962.

20. Michael Quirk, "Beyond Sectarianism?" *Theology Today* 44 (1987): 83.

21. Edmund Arens, *Christopraxis: A Theology of Action*, trans. by John F. Hoffmeyer (Fortress Press: Minneapolis, 1995), 51.

22. Ibid., 52.

23. Vigen Guroian, "Liturgy and the Lost Eschatological Vision of Christian Ethics," *The Annual of the Society of Christian Ethics* 20 (2000): 233.

24. Scripture in many places shows a productive tension between justice and worship. Doing justice is considered a worshipful act, just as a truthful worship (or worship in spirit and in truth) is the ground for justice. In the prophets of the Old Testament, one sees a constant attempt to overcome the gap between liturgy and ethics (how to worship and how to live actual life). The Old Testament prophets were critical of the hypocrisy of Israelites in their worship life and social actions. Similarly, Martin Luther King, Jr., during the Civil Rights Movement, lamented on the passivity of white churches toward the freedom of blacks. His lament was also directed toward the discrepancy of white churches between their worship life and ethics.

25. Michael Downey, *Understanding Christian Spirituality* (New York: Paulist Press, 1997), 14.

26. Cf. Colin Gunton, *The One, the Three and the Many*, 182-183.

27. LaCugna, *God for Us*, 296.

28. The Spirit's particularizing and differentiating work is operative in the incarnation of Jesus in the womb of Mary. The Nicene Creed says that Jesus is fully God and fully human at the same time. This signifies that Jesus is the communion of divine and human. Through communicative *idiomatum*, Jesus unites two natures, divine and human, "without separation, without mingling, without confusion."

29. LaCugna, *God for Us*, 296.

30. Moltmann, *The Trinity and the Kingdom*, 154.
31. H.R. Niebuhr, "The Idea of Covenant and American Democracy," 134.

32. Mount, *Covenant, Community and the Common Good*, 158.

33. Ibid., 158.

34. Ibid., 133.

35. Ibid.

36. I call this a rational dimension of character and virtue. It refers to a universalistic aspect of character or virtue intrinsic to the nature of vocational obligation. There is a discrepancy among various religious traditions and communities in terms of the maturity of this vocational moral consciousness. Some narrative communities and traditions have never fully developed this vocational understanding.

37. Vocations and spiritual gifts are intimately related to each other in the covenantal framework. What vocations are for social spheres, spiritual gifts are for the church. Christian life in the *ecclesia* is not an undifferentiated whole. One may understand vocations as the extensions of spiritual gifts. Gifts take a highly complex and differentiated form to serve and build a *corpus Christi*. The spiritual gifts and vocations provide the significant loci through which Christian virtues are concretely formed and practiced.

38. David Hollenbach's ethics, in many ways, continue the Vatican II moral tradition in a global, pluralistic social context.

39. David Hollenbach, "The Common Good Revisited," *Theological Studies* 50 (1989): 70-94.

40. David Hollenbach, "A Communitarian Reconstruction of Human Rights," in *Catholicism and Liberalism: Contributions to American Public Philosophy,* 133.

41. David Hollenbach, *Claims in Conflict: Retrieving and Renewing the Catholic Human Rights Tradition* (New York: Paulist Press, 1979), 42.

42. Ibid., 108.

43. Ibid., 69-70.

44. David Hollenbach, *Justice, Peace, and Human Rights: American Catholic Social Ethics in a Pluralistic Context* (New York: Crossroad, 1988), 98.

45. Ibid., 93.

46. Hollenbach, "Liberalism, Communitarianism, and the Bishops' Letter on Economy," 33.

47. Hollenbach, "The Common Good Revisited," 88.

48. Hollenbach, *Justice, Peace, and Human Rights*, 91.

49. Paul Lakeland also points out that a major problem for Catholic ethics is its piecemeal approach to social criticism, which often adopts an uncritical attitude to the Catholic "house of authority," and defensiveness about the place of the church in society (Paul Lakeland, "Ethics and Communicative Action: The Need for Critical Theory in Catholic Social Teaching," *Thought* 62 (1987): 59-73).

50. Margaret Farley, "New Patterns of Relationship," *Theological Studies* 36 (1975): 645-646.

51. Jürgen Moltmann, "Human Rights, the Rights of Humanity and the Rights of Nature," in *Ethics of World Religions and Human Rights*, ed. Hans Küng and Jürgen Moltmann (London: SCM Press; Philadelphia: Trinity Press International, 1990), 122.

52. Ibid., 121.

53. Quoted in Sumner B. Twiss, "Comparative Ethics and Intercultural Human-Rights Dialogues: A Programmatic Inquiry," in *Christian Ethics: Problems and Prospects,* ed. Lisa Sowle Cahill and James F. Childress (Cleveland: Pilgrim Press, 1996), 359.

54. Sumner B. Twiss & Bruce Grelle, "Human Rights and Comparative Religious Ethics: A New Venue," *The Annual of the Society of Christian Ethics* 15 (1995): 27.

55. Twiss, "Comparative Ethics and Intercultural Human-Rights Dialogues: A Programmatic Inquiry," 371.

56. Cf. Stackhouse, *Creeds, Society, and Human Rights.*

57. Allen, *Love and Conflict*, 40.

58. Ibid., 66.

59. Stackhouse, *Creeds, Society, and Human Rights*, 59.

60. Habermas, "Struggles for Recognition in the Democratic Constitutional State, in *Multiculturalism*, ed. & introduced by Amy Gutmann (Princeton: Princeton University Press), 108. One could easily remember the civil rights movements in the 1960s in America. They were a democratic "struggle for rec-

ognition" as equal citizens, not secondary ones. They were the struggles of
Blacks to demand basic freedom, equality, and basic human rights for political
participation. Also, various liberation movements of oppressed peoples, minor-
ity groups, such as women, native people, and independence movements in
African and Asian nations present concrete historical examples of "struggle for
recognition."

61. Allen, *Love and Conflict*, 41.

62. Ibid.

63. Michael Walzer, *Spheres of Justice*, 1995.

64. Jürgen Moltmann, "The Destruction and Healing of the Earth: Ecology and
Theology," in *God and Globalization: The Spirit and the Modern Authorities*,
vol. 2. Max L. Stackhouse and Don S. Browning (eds.) (Harrisburg, PA: Trinity Press International, 2001), 183ff.

65. Christopher J. H. Wright, *An Eye for an Eye: The Place of Old Testament
Ethics Today* (Downers Grove, IL: InterVarsity Press, 1983), 47.

66. Susan Thistlethwaite and Mary Engel, eds., *Lift Every Voice: Constructing
Christian Theologies from the Underside* (New York: HarperCollins, 1990),
293.

67. Ibid., 294.

CONCLUSION

This study has proposed a new methodology of Christian ethics to liberal political institutions (democracy and human rights) in a global, pluralistic society, called covenantal-communicative ethics. Covenantal-communicative ethics refers to a reconstructive Christian ethics which synthesizes Habermas' formal-pragmatic communicative methodology and a trinitarian-covenantal theology. I have shown that Habermas' theory of communicative ethics offers methodological insights which could be creatively appropriated into a trinitarian-covenantal theology for a constructive Christian ethics today. Specifically, through a critical dialogue between Habermas and a trinitarian-covenantal theology, I have identified prominent communicative thrusts and motifs within Christianity, and their significance and implications for a Christian ethical methodology. I have demonstrated that the idea of communication discloses something strikingly congruent with the Reformed Christian idea of covenant, especially a bilateral covenanting process, and with a social trinitarian notion of perichoresis. Habermas' communicative methodology could be incorporated by a trinitarian-covenantal theology because both communicative ethics and trinitarian-covenantal theology share similar emphases on the moral values of freedom, equality, and reciprocity.

The idea of communicative interaction offers a critical clue for a constructive Christian ethics because it refers to a structure and procedure of a fair human interaction in search for mutual understanding, justice, and reconciliation. Communicative interaction is couched in the moral requisites of a fair procedure and the free and equal participation of all concerned. These principles stipulate that if a conflict resolution is to rely on a dialogue rather than oppression and domination, then the participation of all concerned and their freedom and equal opportunity to speak must be guaranteed. I refer to these indispensable elements of a fair human interaction as "communicative requisites." These requisites may be regarded as the products of philosophical analysis as persuasively espoused by Habermas in his theory of communicative ethics. Yet they also present the collective moral wisdom and experience of the modern western civilization, gleaned from a long history of political struggles, religious wars, experiences of atrocities, persecutions, and oppressions. Any meaningful discussion of social order, justice, and democracy in a global society does not permit us to easily dismiss these communicative elements.

The discovery of communicative rationality as the centerpiece of ethical methodology, accepted by both Christian theology (covenant and the Trinitarian doctrine) and a contemporary philosophical moral theory (viz. Habermas' communicative ethics), has a profound implication for the constructive relationship of Christians with liberal political institutions. This discovery means that Christians may now approach and justify liberal political institutions on the basis of their theological convictions. Passively, it might suggest that Christianity is not inimical to liberal political institutions. More positively, Christianity has some valuable insights to offer for the reconstruction and revitalization of these institutions. That is, as our discussion of the constructive relationship of Puritan covenantal theology and American political institutions has shown, Christians, through a covenantal-communicative action, could make a significant contribution to revitalizing civic and public institutions and the lifeworld against the colonizing system of political administration and the commodifying force of capitalism.

Unlike Habermas, who refuses to acknowledge any positive role of a religious community for the betterment of a civil society, a covenantal-communicative ethics upholds a constructive role of a Christian community for public discourse and public policy formation. Covenantal-communicative ethics is grounded in the conviction that without the retrieval and reconstruction of this rich communicative rationality within deeply rooted religious traditions, rituals, and practices, any fight against the colonizing power of the system (intrusive administration and commodifying global economy) will not stand long. Religion has been a culture-constitutive power in human history. The lifeworld has been informed by religion. Molding the deepest dimension of human aspirations and moral expectations, it has constituted the backbone of the lifeworld. This contention is warranted by the fact that many of today's new movements of resistance to colonization of the lifeworld are inspired and organized most assiduously by religious communities. Of course, not all religious resistance movements are democratic in nature. Yet one cannot deny that when properly identified and directed, their religious energy, practices, and dedication could be used creatively for the revitalization and empowerment of the public sphere and the lifeworld.

For Christians, this study has shown that the trinitarian Kingdom presents a theologico-ethical vision and context in which Christian communicative public engagements are enacted. As the compatibility between communicative action and the trinitarian perichoretic action demonstrate, communicative ethics attains a higher degree of plausibility and practicality when it acknowledges the triune God as its foundation and goal, and the church as a collective moral agency. Every human communication points toward the unity in the universal communicative community of the trinitarian Kingdom. The trinitarian Kingdom indicates a fully reconciled community that advances through the work of the Logos and the Holy Spirit.

A trinitarian-covenantal approach to public discourse effectively addresses some critical concerns raised by communitarians against Habermas. Without diminishing a genuine contribution of his intersubjectivist idea of rationality and the dialogical method of practical reasoning toward a constructive ethics, one must acknowledge that Habermas presents an overly cognitivistic and anthropocentric view of human agency. By recognizing the significance of passion, virtue, desire, and aesthetic imagination for a robust moral agency, covenantal-communicative ethics synthesizes the communitarian sensibility toward virtue and the shared vision with the liberal concern for freedom, equality, and fairness.

On the other hand, a communicative dimension, appropriated from Habermas' theory, adds a political and practical edge to a covenantal theology. For Christians, communicative action means a procedural methodology of covenant. Covenant is established and renewed through a communicative discourse. A common morality is understood as a commonly (or covenantally) achieved moral consensus. By embracing communicative methodology, the Christian endeavor to reach communion becomes a more self-conscious, self-critical, and other-respecting process.   Accordingly, covenantal-communicative ethics overcomes the exclusivistic tendency of a traditional covenantal theology. It emphasizes a procedural dimension of justice. Justice is tied with the protection of a fair and equal opportunity of all concerned parties to participate and debate in a covenant-making process. It stipulates a communicative interaction (free, open, and equal intersubjective critique) as the core process of covenanting on the basis of the belief that for the achievement of justice in a society, the communicative requisite (the participation of all concerned, and free, equal, and reciprocal opportunity to participate) must be satisfied. Covenantal-communicative ethics, by benchmarking these requisites in its core methodology, makes the process of covenanting more open, fair, and just than the traditional covenantal theology.

Within the framework of covenantal-communicative ethics, the church understands itself as the sacrament of the trinitarian Kingdom of God. Its ministry and witness manifest a perichoretic sociality of the triune God. Through the practices of the open, liberated form of life and engagement, the church needs to witness to the Kingdom. The mission of the church is to sustain the practice of communication by its own ecclesial practices, and to help to expand this open, free, universal, and intersubjective form of sociality in our society. It is a way to continue the theological tradition and vision of a trinitarian covenant.

If history is the theatre of the triune God who works to bring about the completion of God's redemptive work by inviting humanity into the righteous and loving communion of trinitarian life, then covenant, as the agreement between different parties concerning the common morality, is the penultimate achievement of this ultimate communion. A human moral achievement, such as covenant, is always limited and vulnerable to distortion. As a methodology of conflict resolution, communicative-covenant means a tentative, provisional realization of communion. As a political praxis of critique of systematic distortion, it represents the reestablishment of justice. In history, communion is approximated and partially realized through various forms of covenants.

By incorporating the methodological insights of Habermas' ethics into a covenantal-trinitarian theological framework, covenantal-communicative ethics provides a practical methodology for Christian public engagement and interreligious dialogue. In a global, pluralistic context, communicative-covenantal ethics leads Christians into a cooperative, ecumenical dialogue with other religious or secular groups in search of global peace and justice. Christians present their validity claims to the public realm informed by scripture, religious experience, and tradition, with prayerful hearts and much reflection. Dialogue and engagement are important because Christians still believe, as did the covenantal theologians, that God is the author of the universe and God's grace works in every realm of society to bring about reconciliation and justice. Intersubjective critique and argumentation are indispensable for discernment of the right from the wrong, but also the good from the bad, and the relevant from the irrelevant. Dialogue may open the possibility of overlap and mutual understanding among different groups concerning common moral interests.

The process of conversation to reach mutual moral understanding could also serve the process of retraditioning, retrieving and articulating once suppressed, forgotten, or ignored doctrines, symbols, values, expectations, and practices of a particular tradition.

The process of constructing the common morality, such as human rights, may be long and painstaking, and irritating for some. Yet the process of communicative mutual engagement is indispensable for what Francis Fukuyama calls the renorming of a global society which is exploitative and conflictual in many aspects.[1] The renorming of a global society in justice is not possible without certain shared moral criteria, without the institutional protection to guarantee the participation of all concerned, respect for diverse expression of human freedom and ultimate concerns, and collective resistance to domination. These concerns all point and converge toward the significance of the communicative process in forging the commonly acceptable principles of rules of mutual regulation and transaction. The encounter and engagement will offer the opportunity of mutual learning, understanding, and questioning. Communicative conversation and covenant are alternatives to violence. If humanity refuses to take these divinely ordained routes, a global society will be an animalistic jungle, fulfilling the Darwinian prophecy of the survival of the fittest through domination.

Notes

1. Francis Fukuyama, *The Great Disruption: Human Nature and the Reconstruction of Social Order* (New York: Simon & Schuster, 1999).

BIBLIOGRAPHY

Abott, Walter M., ed. *The Documents of Vatican II*. New York: American Press, 1966.

Allen, Joseph L. *Love and Conflict: A Covenantal Model of Christian Ethics*. Lanham, New York, and London: University Press of America, 1995.

Alstrom, Sydney E. "The Puritan Ethics and the Spirit of American Democracy." In *Calvinism and the Political Order*, ed. George L. Hunt. Philadelphia: Westminster Press, 1965.

Althusius, Johannes. *The Politics of Johannes Althusius*. Abridged and translated by Frederick S. Carney. Boston: Beacon Press, 1964.

An-na'im, Abdullahi A, et al., eds. *Human Rights and Religious Values: An Uneasy Relationship?* Grand Rapids: W. B. Eerdmans Publishing Co.; Amsterdam: Editions Rodopi, 1995.

Apel, Karl-Otto. *Towards a Transformation of Philosophy*. London: Routledge & Kegan Paul, 1980.

Arblaster, Anthony. *The Rise and Decline of Western Liberalism*. New York: Basil Blackwell, 1984.

Arens, Edmund. *Christopraxis: A Theology of Action*. Trans. John F. Hoffmeyer. Minneapolis: Fortress Press, 1995.

Baker, J. Wayne. *Covenant and Community in the Thought of Heinrich Bullinger*. Philadelphia: Center for the Study of Federalism, Temple University, 1980.

Baron, Hans. "Calvinist Republicanism and Its Historical Roots." *Church History* 8 (1939): 30-42.

Barth, Karl. *Church Dogmatics*. vols. I/1, II/2, III, and IV/1. ed. G.W. Bromiley and T. F. Torrance. Edinburgh: T. & T. Clark, 1949ff.

Baum, Gregory, and Robert Ellesberg, eds. *The Logic of Solidarity*. Maryknoll, New York: Orbis Books, 1986.

Beauchamp, Tom L., and James F. Childress. *Principles of Biomedical Ethics*, 2nd ed. Oxford: Oxford University Press, 1983.

Bellah, Robert N. *The Broken Covenant: American Civil Religion in Time of Trial*. New York: Seabury Press, 1975.

Benhabib, Seyla. *Critique, Norm and Utopia: A Study of the Foundations of Critical Theory*. New York: Columbia University Press, 1986.

———. *Situating the Self: Gender, Community and Postmodernism in Contemporary Ethics*. New York: Routledge, 1992.

Benhabib, Seyla, and Fred Dallmayr, eds. *The Communicative Ethics Controversy*. Cambridge: M.I.T. Press, 1990.

Benne, Robert. *The Paradoxical Vision: A Public Theology for the Twenty-First Century*. Minneapolis: Fortress Press, 1995.

Berger, Peter L. *The Sacred Canopy: Elements of a Sociological Theory in Religion*. New York: Anchor Books, 1990.

Bernstein, Richard J., ed. *Habermas and Modernity*. Cambridge: M.I.T. Press, 1985.

Bierma, Lyle D. "Federal Theology in the 16th Century: Two Traditions?" *Westminster Theological Journal* 45 (1983): 304-321.

Braaten, Carl E. *No Other Gospel: Christianity among the World's Religions*. Minneapolis: Fortress Press, 1992.

Brown, Harold I. *Rationality*. London: Routledge, 1988.

Browning, Don S., and F. S. Fiorenza, eds. *Habermas, Modernity, and Public Theology*. New York: Crossroad, 1992.

Burrell, Sidney A. "The Covenant Idea as a Revolutionary Symbol: Scotland 1596-1637." *Church History* 27 (1958): 338-350.

Butler, Charles J. *Covenant Theology and the Development of Religious Liberty*. Philadelphia: Center for the Study of Federalism, Temple University, 1980.

Cahill, Lisa Sowle. "Toward a Christian Theory of Human Rights." *Journal of Religious Ethics* 8 (1980): 277-301.

Calhoun, Craig, ed. *Habermas and the Public Sphere*. Cambridge: M.I.T. Press, 1992.

Calvin, John. *The Institutes of the Christian Religion*. 2 vols, ed. John T. McNeil. Philadelphia: Westminster Press, 1960.

Chambers, Simone. *Reasonable Democracy: Jürgen Habermas and the Politics of Discourse*. Ithaca and London: Cornell University Press, 1996.

Cohen, Jean L., and Arato Andrew. *Civil Society and Political Theory*. Cambridge: M.I.T. Press, 1992.

Coleman, John A. *An American Strategic Theology*. New York: Paulist Press, 1982.

————, ed. *One Hundred Years of Catholic Social Thought: Celebration and Challenge*. Maryknoll, New York: Orbis Books, 1991.

Cooper, John W. *The Theology of Freedom: The Legacy of Jacques Maritain and Reinhold Niebuhr*. Macon, GA: Mercer University Press, 1985.

Cranston, Maurice. "Liberalism," *The Encyclopedia of Philosophy*. New York: MacMillan and Company, Inc./ Free Press, 1967.

Cunningham, David S. *These Three Are One: The Practice of Trinitarian Theology*. Malden: Blackwell Publishers, 1998.

Curran, Charles E., and Richard A. McCormick, eds. *Readings in Moral Theology No. 5: Official Catholic Social Teaching*. New York: Paulist Press, 1985.

D'Costa, Gavin. *The Meeting of Religions and the Trinity*. Maryknoll: Orbis Books, 2000.

De Jong, Peter Y. *The Covenant Idea in New England Theology 1620-1847*.
    Grand Rapids: W. B. Eerdmans Publishing Co., 1945.

d'Entreves, A. P. *Natural Law: An Introduction to Legal Philosophy*. London:
    Hutchinson University Library, 1951.

Douglass, R. Bruce, Gerald M. Mara, and Henry S. Richardson, eds. *Liberalism
    and the Good*. New York: Routledge, 1990.

Downey, Michael. *Understanding Christian Spirituality*. New York: Paulist
    Press, 1997.

Duff, Nancy J. *Humanization and the Politics of God: The Koinonia Ethics of
    Paul Lehmann*. Grand Rapids: W. B. Eerdmans Publishing Co., 1992.

Dyck, Arthur. *Rethinking Rights and Responsibilities: The Moral Bonds of
    Community*. Cleveland: Pilgrim Press, 1994.

Elazar, Daniel J. *Covenant and Polity in Biblical Israel*. The Covenant
    Tradition in Politics. Vol. 1. New Brunswick, N.J.: Transaction Publishers,
    1995.

———. *Covenant and Commonwealth*. The Covenant Tradition in Politics.
    Vol. 2. New Brunswick, N.J.: Transaction Publishers, 1996.

———. *Covenant & Constitutionalism*, The Covenant Tradition in Politics.
    Vol. 3. New Brunswick, N.J.: Transaction Publishers, 1998.

Emerson, Everett H. "Calvin and Covenantal Theology." *Church History* 25
    (1956): 136-144.

Evans, Donald. *The Logic of Self-Involvement*. New York: Herder & Herder,
    1969.

Everett, William J. *God's Federal Republic: Reconstructing Our Governing
    Symbol*. New York/Mahwah: Paulist Press, 1988.

Farley, Margaret A. "New Patterns of Relationship: Beginnings of a Moral
    Revolution." *Theological Studies* 36 (1975): 627-646.

Fiorenza, Francis S. *Foundational Theology: Jesus and the Church*. New York:
    Crossroad, 1992.

Friedrich, Carl. *Trends of Federalism in Theory and Practice*. New York:

Frederick A. Praeger, 1968.

Fukuyama, Francis. *The End of History and the Last Man*. New York: Free Press, 1992.

———. "The End of History?" *National Interests* (1989): 3-18.

Gadamer, Hans-Georg. *Truth and Method*. New York: Seabury Press, 1975.

George, Robert P., ed. *Natural Law Theory:Contemporary Essays*. Oxford: Clarendon Press, 1992.

Giddens, Anthony. *Central Problems in Social Theory: Action, Structure and Contradiction in Social Analysis*. London: Macmillan Press, 1979.

———. *The Constitution of Society: Outline of the Theory of Structuration*. Berkeley: University of California Press, 1984.

Gray, John. *Liberalism*. Minneapolis: University of Minnesota Press, 1995.

Greaves, Richard L. "The Origins and Early Development of English Covenant Thought." *The Historian* 31 (1968): 21-35.

Griffioen, Sander. "The Metaphor of the Covenant in Habermas." *Faith and Philosophy* 8, no. 4 (1991): 524-540.

Gunnemann, Jon P. "Habermas and MacIntyre on Moral Learning." *The Annual of the Society of Christian Ethics* (1994): 83-110.

Gunton, Colin E. *The One, The Three, and the Many: God, Creation and the Culture of Modernity*. New York: Cambridge University Press, 1993.

———."Trinity, Ontology, and Anthropology: Toward a Renewal of the Doctrine of the Imago Dei." In *Persons, Divine and Human: King's College Essays in Theological Anthropology*, ed. Christoph Schwöbel and Colin E. Gunton, 47-61. Edinburgh: T & T Clark, 1991.

Guroian, Vigen. "Liturgy and the Lost Eschatological Vision of Christian Ethics," *The Annual of the Society of Christian Ethics* 20 (2000): 227-238.

Gutmann, Amy. "Communitarian Critique of Liberalism." *Philosophy and Public Affairs* 14 (1985): 308-322.

Habermas, Jürgen. *Autonomy and Solidarity: Interviews*, ed. Peter Dews. London: Verso-New Left Books, 1986.

———. *Communication and the Evolution of Society*. Boston: Beacon Press, 1979.

———. *Faktizitat und Geltung: Beitrage zur Diskurstheorie des Rechts und des demokratischen Rechtsstaats*. Frankfurt: Suhrkamp, 1992.

———. "Further Reflections on the Public Sphere." In *Habermas and the Public Sphere*, ed. Craig Calhoun, 421-461. Cambridge: M.I.T. Press, 1992.

———. *Justification and Application: Remarks on Discourse Ethics*. Cambridge: M.I.T. Press, 1993.

———. "Law and Morality," *The Tanner Lectures on Human Values*. vol. 8, ed. Sterling M. McMurrin, and trans. Kenneth Baynes. 217-279. Salt Lake City: University of Utah Press, 1988.

———. *Legitimation Crisis*. Boston: Beacon Press, 1975.

———. *Moral Consciousness and Communicative Action*. Cambridge: The M.I.T. Press, 1990.

———. *On the Logic of the Social Sciences*. Cambridge: M.I.T. Press, 1988.

———. *The Philosophical Discourse of Modernity*. Cambridge: M.I.T. Press, 1987.

———. *Postmetaphysical Thinking: Philosophical Essays*. Cambridge: The M.I.T. Press, 1992.

———. "Reply to My Critique." In *Habermas: Critical Debate*, ed. John B. Thompson and David Held, 219-283. Cambridge: M.I.T. Press, 1982.

———. *The Structural Transformation of the Public Sphere: An Inquiry into a Category of Bourgeois Society*. Cambridge: M.I.T. Press, 1989.

———. "Struggle for Recognition in the Democratic Constitutional State." In *Multiculturalism: Examining the Politics of Recognition*, ed. and intro. Amy Gutmann, 107-148. Princeton: Princeton University Press, 1994.

————. *The Theory of Communicative Action.* 2 vols. Boston: Beacon Press, 1984, 1988.

————. "Toward a Communication-Concept of Rational Collective Will-Formation: A Thought Experiment," *Ratio-Juris* 2 (1989): 144-154.

Harvey, Barry. *Politics of the Theological: Beyond the Piety and Power of a World Come of Age.* New York: Peter Lang, 1995.

Hauerwas, Stanley. *After Christendom: How the Church Is to Behave If Freedom, Justice, and a Christian Nation Are Bad Ideas.* Nashville: Abingdon Press, 1991.

————. *Against The Nations: War and Survival In a Liberal Society.* Minneapolis, Chicago, and New York: Winston Press, 1985.

————. *A Better Hope: Resources for a Church Confronting Capitalism, Democracy, and Postmodernity.* Grand Rapids: Brazos Press, 2000.

————. "Can Aristotle Be a Liberal? Nussbaum on Luck." *Soundings* 72 (1989): 675-691.

————. *Character and The Christian Life: A Study in Theological Ethics.* San Antonio, Texas: Trinity University Press, 1975.

————. "Characterizing Perfection: Second Thoughts on Character and Sanctification." In *Wesleyan Theology Today: A Bicentennial Theological Consultation*, ed. Theodore Runyon, 251-263. Nashville: Kingswood Books, United Methodist Pub. House, 1985.

————. "A Christian Critique of Christian America." In *Community in America: The Challenge of Habits of Heart*, ed. Charles H. Reynolds and Ralph V. Norman, 250-265. Berkeley: University of California Press, 1988.

————. *Christian Existence Today.* Durham, NC: Labyrinth Press, 1988.

————. *A Community of Character: Toward a Constructive Christian Social Ethic.* Notre Dame: University of Notre Dame Press, 1981.

————. *Dispatches from the Front: Theological Engagement with the Secular.* Durham and London: Duke University Press, 1994.

————. *In Good Company: The Church as Polis.* Notre Dame: University of Notre Dame Press, 1995.

————. *The Peaceful Kingdom: A Primer in Christian Ethics*. Notre Dame: University of Notre Dame Press, 1983.

————. "Should Christians Talk So Much About Justice?" *Books and Religion* 14 (1986): 15-16.

————. *Should War Be Eliminated? Philosophical and Theological Investigations*. Milwaukee: Marquette University Press, 1984.

————. *Suffering Presence: Theological Reflections on Medicine, the Mentally Handicapped, and the Church*. Notre Dame and London: University of Notre Dame Press, 1986.

————. *Truthfulness and Tragedy*. Notre Dame: University of Notre Dame Press, 1977.

————. *Unleashing the Scripture: Freeing the Bible from Captivity to America*. Nashville: Abingdon Press, 1993.

————. *Vision and Virtue: Essays in Christian Ethical Reflection*. Notre Dame: University of Notre Dame Press, 1974.

————. "Will the Real Sectarian Stand Up?" *Theology Today* 44 (1987): 87-94.

————. *With the Grain of the Universe: The Church's Witness and Natural Theology*. Grand Rapids: Brazos Press, 2001.

Hauerwas, Stanley, and L. Gregory Jones, eds. *Why Narrative?: Readings in Narrative Theology*, Grand Rapids: W. B. Eerdmans Publishing Co., 1989.

Hauerwas, Stanley, Sanford Levinson, Mark V. Tushnet, et al. "Faith in the Republic: A Frances Lewis Law Center Conversation." *Washington and Lee Law Review* 45 (1988): 467-534.

Hauerwas, Stanley, and Alasdair MacIntyre, eds. *Revisions: Changing Perspectives in Moral Philosophy*. Notre Dame: The University of Notre Dame Press, 1983.

Hauerwas, Stanley, Nancy Murphy, and Mark Nation, eds. *Theology Without Foundations: Religious Practice & the Future of Theological Truth*. Nashville: Abingdon Press, 1994.

Hauerwas, Stanley, and William Willimon. *Preaching to Strangers:*

Evangelism in Today's World. Nashville: Abingdon Press, 1989.

———. *Resident Aliens: Life in the Christian Colony.* Nashville: Abingdon Press, 1989.

———. *The Truth About God: The Ten Commandments in Christian Life.* Nashville: Abingdon Press, 1999.

Hebblethwaite, Peter. "The Popes and Politics: Shifting Patterns in 'Catholic Social Doctrine.'" In *Readings in Moral Theology No.5: Official Catholic Social Teaching,* ed. Charles E. Curran & Richard A. McCormick, 264-284. New York: Paulist Press, 1985.

Hoeksema, Anthony A. "The Covenant of Grace in Calvin's Teaching." *Calvin Theological Journal* 2 (1967): 133-161.

Hollenbach, David. "Christian Social Ethics after the Cold War." *Theological Studies* 53 (1992): 75-95.

———. *Claims in Conflict: Retrieving and Renewing the Catholic Human Rights Tradition.* New York: Paulist Press, 1979.

———. "Common Good." In *The New Dictionary of Catholic Social Thought,* ed. Judith A. Dwyer, 192-197. Collegeville, MN: Liturgical Press, 1994.

———. *The Common Good and Christian Ethics.* Cambridge, UK; New York: Cambridge University Press, 2002.

———. *The Common Good in a Divided Society.* Santa Clara, CA: Santa Clara University, 1999.

———. "The Common Good Revisited." *Theological Studies* 50 (1989): 70-94.

———. "Contexts of the Political Role of Religion: Civil Society and Culture." *San Diego Law Review* 30 (1994): 879-901.

———. "Fundamental Theology and the Christian Moral Life." In *Faithful Witness:Foundations of Theology for Today's Church,* ed. Leo J. O'Donovan and T. Howland Sanks, 167-184. New York: Crossroad, 1989.

———. "Human Rights." *New Catholic Encyclopedia,* vol. 17

(supplementary volume), 1979.

———. "Human Rights and Interreligious Dialogue: The Challenge to Mission in a Pluralistic World." *International Bulletin of Missionary Research* 6 (1982): 98-101.

———. "Intellectual and Social Solidarity." In *Catholic Universities in Church and Society: A Dialogue on Ex Corde Ecclesiae*, ed. John P. Langan, 90-94. Washington D.C.: Georgetown University Press, 1993.

———. *Justice, Peace, and Human Rights: American Catholic Social Ethics in a Pluralistic Context*. New York: Crossrord, 1988.

———. "Liberalism, Communitarianism, and the Bishops' Pastoral Letter on the Economy." *The Annual of the Society of Christian Ethics* (1987): 19-40.

———. "The Politics of Justice." *Theology Today* 38 (1982): 489-493.

———. "Public Reason/Private Reason? A Response to Paul J. Weithman." *Journal of Religious Ethics* 22.1 (1994): 39-46.

———. "Plural Loyalties and Moral Agency in Government." In *Personal Values in Public Policy: Conversations on Government Decision-Making*, ed. John Haughey, 91-122. New York: Paulist Press, 1979.

———. "Public Theology in America: Questions for Catholicism after John Courtney Murray." *Theological Studies* 37 (1976): 290-303.

———. "Religion and Political Life." *Theological Studies* 52 (1991): 87-106.

———. "The Role of the Churches in the American Search for Peace." In *The American Search for Peace: Moral Reasoning, Religious Hope, and National Security*, ed. George Weigel and John P. Langan, 237-65. Washington, D.C.: Georgetown University Press, 1991.

Hollenbach, David, Drew Christiansen, Ronald Garret, and Charles Powers. "Moral Claims, Human Rights, and Population Policies." *Theological Studies* 35 (1974): 83-113.

Hollenbach, David, John A. Coleman, J. Bryan Hehir, and Robin W. Lovin. "Theology and Philosophy in Public: A Symposium on John Courtney Murray's Unfinished Agenda." *Theological Studies* 40 (1979): 700-715.

Hollenbach, David and R. Bruce Douglass, eds. *Catholicism and Liberalism: Contributions to American Public Philosophy*. Cambridge: Cambridge University Press, 1994.

Hollenbach, David, Richard A. McCormick, Lisa Sowle Cahill, and John P. Langan. "Notes on Moral Theology: 1984." *Theological Studies* 46 (1985): 50-114.

Hollenbach, David, Richard A. McCormick, William C. Spohn, and Lisa Sowle Cahill. "Notes on Moral Theology: 1985." *Theological Studies* 47 (1986): 69-133.

Hollenbach, David, William C. Spohn, Edward C. Vacek, and John P. Langan. "Notes on Moral Theology: 1987." *Theological Studies* 49 (March 1988): 67-150.

Honneth, Axel, et al., eds. *Philosophical Interventions in the Unfinished Project of Enlightenment*. Trans. William Rehg. Cambridge: M.I.T. Press, 1992.

Hutter, Reinhard. "The Ecclesial Ethics of Stanley Hauerwas." *Dialog* 30 (1991): 231-241.

Ingram, David. *Habermas and the Dialectic of Reason*. New Haven: Yale University Press, 1987.

Jenson, Robert W. "The Hauerwas Project." *Modern Theology* 8:3 (1992): 285-295.

Jones, L. Gregory. "A Response to Sykes: Revelation and the Practices of Interpreting Scripture." *Modern Theology* 5:4 (1989): 343-348.

Krieger, David J. *The New Universalism: Foundations for a Global Theology*. Maryknoll, New York: Orbis Books, 1991.

Kuhn, Thomas S. *The Structure of Scientific Revolutions*. 2nd ed. Chicago: University of Chicago Press, 1970.

Küng, Hans, and Karl-Josef Kuschel, eds. *A Global Ethic*. New York: Continuum, 1993.

Kuyper, Abraham. *Abraham Kuyper: A Centennial Reader*. ed. James D. Bratt. Grand Rapids: W. B. Eerdmans Publishing Co., 1998.

Kymlicka, Will. *Liberalism, Community, and Culture*. Oxford: Clarendon Press,
    1989.
LaCugna, Catherine Mowry. *God for Us: The Trinity and Christian Life*. New
    York: HarperSanFrancisco, 1991.

Lakeland, Paul. "Ethics and Communicative Action: The Need for Critical
    Theory in Catholic Social Teaching." *Thought* 62 (1987): 59-73.

———. "Providence and Political Responsibility: The Nature of Praxis in an
    Age of Apocalypse." *Modern Theology* 7:4 (1991): 351-362.

———. *Theology and Critical Theory: The Discourse of the Church*.
    Nashville, Abingdon Press, 1990.

Langan, John. "Human Rights in Roman Catholicism." *Journal of Ecumenical
    Studies* 19 (1982): 25-39.

Lehmann, Paul. *The Decalogue and a Human Future: The Meaning of the
    Commandments for Making and Keeping Human Life Human*. Grand
    Rapids: W. B. Eerdmans Publishing Co., 1994.

———. *Ethics in a Christian Context*. New York: Harper & Row, 1963.

———. *The Transfiguration of Politics*. New York: Harper & Row, 1975.

Lindbeck, George. *The Nature of Doctrine: Religion and Theology in a
    Postliberal Age*. Philadelphia: Westminster Press, 1984.

Little, David. *Religion, Order, and Law: A Study in Pre-Revolutionary
    England*. New York, Evanston, and London: Harper Torchbook, Harper &
    Row Publishers, 1969.

Little, David, and Sumner B. Twiss. *Comparative Religious Ethics: A New
    Method*. San Francisco: Harper and Row, 1978.

Locke, John. *A Letter Concerning Toleration*. Indianapolis: Bobbs-
    Merrill/Library of Liberal Arts, 1955.

———. *Two Treatises of Government*. ed. Peter Laslett. New York:
    New American Library, 1960.

Love, Thomas T. *John Courtney Murray: Contemporary Church-State Theory*.
    Garden City, N.Y.: Doubleday & Company, 1965.

Lovin, Robin W. *Christian Ethics: Essential Guide*. Nashville: Abingdon Press, 2000.
————. "Equality and Covenant Theology." *Journal of Law and Religion* 2 (1984): 241-262.

MacIntyre, Alasdair. *After Virtue*. Notre Dame: University of Notre Dame Press, 1981.

————. *Whose Justice? Which Rationality?* Notre Dame: University of Notre Dame Press, 1988.

Maritain, Jacques. *Christianity and Democracy & The Rights of Man and Natural Law*. San Francisco: Ignatius Press, 1986.

————. *Man and the State*. Chicago: University of Chicago Press, 1951.

————. *The Person and the Common Good*. New York: Charles Scribner's Sons, 1947.

McCann, Dennis. "The Good to be Pursued in Common." In *The Common Good and the U. S. Capitalism*, ed. Oliver F. Williams and John W. Houck. Lanham: University Press of America, 1987.

McCann, Dennis P., and Charles R. Strain. *Polity and Praxis: A Program for American Practical Theology*. Minneapolis, Chicago, New York: A Seabury Book, Winston Press, 1985.

McCarthy, Thomas. *The Critical Theory of Jürgen Habermas*. Cambridge: M.I.T. Press, 1978.

————. *Ideas and Illusions: On Reconstruction and Deconstruction in Contemporary Critical Theory*. Cambridge: M.I.T. Press, 1991.

————. "A Theory of Communicative Competence." *Philosophy of the Social Sciences* 3 (1973): 181-199.

McClain-Taylor, Mark. *Remembering Esperanza: A Cultural-Political Theology for North American Praxis*. Maryknoll: Orbis Books, 1990.

McCoy, Charles S. "The Federal Tradition of Theology and Political Ethics: Background for Understanding the U.S. Constitution and Society." *The Annual of the Society of Christian Ethics* (1988): 113-132.

McCoy, Charles S., and Wayne J. Baker, eds. *Fountainhead of Federalism: Heinrich Bullinger and the Covenantal Tradition.* Louisville, K.Y.: Westminster/John Knox Press, 1991.

McFague, Sallie. *Metaphorical Theology: Models of God in Religious Language.* London: SCM Press, 1983.

McKim, Donald K., ed. *Major Themes in the Reformed Tradition.* Grand Rapids: W. B. Eerdmans Publishing Co., 1992.

McNeill, John T. "Natural Law in the Teaching of the Reformers." *Journal of Religion* 26 (1946): 168-182.

Meehan, Johanna, ed. *Feminists Read Habermas: Gendering the Subject of Discourse.* New York and London: Routledge, 1995.

Migliore, Daniel L. *Faith Seeking Understanding: An Introduction to Christian Theology.* Grand Rapids: W. B. Eerdmans Publishing Co., 1991.

Miller, Perry. *Errand into Wilderness.* New York: Harper & Row, 1964.

————. *The New England Mind: From Colony to Province.* Cambridge: Belknap Press, 1953.

————. *The New England Mind: The Seventeenth Century.* New York: Macmillan Co., 1939.

Miller, Perry, ed. *The American Puritans.* Garden City, N.Y.: Doubleday & Co., 1946.

Miscamble, Wilson D. "Sectarian Passivism?" *Theology Today* 44 (1987): 69-77.

Moltmann, Jürgen. "The Destruction and Healing of the Earth: Ecology and Theology." In *God and Globalization: The Spirit and the Modern Authorities*, vol. 2, ed. Max L. Stackhouse and Don S. Browning. Harrisburg, PA: Trinity Press International, 2001.

————. "Human Rights, the Rights of Humanity and the Rights of Nature." In *Ethics of World Religions and Human Rights*, ed. Hans Küng and Jürgen Moltmann. London: SCM Press; Philadelphia: Trinity Press International, 1990.

————. *The Trinity and the Kingdom: The Doctrine of God.* New York: HarperSanFrancisco, 1991.

Morgan, Edmund S. *Puritan Political Ideas 1558-1794*. Indianapolis: Bobbs-Merrill Co., 1965.

Mount, Eric, Jr. "The Currency of Covenant." *The Annual of the Society of Christian Ethics* (1996): 295-310.

Mouw, Richard J., and Sander Griffioen. *Pluralism & Horizons: An Essay in Christian Public Philosophy*. Grand Rapids: W. B. Eerdmans Publishing Co., 1993.

Muller, Richard A. "Covenant and Conscience in English Reformed Theology: Three Variations on a 17th Century Theme." *Westminster Journal of Theology* 42 (1980): 308-334.

Nelson, Paul. *Narrative and Morality: A Theological Inquiry*. University Park, London: Pennsylvania University Press, 1987.

Newman, John Henry. *An Essay in Aid of a Grammar of Assent*. ed. Charles F. Harold. New York: Longmans, Green and Co., 1947.

Nichols, James H. *Democracy and the Churches*. New York: Greenwood Press & Publishers, 1969.

Niebuhr, H. R. *Christ and Culture*. New York: Harper and Row, 1951.

———. "The Idea of Covenant and American Democracy." *Church History* 23 (1954): 126-135.

———. *The Kingdom of God in America*. New York: Harper and Brothers, 1935.

———. *The Meaning of Revelation*. New York: Macmillan Co., 1941.

———. "The Protestant Movement and Democracy in the United States." In *The Shaping of American Religion*, ed. James W. Smith and A. L. Jamison, 111-123. Princeton: Princeton University Press, 1961.

———. *Radical Monotheism and Western Culture*. New York: Harper and Brothers, 1960.

———. *The Responsible Self*. New York: Harper and Row, 1963.

Novak, Michael. *Freedom with Justice: Catholic Social Thought and Liberal Institutions*. San Francisco: Harper and Row, 1984.

Outhwaite, William. *Habermas: A Critical Introduction*. Stanford: Stanford University Press, 1994.

Outka, Gene. "Character, Vision, and Narrative." *Religious Studies Review* 6 (1980): 110-118.

Outka, Gene, and John P. Reeder, eds. *Prospects for a Common Morality*. Princeton: Princeton University Press, 1993.

Pedersen, Johannes. *Israel: Its Life and Culture*. 4 vols. London: Oxford University Press, 1926-1940.

Perry, Michael J. *Morality, Politics, and Law*. Oxford, New York: Oxford University Press, 1988.

Perry, Ralph Barton. *Puritanism and Democracy*. New York: Vanguard Press, 1944.

Quirk, Michael. "Beyond Sectarianism?" *Theology Today* 44 (1987): 78-86.

Rasmussen, David, ed. *Reading Habermas*. Cambridge: Basil Blackwell, 1990.

———. *Universalism vs. Communitarianism: Contemporary Debates in Ethics*. Cambridge: M.I.T. Press, 1990.

Rasmusson, Arne. *The Church as Polis: From Political Theology to Theological Politics as Exemplified by Jürgen Moltmann and Stanley Hauerwas*. Lund: Lund University Press; Bromley, Kent, England: Chartwell-Bratt, 1994.

Rawls, John. "The Idea of an Overlapping Consensus." *Oxford Journal of Legal Studies* 7 (1987): 1-25.

———. "Justice as Fairness: Political not Metaphysical." *Philosophy and Public Affairs* 17 (1985): 223-251.

———. *A Theory of Justice*. Cambridge: Harvard University Press, 1971.

Rehg, William. *Insight & Solidarity: The Discourse Ethics of Jürgen Habermas*. Berkeley, Los Angeles, London: University of California Press, 1994.

Riley, Patric. "Three 17th Century German Theorists of Federalism: Althusius, Hugo, and Leibniz." *Publius* 6 (1976): 7-41.

Robertson, D. B., ed. *Voluntary Associations: A Study of Group in Free Societies*. Richmond: John Knox Press, 1966.

Robertson, Roland, and Thomas Robbins, eds. *Church-State Relations: Tensions and Transitions*. New Brunswick (U.S.A.) and Oxford (U.K.): Transaction Books, 1987.

Sabine, George H. *A History of Political Theory*. 3rd ed. New York: Holt, Rinehart and Winston, 1961.

Sandel, Michael. *Liberalism and the Limits of Justice*. Cambridge: Cambridge University Press, 1982.

Scott, J. L. "The Covenant Theology of Karl Barth." *Scottish Journal of Theology* 17 (1964): 182-198.

Seidman, Steven. *Jürgen Habermas on Society and Politics: A Reader*. Boston: Beacon Press, 1989.

Shapiro, Ian. *The Rule of Law*. New York: New York University Press, 1994.

Shipton, Clifford K. "Puritanism and Modern Democracy." *New England Historical and Genealogical Register* 101 (July 1947): 181-198.

Siebert, Rudolf J. *The Critical Theory of Religion: The Frankfurt School: From Universal Pragmatic to Political Theology*. Berlin, New York, Amsterdam: Mouton Publishers, 1985.

Skillen, James W. "From Covenant of Grace to Equitable Public Pluralism: The Dutch Calvinist Contribution." *Calvin Theological Journal* 31 (1996): 67-96.

Smith, Tony. *The Role of Ethics in Social Theory: Essays from a Habermasian Perspective*. Albany: State University of New York Press, 1991.

Stackhouse, Max L. *Creeds, Society and Human Rights*. Grand Rapids: W. B. Eerdmans Publishing Co., 1984.

———. "Liberalism Dispatched vs. Liberalism Engaged." *Christian Century* 112, no. 29 (1995): 962-967.

———. "The Moral Meanings of Covenant." *The Annual of the Society of Christian Ethics* (1996): 249-264.

Stout, Jeffrey. *Ethics After Babel: Languages of Morals and Their Discontents.* Boston: Beacon Press, 1988.

Sykes, John. "Narrative Accounts of Biblical Authority: The Need for a Doctrine of Revelation." *Modern Theology* 5:4 (1989): 327-342.

Taylor, Charles. *Sources of the Self: The Making of the Modern Identity.* Cambridge, MA.: Harvard University Press, 1985.

Tracy, David. *The Analogical Imagination: Christian Theology and the Culture of Pluralism.* New York: Crossroad, 1991.

Trinterud, Leonard J. "The Origins of Puritanism." *Church History* 20 (1951): 37-57.

Twiss, Sumner B., and Bruce Grelle. "Human Rights and Comparative Religious Ethics: A New Venue." *The Annual of the Society of Christian Ethics* 15 (1995): 21-48.

———. *Philosophical Papers. 2 vols.* Vol. 1: *Human Agency and Language.* Vol. 2: *Philosophy and the Human Sciences.* Cambridge: Cambridge University Press, 1985.

Vanhoozer, Kevin J., ed. *The Trinity in a Pluralistic Age: Theological Essays on Culture and Religion.* Grand Rapids: W. B. Eerdmans Publishing Co., 1997.

van Huyssteen, Wentzel. *Theology and the Justification of Faith: Constructing Theories in Systematic Theology.* Grand Rapids: W. B. Eerdmans Publishing Co., 1989.

Walzer, Michael. *Spheres of Justice: A Defense of Pluralism and Equality.* New York: Basic Books, 1983.

Welker, Michael. *God the Spirit.* Minneapolis: Fortress Press, 1994.

———. ""...And also upon the Menservants and the Maidservants in Those Days will I Pour out My Spirit": On Pluralism and the Promise of the Spirit." *Soundings* 78 (1995): 49-67.

Wellmer, Albrecht. "Ethics and Dialogue: Elements of Moral Judgment in Kant and Discourse Ethics." In *The Persistence of Modernity: Essays on Aesthetics, Ethics, and Postmodernism*, trans. David Midgley, 113-231. Cambridge: M.I.T. Press, 1991.

West, Cornel. *The American Evasion of Philosophy: A Genealogy of Pragmatism*. Madison: University of Wisconsin Press, 1989.

White, Stephen K. *The Recent Work of Jürgen Habermas: Reason, Justice & Modernity*. Cambridge: Cambridge University Press, 1988.

Williams, Rowan. "Trinity and Revelation." *Modern Theology* 2:3 (1986): 197-212.

Witte, John, and Johan van der Vyver, eds. *Religious Human Rights in Global Perspective*. 2 vols. Hague, Boston, London: Martinus Nijhoff Publishers, 1996.

Woodhouse, A.S.P., ed. *Puritanism and Liberty: Being the Army Debates (1647-9) from the Clarke Manuscripts with Supplementary Documents*. London: J. M. Dent and Sons Limited, 1938.

Zizioulas, John. *Being as Communion: Studies in Personhood and the Church*. Crestwood, N.Y.: St. Vladimir's Seminary Press, 1993.